The Ugli Fruit

The Ugli Fruit

Tapping the Inner Spirit for
Greater Mental Health

Dr. Al L. Holloway

THE UGLI FRUIT
TAPPING THE INNER SPIRIT FOR GREATER MENTAL HEALTH

Scripture quotations marked NIV are taken from THE HOLY BIBLE, NEW INTERNATIONAL VERSION®, NIV® Copyright © 1973, 1978, 1984, 2011 by Biblica, Inc.® Used by permission. All rights reserved worldwide.

Scripture quotations marked NKJV are taken from the New King James Version. Copyright © 1982 by Thomas Nelson, Inc. Used by permission. All rights reserved.

Scripture quotations are marked NRSV are taken from the New Revised Standard Version Bible, copyright © 1989 the Division of Christian Education of the National Council of the Churches of Christ in the United States of America. Used by permission. All rights reserved.

Scripture quotations marked RSV are taken from the Revised Standard Version of the Bible, copyright © 1946, 1952, and 1971 the Division of Christian Education of the National Council of the Churches of Christ in the United States of America. Used by permission. All rights reserved.

iUniverse books may be ordered through booksellers or by contacting:

iUniverse
1663 Liberty Drive
Bloomington, IN 47403
www.iuniverse.com
1-800-Authors (1-800-288-4677)

Because of the dynamic nature of the Internet, any web addresses or links contained in this book may have changed since publication and may no longer be valid. The views expressed in this work are solely those of the author and do not necessarily reflect the views of the publisher, and the publisher hereby disclaims any responsibility for them.

Any people depicted in stock imagery provided by Thinkstock are models, and such images are being used for illustrative purposes only. Certain stock imagery © Thinkstock.

ISBN: 978-1-5320-0478-0 (sc)
ISBN: 978-1-5320-0477-3 (e)

Library of Congress Control Number: 2016913205

Print information available on the last page.

iUniverse rev. date: 08/18/2016

Contents

Acknowledgements

I could not begin, follow through with or complete any writing endeavor (or any life endeavor for that matter) without the Goodness and Grace of God. To which, anything substantial or beneficial that the reader gleans from this book, all credit is given to God. Any errors, missteps or confounding ideas are totally mine to own. In addition, the creative ideas that are expressed in this book and the descriptive narratives could have only been made possible through my work at Western Mental Health Center (WMHC). During my ten year stint at WMHC I have been associated with both current and past colleagues that have exhibited the height of spiritual advancement into the "pure-heart realm." They are thoughtful, considerate, compassionate and kind. They are intelligent and humble; dedicated to the service of others. The very moment that I acknowledge one person here, I realize that I would do a tremendous disservice to those I may have inadvertently overlooked. In serving humanity, whether it is the professionalism and kindness of our intake workers or the appointment reminders from our receptionists (on the frontlines of dealing with some clients with very significant needs), supported by information technology (IT), administration, billing or in the "trenches" with our clients assuming roles as therapists, prescribers, adult rehabilitative mental health service (ARMHS) workers, assertive community treatment (ACT) teams, etc., we are often "unsung heroes" in the service that we do. Therefore, I thank you here!

With one exception, I must specifically acknowledge one of my colleagues here. To Jen Gregoire, MSW, LICSW and ACT Team Leader, who is "tough as a rusty nail" and exemplifies well the essence of "The Ugli Fruit." She is tirelessly committed to the service of those with serious and persistent mental illness (SPMI), where many others would overlook them, ignore them or discount them. She has gone beyond the limitations of her job to serve, advocate for and protect these most vulnerable people. She and her team have gone into bedbug-filled, dilapidated houses and apartments, serving a clientele who may have not bathed in a month and caring for these vulnerable people with great dignity and respect. She is mindful of the little things (e.g., a phone call, a birthday card, a Christmas gift, etc.), letting those know (with absolutely no one else in their lives) that they matter. Jen has sparred with me often but beneath it all, I've known her to be a true servant of God and she didn't hesitate one second to read and respond to the manuscript for this book. Thank you Jen!

We are touching the lives of people and we don't always know what our "seeds" have produced. To this, I wish to express a heartfelt thank you to Carmen Love, the author of "*They Loved with a Closed Fist*," who reminds me that the seeds we sow can take root in the lives of others and produce tremendous change. In addition to the service providers, there are some spiritually evolved clients (and those in the process of evolving) who have come through Westerner's doors seeking guidance, support and healing from mental health providers and unbeknownst to them, shared their stories that have guided, supported and provided healing for us as we were serving them—Thank you!

Preface

What strikes me as a therapist in a rural community mental health center is the pervasiveness and intensity of those in psychological and emotional pain. Having previously worked primarily with a skewed population of largely improvised minorities within a large urban, inner-city community, with those suffering from severe and persistent mental illness (SPMI) referred on to regional hospitals, I have been awestruck by the enormity of mental illness in such a small community. The "floodgates" have opened at Western Mental Health Center and the clients just keep coming. Within my ten years of service to this community, I have provided mental health services to medical doctors, chiropractors, dentists, chemical dependency counselors and even other therapists. I've worked with corporate executives and employees, USDA Agricultural workers, FBI agents, ministers, K-12 teachers, college professors and students. I've met with farmers and farm wives, immigrants (both legal residency and undocumented), factory workers, retail workers and the unemployed. I've seen felons, ex-felons and those yet to have been adjudicated. I've seen prosecutors, defense attorneys and correctional officers. I've seen the elderly, the young, males, females, Caucasians, African Americans, Mexicans, Hmong, Native Americans, East Indians, Asians, Somolians; indeed people from all over the world.

What I've received by such a rich and diverse client population is a wealth of equally rich and diverse client narratives! I have no doubt that service within any capacity is noble but therapy provides one with a unique opportunity to join with the client in an extremely intimate way for the purpose of change and healing. Therapists bear witness to the individual atrocities that clients have endured. We are privileged to have a "front row seat" for clients to reveal their triumphs and tragedies, their joys and sorrows, their courageousness and fears; along with their successes and defeats. We have an opportunity to impart a new vision for clients that directs them out of their morass to quality life experiences.

Many of us feel that we are ruled by events in the physical world. We are ruled by the limitations of our physical being. We are ruled by our wants and lack; thus, craving for physical sensations that are far from satiating. We are ruled by the histories of perceived interactions that have long since gone by. We are ruled by the perceptions and influences of others who erect "monuments and statues" of what we are not. The physical world lulls us into notions of permanency where nothing permanent exists. Our *minds*, which should receive instruction from the *spirit* to create a strategic plan to be carried out by the physical *body*, are woefully misaligned. The mind is taking its cue from the body and all but denying agency or authority from the spirit. The spirit is prostrated before the "all-mighty body" which believes it has preeminence in the physical world.

In working with this group of diverse individuals at Western Mental Health Center (a community mental health facility in rural, Southwest Minnesota), it is clear to me that the many sufferers are not taking their cue from spirit. It is clear to me, even though many are "religious," many have little knowledge about the operation of spirit. This concept was clearly represented to me in the produce aisle in the not so popular fruit called the "Ugli fruit." Like the fruit itself, we tend to view ourselves by the physical image we project verses the true substance of what resides inside. Indeed, we often peel fruit, throwing the peel away and consume the juicy, sweet pulp within. If nature relishes the substances within, it should convey for us how much more precious and powerful the spirit is that resides within each of us.

The spirit is the "juicy, sweet stuff" or the "substantive stuff" that directs our mind and body; and not the other way around. When we don't know spirit and the importance of spirit, we give credence to our lessor self to run our lives. In "*The Ugli Fruit: Tapping the Inner Spirit for Greater Mental Health,*" I identify how we can be compromised by our faulty perceptions and our allegiance to anything other than God. As a clinician and one who truly does appreciate the role of therapy in the lives of people, I also realize that therapy is a method, an approach or a tool to facilitate change and healing within individuals. However, the real catalyst for change and healing comes from the Almighty God. Therapy is akin to taking over the counter (OTC) flu medication when stricken by the flu virus. We do get some symptom relief from our medicinal efforts, but the flu itself is tackled and defeated by our internal immune system that fights off and destroys the invading flu virus. Thus God has already inculcated healing within His wonderful design.

What is in us comes out of us and the things that are spiritual are activated by our faith. Christ shared with his disciples, *"For a good tree does not bear bad fruit, nor does a bad tree bear good fruit. For every tree is known by its own fruit. For men do not gather figs from thorns, nor do they gather grapes from a bramble bush"* (Luke 6:43-44-NKJV). If we don't have a sense of our worthiness, we tend to bear "bad fruit." We represent to the world the ugliness that we feel inside that is manifested in the stories we tell. Every human being has a story that matters! We can give our testimony in a confessional, to a church congregation, to a family member or friend or within a confidential, therapeutic setting in a clinician's office but the important thing is to tell our stories. James (5:16-NKJV) writes, *"Therefore confess your sins to each other and pray for each other so that you may be healed. The prayer of a righteous person is powerful and effective."*

Given the importance of a person's story, I've highlighted many stories to illustrate points throughout this book. However, I am mindful of a small community and the propensity for gossip. To protect privacy and to honor confidentiality, all names are assumed, descriptive features have been augmented; along with knitting together a compilation of narrative details that would not expose anyone. If there is a wisp of familiarity in the stories within this book it is only due to so many people that have been similarly hurt, harmed and abused along the way.

The Ugli Fruit: Tapping the Inner Spirit for Greater Mental Health is just a reminder that we are more than our outer layer projections; along with a reminder for therapists that there is something more that we must minister to (spirit) that facilitates good mental health. If spiritual development is not considered by client or therapist, there is little healing and no fundamental and lasting change. No matter what is reflected on the outside of us and no matter what type of life circumstances we find ourselves in, we are all made in the image of All Mighty God. As a result, we have a prestigious heritage and our birthright grants us access to the "Kingdom of God" right here on Earth. God has not bestowed upon any of us a disturbed mind, discord within our families or disharmony within the world. Among the Fruit of the Spirit, God has granted us peace. There is a spiritual prescription for peace; which is faith in and obedience to God. Apostle Paul wrote, *"Become complete. Be of good comfort, be of one mind, live in peace; and the God of love and peace will be with you."* (2 Corinthians 13:11-NKJV)

I

Recognizing Worthy Fruit

For the kingdom of God is not meat and drink; but
righteousness, and peace, and joy in the Holy Spirit.
(Romans 14:17-KJV)

Ahhh, the Ugli fruit! Have you seen it in the produce section at your local supermarket? While pushing your metal grocery cart through the wide aisles of the brightly-lit grocery store, just a bit annoyed that the left front wheel appears to be having an epileptic convulsion, rapidly whipping itself back and forth, seemingly trying to redirect your purposeful journey throughout the store and you happen upon the fruit. The Ugli fruit. Unless you've had this delectable fruit before, it will probably raise a singular eyebrow as you gaze upon this pyramid mound of oddly shaped fruit; both curiously and perplexed.

The Ugli fruit has its origins in Jamaica. It is about 6" in diameter with an uneven surface. It may be greenish, yellowish or a strange looking orange in color. It has characteristically puffy skin that is often marred, scarred or with pockmarks. "Who would put this strange looking fruit into their mouths," you wonder? Yet, your curiosity pulls you toward this misbegotten fruit. You feel it in your hands…give it a good sniff. You are just about to put one in your cart. "What the heck," you reason, "I'll give it a try." Just as you are about to commit by placing this bizarre oddity in your cart, you change your mind yet again, "Well, maybe next time," as your cart squeaks away from the mound, with your left front wheel resuming its uncontrollable fit.

The fact of the matter, this is a refreshing, sweet (yet, tart), juicy, and delicious fruit that is the cross between a grapefruit or pomelo and tangerine. It is high in potassium, vitamin A, vitamin C and folic acid. The labeling of this fruit ("Ugli") is consistent with its exterior, but the exterior belies what is contained within. We have notions of beauty that are symmetrical and certainly without blemish. There is a beauty in nature and a beauty in the Spirit of God that is awe inspiring and can simply take our breaths away! The Ugli fruit doesn't meet this standard of beauty; thus, we are inclined to not see what we deem as ugly (or choose to be critical of in our assessment) as a thing of beauty or worth. The Ugli fruit is the "Rodney Dangerfield" of fruit…it gets no respect.

I have found the Ugli fruit to be nature's metaphor in how we see ourselves. As a psychologist and clinical social worker, I have noticed that virtually everyone who enters into a therapeutic setting sees themselves as "marred," "scarred" or "blemished" in some way. Rebecca is a 28 year old, Native American woman. She has a swarthy complexion; perhaps a bit darker than typical Native American women. Her almond shaped eyes and raven black hair presents a woman who is striking in her appearance but she discounts her value because she is not able to mimic the features she associates with beauty represented by the Caucasian celebrities that she so greatly admires. Sarah is Caucasian and a 22 year old, local beauty pageant winner who is stricken by anxiety and riddled with insecurities about her perceived flaws that no one else sees. Thomas, a 50 year old, intelligent, Caucasian man, who isolates and avoids interaction with others due to his perceived intellectual deficiencies and as Yogi would say, "I am smarter than the average bear," Thomas is smarter than the average person. Reggie is a kind-hearted, responsible, 42 year old, Caucasian married, family man who feels inadequate and flawed because his neighbors appear to be doing financially better than him. Oh, I would love to say that there are those who represented well the image of beauty that society clamors for, but even the generally accepted "good looking" people are trapped by the distortions of their marred, scarred and blemished selves.

It should be noted that this distorted image of ourselves and others is not simply relegated to those in need of clinical mental health help. Most of us see, react to and relate with the notion of the person's outer self; thus, few of us go beyond the curious stare, the cursory pinch, or the obligatory squeeze and sniff as we set others back upon the "mound" of which we found them. In today's world, we are clustering people into negatively labeled groups (i.e., "Muslim terrorists," "angry blacks," "racist whites," "illegal Mexican immigrants," "deviant gays & lesbians," "fundamental/bigoted Christians," etc.). Perhaps…just perhaps we can make a justification or rationalization for the rejection of others in an exclusionary fashion, but the real travesty is the rejection that we have of ourselves. We are the Ugli fruit! It is out of our own perception of ugliness that we project ugliness upon the world.

When I wrote my previous book, *"The Fruit of the Spirit: A Primer for Spiritual Minded Social Workers,"* I was placing the emphasis of spiritual differentiation on clinicians. As a clinician (psychologist and clinical social worker) and a former educator (assistant professor in the school of social work) I was (and remain) concerned about the lack of spiritual differentiation on the part of clinicians and students who are studying to become human service providers (e.g., psychologists, social workers, marriage and family therapists, and the like). In this book, I am focusing upon the lack of spiritual differentiation that many of us are experiencing despite our titles or roles. It is laypeople's evolution verses that of "wounded warriors" I am focusing on this time around (though there is really little distinction or separation between the two). Indeed, we tend to develop notions of distinction and separation to our own folly. *"The wisdom of the prudent is to understand his way, but the folly of fools is deceit."* (Proverbs 14:8-NKJV)

The concept of spirituality, though not readily understood by many, has a remote appeal for just about all human beings. Though the notions of spirituality, and the things related to spirit, have such layers of abstraction that we tend to store these notions in the recesses of our minds verses daily, mindful focus, it appears all of humanity has a yearning for spirit. Every human being has an innate spiritual longing for the integration of him or herself. Every human being has a sense of belonging; whether it is an inner-city gang member or the person with paranoid schizophrenia who has elaborate conversations with a bucket of dirty mop water. Every human being aspires to something greater, as reflected in our human endeavors and accomplishments; yet, in the stillness of our being, our heart (spirit) yearns for something more. If this were not the case we would not see the promulgation of religious expression exhibited in all "four corners" of the world.

This longing aligns us with all the religiously faithful in pursuit of our understanding of God. We aspire for a relationship with the Ultimate and we attempt to replicate that relationship with our fellow human beings. We long to see greatness in that celebrity movie star, politician, minister or therapist and equally saddened by the notion that all human relationships will fail us. In some ways this is a good thing because we learn to trust in God instead of other human beings or even ourselves. I can't tell you how many times I've let myself down in pursuing a pathway or a relationship that steered me in the "wrong direction." Well…I want to qualify this last statement a bit. There are lots of wrong directions in life and when we take one of them and recognize that we are off course, we then conclude that we are failures. This is a patently false notion!

We are not "failures" in this journey of life. We are spiritual beings having a human experience; thus, our human experience can take us in all kinds of different directions. A desolate, backwoods type of road can also lead us to God. The Apostle Paul informs us that, *"And we know that all things work together for good to those who love God, to those who are the called according to His purpose."* (Romans 8:28-NKJV) In our human understanding, "the quickest path between two points is a straight line"; however, God is not in a hurry and the quickest path for our experience could be a meandering road.

To have failed doesn't make us failures and failure is not fatal. Failure is often the result of having insufficient data, or if we have sufficient data, we are not implementing the data that we inherently know to be true. Many of us struggle with the implementation of data that we intuitively know to be true; rather, we accept data that we intuitively know to be false. Instead of being god-like, we are shame-based; thereby, endorsing the notion that we are "Ugli fruit." If we accept the faulty premise that we are blemished or flawed (shame-based), we can easily conclude that we are failures and replicate life experiences causing deliberate failings. That is, shame-based people will either consciously or subconsciously pursue a life path to sabotage their opportunities for successful outcomes because the "success" doesn't match their skewed notions that they are failures.

This is a daunting task for therapists. As a change-agent and healer I don't see my role as one that necessarily "changes" the individual that seeks out therapeutic intervention, as the core of humanity (spirit) is good. It is "good" because God is Good and ultimately, we can't be anything other than what we are. However, whether our roles as therapists is to provide avenues for change or modalities for healing, we must create an environment where the client's perception of "self" changes; thus, healing flows from the client's perception of change (i.e., "I am not a failure!). We, as therapists or concerned others, cannot impose change upon the client, a family member or a friend that we like to see occur. Try, as you might, to have someone give up alcohol, drugs, sexual indiscretions, work, bigoted views, hoarding and the like when they are not ready for change and witness the futility of your efforts. Christ informs us that the salvation of "man" is not in the hands of another, as referenced in the Book of Mark, *"Jesus looked at them and said, 'With men it is impossible, but not with God; for with God all things are possible.'"* (10:27-NKJV)

It is interesting to me to observe how so many people see themselves as the inverse of Ugli fruit. Obviously, there are people in this world that others know to be gorgeous and they know it too. With a degree of calculation in how beauty is measured in a particular society, along with comparison to others, some may not see themselves as pitted, blemished or marred on the outside. Indeed, ask them to pick a fruit that best represents them and virtually none of them would say, "I'm an Ugli fruit." They are tangerines and mangos, cherries and strawberries, apples, pears and bananas, but not the Ugli fruit. Yet, even with a proclamation that they may outshine others in the way of physical beauty, they will inevitably see themselves as being flawed on the inside. Psychologically, emotionally and spiritually they feel flawed; and I am not just relegating this perception to just those seeking clinical intervention.

How is it that an icon, like Marilyn Monroe, the '50's film goddess...the pinup girl for servicemen throughout the world...whose beauty captivated other famous icons of her time (e.g. Joe DiMaggio of baseball fame and John F. Kennedy, our 35th president), saw herself as flawed, unworthy and killed herself? How is it that another celebrity beauty and icon for another generation, Angelina Jolie, engaged in self-mutilating behaviors; thus, deliberately marring herself? Why is it that the local beauty pageant winner that I mentioned earlier is unable to see the beauty that the community sees and the pageant officials saw; thus making her the winner? How is it that my niece, whom I see with extraordinary beauty, is in constant "achievement-oriented" mode because she doesn't believe that she is "good enough?"

What I've come to know as a clinician, academician, and spiritual sojourner or even directly experienced as one among the "walking wounded" throughout various times in my life, is that this world we reside in is socially constructed. Our schema is a psychological construct that is socially created, with which we experience the world. Oh this is not to deny the absolutism of God and His realm, but our human/individualistic experience of the "absolute" is socially constructed. Our social interactions with others edify us and allow us to construct meaning of our world. We can't consume the totality of our worldly experiences in a single moment, so we create categories. Categories are necessary to develop knowledge, seek understanding and to share our limited understandings with others. In reductionist form we then reduce these categories to labels.

Let's look at the way I've conceptualize this for my anger management therapy group (AMTG). Often, (and certainly not always), when I conduct an initial diagnostic assessment on potential group members, they may have been referred by their probation agent, judge, county social worker or perhaps their defense attorney prior to or following adjudication. Whether male or female, being "forced" to see a therapist due to allegations or findings of abuse/violence/assault generates resistance on the part of the clients. They have been adjudicated within a legal system and ascribed a label (e.g., "abuser" or "batterer") per a charge of 5th degree domestic assault and now being labeled by me (or another therapist) with a mental health diagnosis; namely, Adjustment Disorder with a Disturbance of Conduct and/or Physical Abuse of an Adult or Child. Their resistance is also magnified by their denial that they even have "anger issues," having to sit ten weeks in a group with other people they think, *"really do have anger issues,"* along with the notion of having an out of pocket expense of $2,000+ dollars to attend a group with *angry people* when they don't have anger issues. If they weren't angry prior to going through this process, they are certainly angry in the earlier stages of this process.

"Labels" are limiting and in this case, they are relatively shaming. Like the Ugli fruit, these clients have exhibited behaviors that are very "unattractive"; yet, the core of what they are is still "precious" and "good." During the 1st day of therapy, I illustrate a diagram on the board to introduce the notion of "socially constructed realties" to the group members (see figure 1). Indeed, the sum total of who we are (in human form) is our narratives… our histories. I'll illustrate three distinct circles (large, medium and small) on the board, with the largest circle representing our "histories" (which is a collection of "his"-stories and "her"-stories). Our stories/histories are vast, comprehensive and complex. It is the totality of our lived and perceived experiences that is huge. If you happen to be 20, 40 or 80 years old, a comprehensive and complete assessment of your story would take 20, 40, or 80 years to complete. And even then it will still be incomplete as another 20, 40 or 80 years would have gone by with the assessor attempting to glean every nuance representative of your entire story/history.

Every exchange that we have with the world has others making an assessment of the stories/histories that we are creating (or have created). I represent this with a medium circle that is purposefully smaller; therefore, much more limiting than the totality of our comprehensive and full stories/histories. Of course, no one has the time or the inclination to complete a full assessment of our stories/histories, but everyone indeed assesses. We all take "snapshots" (assessments) out of the "reel" of the person's life (histories) and make judgments (labels). The assessment is framed not so much by the person presenting the history but by the person receiving the history. This is important because we are now "socially reconstructing" the history of another person under the prism of our own frame of reference. The author of one's story can be artfully promoted but it is the receiver of that story who reduces it down through the lens of their own assessment criteria.

The third circle falls underneath the first two circles and it is the smallest by design because it becomes the "label." Labels are descriptive. It is a truncated way of reducing our linguistic expressions to a word or two, where others (in this socially constructed world) derive meaning. What is important to consider is that a label, though descriptive, is not predictive of anything. President Barrack Obama is the first African-American president and virtual leader of the entire Western world but was immediately reduced in his first address to congress with a republican congressman yelling that he was a "liar." The decorum of the office itself, if not the man holding the office, was demeaned by a shouted label from a disgruntled congressman. The 2016 presidential campaign is not much different with dehumanizing labels bandied about (e.g., "Lyin' Ted," "Little Marco," "Crooked Hilary," and "Small Hands Trump").

Let's take a closer look at this labeling process and the impact it has on those who are labeled negatively. In my AMT group I take a caption from the history of a small child

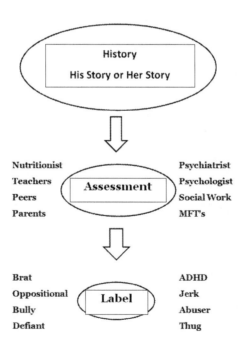

that simply reads, "Johnny hits Sally...Why?" Then I surround the assessment circle with the interpretation of professionals and laypeople alike as they attempt to discern, "Why Johnny hits Sally?" Watch how one's theoretical orientation and frame of reference shapes the assessment of each of the people observing the very same thing-"Johnny hits Sally." The psychiatrist, endowed with medical, biological and pharmaceutical knowledge promotes an assessment that Johnny hits Sally due to chemical imbalances in the brain. Having concluded this assessment, psychiatrists then generate labels of attention deficit hyperactive disorder, depression and the like, with medication to ameliorate the problem.

A psychologist (one of the hats that I wear) scans for internalized traits (perhaps cognitive, emotional and developmental deficits) fostering notions of low self-esteem, low self-worth, or poor impulse control. One school of thought for psychologists was introduced by Sigmund Freud, called "psychoanalysis." According to Charles Zastrow, in his text, *"The Practice of Social Work,"* the goal of psychoanalysis "…is to discover the disturbing unconscious processes and bring them into the conscious part of the patient's mind…" This can generate a cathartic emotional release; thereby, freeing the individual of repressed, pent up and traumatic experiences of childhood. Psychologists may also echo some of the psychiatrists' pronouncements of brain functioning and chemistry but also looks at parent or peer group dynamics in causing some disorders. Therefore, "oppositional defiance disorder" or depending upon the age and history of behaviors that are presenting, "conduct disorder" are among the labels we'll choose.

I wear a clinical social worker's hat as well and the frame of reference provided by this discipline is system's theory. A system is a set of interlocking or interacting parts that represents a whole. A system's paradigm is in play as we try to figure out why Johnny hits Sally because we want to look beyond just Johnny's immediate behaviors. Perhaps we'll look at the influence of poverty or affluence as associated factors for Johnny's acting out behaviors. Perhaps we will view the educational system and the curriculum used or class size. Perhaps it is the political system that needs to be evaluated in terms of where dollars are allocated. Perhaps we'll examine peer alienation or acceptance that may help us explain Johnny's behaviors. Perhaps it is the family constellation that is examined which includes familial construction (e.g. single parent households vs. dual parent households, blended families and sibling birth order, etc.).

The theoretical orientation of system's theory in social work is often paired with a "strength's based perspective" where we tend to frown on pathologizing labels; nevertheless, in the process of communicating, we still have to generate categories that produce labels. In doing so, we may then see Johnny's "acting out" behaviors as a byproduct of a "dysfunctional" family system that continues to produce labels. Even benign labels shift in connotation over time; whereas it was once nice to be known as someone "special" but who now would want to be known as a "special kid."

Marriage and family therapists weigh in with their frame of reference that hones in on the family constellation with more depth. Perhaps Johnny hits Sally because his parents are divorcing…because he is being abused… because mom lost her job…because dad started drinking…perhaps a sibling is chronically ill…perhaps the other sibling is the star of the family and Johnny gets attention by acting out. Whatever the reason, MFTs are keenly focused upon issues related to the family constellation to interpret Johnny's acting out behaviors. Marriage and family therapists are likely to use more benign labels than psychologists would use but they recognize that family dynamics can scapegoat Johnny as the "problem child" thus trying to conceptualize what is going on in the family is still reduced to labeling (e.g., "terrific twos" vs. "terrible twos" and "active/alert child" vs. "brat").

What sustains each and every one of us is our consumption of nutrients in the form of food and drink. It is often said that we are what we eat; so what about nutritionists? What do they have to say about Johnny's behaviors toward Sally? Perhaps Johnny's behaviors are exacerbated by the foods that he eats or the foods that he doesn't eat. Perhaps Johnny is fueled by sugars, caffeine or excessive carbohydrates. Perhaps he has a reaction to food colorings/dyes or vitamin and protein deficiency. Perhaps he is just hungry because his family doesn't feed him breakfast, resulting from Johnny's irritability and he then lashes out at Sally.

Given Johnny's acting out behaviors happens at school, what do the educators' say? Do educators have theories about what causes acting out behaviors in students in general? How about theories about Johnny's behaviors in particular? You bet they do! So how might educators assess the reason why Johnny hits Sally? Perhaps Johnny lacks academic competence and acts out by being the class "bully" or the class "clown." Perhaps he is written off as being incorrigible or labeled with emotional behavioral disturbance (EBD). Perhaps Johnny has a low intellectual quotient (IQ) or emotional quotient (EQ) and is not developmentally on par with the other students in his class. Perhaps he just likes Sally and hasn't developed enough social competence to tell her or riddled by fear as to what would happen if he did tell her.

Laypeople also assess what they see and perhaps have less sophisticated theories about what they are seeing but they have theories nevertheless. What about Johnny's peers? They'll make their own assessments as to why Johnny hits Sally? Maybe they know that even though Johnny is the one that is in trouble it is really Sally that is the bully and Johnny finally defended himself by striking her back. Perhaps both Johnny and Sally are on the periphery of the insider's group and for Johnny to gain entry into the insider's group he needs to lash out and alienate Sally (at which point he becomes labeled "cool" by his peers vs. adhering to the label of "booger nose" he had previously been called).

Family members make their own assessment about the narratives of other family members and Johnny's family is no exception. They may see him as a "troubled kid," "incorrigible" or a "bad seed." I want you to think about this for a moment. Our home is our sanctuary…it is our haven… it is our safe place. It is the place where we are to be edified and nurtured and grow into healthy, whole, spiritually mature individuals. It is the refuge we run to when the world is against us but as you can see, not even family members are beyond using descriptive labels that diminish us. Jesus understood that people in our inner circle can reduce us and limit us. It is illustrated in these verses when Jesus returned home: *"Is this not the carpenter, the Son of Mary, and brother of James, Joses, Judas, and Simon? And are not His sisters here with us?' So they were offended at Him. But Jesus said to them, 'A prophet is not without honor except in his own country, among his own relatives, and in his own house.' Now He could do no mighty work there, except that He laid His hands on a few sick people and healed them."* (Mark 6: 3-5-NKJV)

What flows from everyone making an assessment of Johnny, shaped by their own frame of reference/social constructions, is a plethora of "labels" defining and further limiting Johnny: ADHD, oppositional defiant, bully, jerk, thug, brat, incompetent, stupid, retarded, malnourished, low esteem, and so on. Though it would be a lot more preferable, people can also be reduced or limited by positive labels. To be perceived as being "smart," "beautiful," or "wealthy" can place a burden on someone trying to live up to these labels as well. If labeled a "genius" others are not likely to question what you know or offer up any help due to feeling inferior to the one labeled a "genius." The "genius" is not likely to ask for help because he/she may erroneously presume that others don't know the answer or the fearing that others may know; thus, eroding the prestige of the "genius." Of course, given a preference, most would prefer an affirming and validating label over a negative one but any label reduces the totality of our narratives to whatever notions that others may have of us.

Nevertheless, it is the negative labels that have such powerful influence in shaping our lives. What invariably happens is that people take on internalize negative labels and these negative labels become self-fulfilling prophesies that now eclipses the actual people we've become. We lose the salience of our stories/histories and are reduced to the ugly labels. Once we have adopted these "ugly labels", we project to the world that we are "Ugli fruit" and we forget the true value that lies within. I recall having received similar labels that Johnny has received while I was growing up, and as a young black boy, I was the recipient of labels from blacks and whites that I rather not reiterate here. Suffice to say that all of us have likely experienced and taken in unbecoming and dehumanizing labels that have shaped the vision of ourselves and our perceived value of ourselves.

In my role of therapist, I don't see children in therapy but it wouldn't surprise the reader to know that what is said to children (whether criticism or praise) is stored in the "heart" and carried with them and us throughout our lives. What makes the negative labeling so insidious is that we accept it and repeat it over and over again with our internal and external dialogue. It doesn't take me very long to assess a person's level of esteem and perceived worth. Clients speak their self-perceptions like, "I'm stupid...I'm a failure... I'm a loser." The Disciple Luke didn't know psychological verbiage like "schema development", "fragmented psyche" or "internalized toxic shame" but he did know that what is in our hearts is revealed through our speech. He wrote, *"The good person out of the good treasure of his heart produces good, and the evil person out of his evil treasure produces evil, for out of the abundance of the heart his mouth speaks"* (Luke, 6:45-NKJV).

What I share with my anger management therapy group participants in the very first session (and throughout our ten weeks together) that despite whatever behaviors they've exhibited that has brought them to my group, they are and remain precious souls! You've heard this adage before that, "hurting people hurt others" and "broken people break things." Well, the people that present for my group are "hurting" people and "broken" people. They act out their wounds in their close relationships and more than likely bring hurt and harm to the people they purport to love. Their peace comes in not by trying to manipulate and exploit an arbitrary and socially constructed world; it comes from knowing their value and worth.

The things that we perceive to be worthy, we take care of. The things we deem unworthy, we dismiss. It is easy to dismiss ourselves when we perceive ourselves as "unworthy" or "flawed" in some way and as Luke was implying above that "what is in us comes out of us," we can easily see how someone close to us can be a victim of our pain. It is imperative to the development of ourselves and our interactions with others that we perceive ourselves accurately. We are the offspring of the Most High God; thus, we can't be anything less than the essence of the Most High God. The more we tap into the Essence of the Most High God, the less we'll give credence to our lessor human self.

If we are to grow beyond the labels of anyone's limited assessment of us, we must reconstruct the narratives written about us. "Johnny hits Sally" and we must respond to, care for and protect Sally. That is undeniable and unquestionable! The plethora of labels may point to theoretical constructs that may help us feel more knowledgeable and understand our individual fields better but labeling Johnny is not productive or helpful for Johnny. Johnny won't cease his behaviors simply because parents, peers or even some teachers label him a "brat." Even if we move past the pejorative labels that a layperson might use ("brat") to professional or clinical labels (e.g. "oppositional defiant disorder" or "disruptive behavioral disorder"), these labels don't stop Johnny from hitting Sally. What changes Johnny, (indeed, what changes all of us) is a transformation of his head and heart.

There is no doubt that young children are in the process of developing a capacity for emotional regulation and internal locus of control. There is no doubt that school provides not only an educational function for children but a socialization functioning for children. There is no doubt that our unique individualization will have children excel in this level of development or be delayed in this process. However, the cruelty that emanates in Johnny's head and heart and then exhibited in his behaviors is a projection of how Johnny sees himself. John Bradshaw in his book, *"Healing the Shame that Binds,"* referred to these projections as being, "disowned pieces of ourselves."

Unfortunately, within my anger management group, I am seeing the "Johnnies" and the "Johnnie Mae" that are all grown up and they are still "hitting Sally." In the ten weeks of sessions, I try to let them know (in addition to the educational and therapeutic component of the group) that they are worthy and precious souls! I try to convey to them these sentiments written by Apostle John, *"And we have known and believed the love that God has for us. God is love, and he who abides in love abides in God, and God in him."* (1 John 4:16-NKJV) This can appear to be an "uphill" battle and a bit futile to change the trajectory of someone who may have discounted God or have denied they have any worth throughout their lives but I am obliged to sow these seeds and trust God that there will be fertile ground to receive these seeds.

How we show up in this world is not as important as what is contained within. Physical attractiveness, wealth, and health are wonderful attributes in a physical world but everything physical is fleeting. Spending too much time focusing upon what we do have and what we don't have in this physical world distracts us from what we really are and why we are here upon this Earth. Each of us is responsible for creating "fertile ground" for "seeds" of spiritual fruit to take "root." We are also responsible for the "seeds" that are spewed out of our mouths and the "seeds" that we are willing to accept into our "gardens" and to grow as "fruit." The best "seeds" or word choices that inevitably generate positive labels are selected while in relationship with God. That is, we go to the Source (God) to be fed and nourished (fruit of the spirit) to deposit these seeds (words and actions) in the fertile ground, (minds and hearts) of others. To start seeing ourselves differently, create a regiment to develop a daily relationship with God. This will orientate us daily by directing us to the Most High God in order to receive sustenance that will nourish us for the day.

The older I get the more value I find in prayer as one of the regiments that I use to gain spiritual nourishment to sustain me through my day. Thus, I start my day and end my day with contact with God. In doing so, it becomes harder to think negatively about myself and others. The less negatively I think about myself and others, the less likely I am to use disabling and devaluing labels. The exercise that follows is helpful in connecting you with the Ultimate Source and reshaping your thoughts to honor the divinity within all sentient beings.

Ripening the Fruit-Prayer

If we plan to make purposeful changes to develop ourselves, it is what we focus upon that establishes the destination for our journey. I have often referred to prayer as having a "conversation with God." Additionally, from a psychological perspective, I have found prayer to be a wonderful aid in "cognitive restructuring." Indeed, Paul instructs us in his epistle to the Ephesians *"Let no one deceive you with empty words, for because of these things the wrath of God comes upon the sons of disobedience. Therefore do not be partakers with them. For you were once darkness, but now you are light in the Lord. Walk as children of light (for the fruit of the Spirit is in all goodness, righteousness, and truth), finding out what is acceptable to the Lord."* (5:6-10-NKJV) Establish a daily ritual that will allow you to focus upon the Ultimate. My daily recitation or prayer is as follows:

> *I take refuge in the Heavenly Father*
> *-The Creator and Sustainer of the Entire Universe*
> *I take refuge in the Divine Son*
> *-The Exemplar of our daily living*
> *I take refuge in the Holy Spirit*
> *-The Connector of animate and inanimate objects*
> *I take refuge in the Holy Trinity*
> *-Of the Father, Son and Holy Spirit*
> *Heavenly Father, descend upon this earthly plane*
> *And enter into the minds, hearts and souls of all sentient beings.*
> *Enter into our minds, O'Heavenly Father*
> *That we'll become people of righteous discernment; that*
> *we'll know good from bad & righteousness from evil!*
> *Enter into our hearts, O'Heavenly Father*
> *That we'll extend ourselves in loving kindness*
> *in service to all others.*
> *And, enter into our spirit, O'Heavenly Father*
> *That we'll endeavor to do what our minds*
> *understand and our hearts command.*

II

Who Am I?

He who forms the mountains, who creates the wind,
and who reveals his thoughts to mankind, who turns
dawn to darkness, and treads on the heights of the
earth— the Lord God Almighty is his name.
(Amos 4:13-NIV)

"Who am I," is a fundamental and age old question. Philosophers, academicians and theologians have endeavored to answer this existential question; yet, people still seem to be hungry for a definitive answer as it relates specifically to them and they seek out psychotherapy to find an answer. When Moses was being sent back into Egypt to free the Israelites from 400 years of bondage, he asked God whom should he say that has sent him back? God answered in a succinct (and perhaps an idiomatic way that resembles a Zen Koan), *"Tell them I Am Who I Am"* (Exodus 3:14-NKJV). Now I can imagine Moses saying (if he didn't have that stuttering problem and God sending Aaron along with him to help him speak), "Yeah, right God. You want me to go up to my 'brother' the Pharaoh, whom we now know is not my brother and banished me in the desert for 40 years and tell the people that have been brutally enslaved that 'I Am' sent me? Give me a name that is powerful and distinguish, like 'Jehovah' or 'Yahweh' or 'He Whose Voice Ignites Bushes and Causes the Earth to Tremble!'"

Interestingly, we don't see in the Bible where Moses brings up this "I Am" business again; however, God is still Brilliant and Prophetic in His "simplicity." If God is the definitive, "I Am" and each of us are made in the image of God *("Let Us make man [and woman] in Our own image"* Genesis 1:26-NKJV), then the answer to our existential hunger (Who am I?) has indeed already been answered. Because we've been inundated with confusion, ignorance and doubt, we've been on this perpetual quest for self-discovery. That is what brings clients into therapy. Their "history/ narrative" has been fragmented and "they know not who they are." Of course, most with lack of accesses or financial resources or lacking confidence in the credibility of psychotherapy do not enter into therapy as a method of self-discovery; yet, everyone incessantly seeks the answer to "Who am I?"

We are Tri-fold beings (spiritual, mental and physical) with each aspect of "self" working in tandem to have this earthly experience. Our births are gifts from God where we have the capacity to take on some "authorship" in "writing the narratives" of our own life journeys. No other creature has that capacity! No other creature has the capacity to replicate God's process of speaking into being the creation of the heavens and the Earth. This is not to place humans on par with God, as a "creation" is never as great as the "Creator"; however, we are made in the image of God and our human capacity for creation is only limited by our imaginations.

In a preceding book, "*The Fruit of the Spirit: A Primer for Spiritual Minded Social Workers*," I tackled the notion of "spirit" with esoteric and perhaps confounding language. That is, I wanted to conceptualize and operationalize this nebulous thing called, "spirit" with descriptive words like "amorphous" and "ephemeral." In targeting professionals in the field of service like social workers or psychologists with an academic or theoretical knowledge base; thus, this was indeed appropriate. But what does this mean to laypeople in general and those hungering for the knowledge of self; while seeing themselves as scarred, marred or blemished as symbolized in the Ugli fruit? What does this all mean for those who are hurting and languishing in pain?

What does it mean to be of spirit in rudimentary or basic terms? I attest that the *spirit* is the ultimate essence of who we are. It is the permanent essence of our being that will return to its original source (God Consciousness); whereas, the other aspects of who we are (mental and physical) will fade away in the material world of impermanence. I realize that this is a daunting statement as our inclination is to try to hang onto that which we delude ourselves is permanent (our minds and body). Indeed, I have met many people that can't wait to get to Heaven to walk on "streets made of gold" and to move into their individual "mansions" and to reclaim the bodies of their youth where they strut their stuff with envious ogling and admiration from others. They project upon Heaven their limited understanding that is experienced in the material world.

When we are young in our spiritual maturity we strive to understand by using concrete concepts of familiarity, affluence and esthetics. That is, we much rather think of the ultimate "resting place" like Heaven made of "golden streets" vs. "cobblestone"; "mansions" vs. "flophouses"; and attractive physical qualities like represented in "Angelina Jolie and Brad Pitt" vs. "Bertha the barmaid" and "Buster her belching, beer-bellied boyfriend." As we develop in our spiritual maturity we shift from concrete understandings to higher developed abstract thought and reasoning. Jesus spoke in "concrete" language of the time when he was physically present upon the Earth but his stories were often allegories with the use of metaphors; therefore, with greater levels of abstraction, designed for people with spiritual knowledge and "ears to hear." Apostle Paul wrote, *"When I was a child, I spoke as a child, I understood as a child, I thought as a child; but when I became a man, I put away childish things."* (I Corinthians 13:11-NKJV)

God is very clear about who He is. He proclaims, "I Am Who I Am!" We, of course, have great uncertainty and throughout the generations, we are constantly asking, "Who am I?" This lack of knowledge comes from being separated from God. Some think of this as a curse upon humanity by the original sin of disobedience perpetrated by Adam and Eve. But I purport that it is all blessing and part of God's Ultimate Design, *"...all things work together for the good to them that love God, to them that are called for His purpose"* (Romans 8:28-NKJV). If we are indeed spiritual beings having a human experience upon this Earth, then we had to have had this separation from God that generated an individualized ego. We could not have received the gift of our "human" experience unless we were separated. So, we have been empowered, even above the angels, to have freedom of choice. When freedoms are granted, the risk of abuse/ sin is ever present. Nevertheless, the gift of empowerment invites us to choose what direction to follow, *"I call heaven and earth as witnesses today against you, that I have set before you life and death, blessing and cursing; therefore, choose life that you and your descendants may live."* (Deuteronomy 30:19-NKJV)

Spirit is at the apex of our trifold selves. Its function is not unlike the Board of Directors for a corporation. It sets up a vision or direction for the corporation. The Board (spirit) brings in a CEO (mind) to create a strategic plan to carry out the vision of the Board. Corporations will then need the physical capital of their employees to carry out the planning of the CEO and the vision of the Board. Moses provided a simpler construct for spirit, *"And the Lord God formed man of the dust of the ground, and breathed into his nostrils the breath of life; and man became a living being."* (Genesis 2:7-NKJV) From that point and onward our theosophical understanding of spirit is often aligned with our religious affiliation and though indoctrination into a specific religious belief is not the purview of mental health professionals, helping others recognize their spiritual essence is germane to healing. I assert, in simplistic terms, that spirit encompasses *"meaning, purpose, connection* and *direction."*

Whether one is hurting and seeking therapy or merely contemplating one's existence, the spiritual aspect of who we are searches for meaning. So, "who" we are, are trifold beings made in the image of God and the *meaning* of our spiritual existence results in the "whys." We ponder why are we here? Why are we born male or female? Why were we born in the United States or some other part of the world? Why are we the race and/or the ethnicity we happen to be? Why were we born in affluence or poverty… in an urban area or rural? Why are we the 1st born or the 8th? Why do we have a family system that boasts of love and yet we feel love deprived? Why did our parent(s) abandon us…abuse us…dispatched us to the care of foster homes, detention centers or fictive kin? Why were we sexually abused…incarcerated…mentally ill…physically deformed…socially inept or constantly seeking relationships with emotionally/physically abusive men or women? Why are we ensconced in a particular religion or reject

God altogether? The "whys" are inexhaustible but there is always simplicity to spirit and the basic meaning of our spiritual existence is to form healthy relationships.

In order to forge healthy relationships we must develop an authentic self. I suspect to the reader that it is common sense that those seeking the help of a therapist would be fragmented or wounded in some way and I've yet to find those that have entered into my office that didn't feel marred, scarred or blemished in some way. They are the "Ugli fruit," opting to put themselves back on the supermarket shelf or to walk right past what they erroneously believe themselves to be. They don't know what lies within. We are the offspring of a Loving God. Whatever our physical attributes (or lack thereof), there is absolutely no defect that resides within us because there is no defect in God.

If there is no defect in the eternal nature of spirit, why do we grant so much credence in the impermanent aspects of self (mental and physical)? It is due to the deception of ego, viewing itself as a separate and distinct individual, vying for survival and permanence where no such thing exists for it. Ego relishes in its distinction; whether it deludes itself in notions of superiority or wallowing in faulty notions of inferiority. The ego battles with spirit for top billing and often rules over us in the choices we make and the experiences we are having on this earth. The ego is not superior to spirit. It, like other constructs of the mind, is to work in behest of spirit. The spirit has authority and permanency because it is the only thing linked to an everlasting source. The spirit is the overseer of our lessor functions (mind and body). The goodness of our spiritual essence is forever attached to God.

This is hard for the spiritually immature or uninitiated to accept because we've been told over and over and over again how flawed we are due to the original nature of sin. We embrace the inheritance of "man," the original sin of Adam and Eve, without much thought or discussion but we were never made in the image of Adam and Eve. We are not the benefactors of the legacy left behind by Adam and Eve. The legacy bestowed upon all of us derives from the Original Source of God. Not unlike the "prodigal son" Adam and Eve may have squandered their inheritance but it was a necessary journey to allow each of us the opportunity to experience an individual self. The "coverings" (the "tunics of skins") God clothed Adam and Eve with as they were being expelled from direct fellowship with God, can also be seen as an allegory illustrative of spiritual beings (originally made in the image of God) taking on human form and beginning our individualistic journeys. This was the birth of "ego" (also known as an acronym for "Easing God Out").

"Meaning" changes based upon the level of our spiritual differentiation (indifferent-heart/selfish, craving-heart/self-aware & pure-heart/selfless) and I wrote about this in my book, *The Fruit of the Spirit: A Primer for Spiritual Minded Social Workers.*" Meaning, as viewed through the skewed lens of the indifferent-heart realm, is about self-indulgence, hedonism and intemperance. Residing in the indifferent-heart realm is represented in a client named, "Joe." Joe is a 45 year old, Caucasian, married but currently separated father of two children. I originally met Joe due to a compulsory referral from his probation officer resulting from a charge and conviction of domestic violence. At the time, his oldest daughter (let's call her "Venice") was 17 years old and exhibiting adolescent angst with marginal academic performance, pushing back on parental authority and dating an older, Native American male triggering every stereotype and fear that Joe had about *"those people"* and *"his daughter."*

Venice was out after curfew and hanging out in her boyfriend's home when Joe burst in and manhandled his resistant daughter. The scene got out of control and the police were called, resulting in Joe being arrested for domestic violence (5th degree assault). Joe had issues with authority and often cited that he trusted criminals over the police or government officials. He complied with his physical presence to complete anger management therapy but with defiance and rigidity in his moralistic position throughout each session. When I assess potential clients for the need of anger management therapy, among other things I look for is the client exhibiting ego defenses of minimizing, denial and/or blaming, while scanning for insight, empathy and remorse. Joe presented greatly with the former and absently with the latter.

After completing compulsory anger management therapy, ironically Joe presented willfully for therapy again about a year later because his family was falling apart and he was desperate. He was desperate to hold onto a 20 year marriage despite his wife moving out with the girls and implying to him that she was through with their marriage. Out of his desperation and hurt Joe called his wife the "B"-word and his daughters "whores." Etched in each of the women's minds were their father and husband denigrating their femininity…their humanity…their spirituality. The person obliged to love them the most has hurt them the worst with the utterings from his own mouth. However, Joe endeavored to hang onto the "rightness" of his opinion that he didn't mean his daughters were "whores" but "dressed like whores" and he wasn't calling his wife a "B"-word; "she just acts like it!"

Having amassed a greater history on Joe, I learned that he had over a hundred sex partners prior to marriage, consumed pornography throughout their marriage and even though his wife pulled away from him intimately and sexually, he demanded that his wife be sexually available to him twice a week. She relented to this demand and in lifeless fashion she received his ejaculated discharge dutifully and with disdain. Undoubtedly, Joe would have preferred a more animated sexual partner but he told me in therapy that he didn't care if she was just lying there but she needed to be there twice a week. Clearly, Joe's interaction with his family (or lack thereof) is indicative of someone residing in the indifferent-heart realm. From a psychological point of view, I diagnosed Joe with having a Narcissistic Personality Disorder. Nevertheless, spiritually speaking, Joe's meaning for existence was hedonistic (pleasure seeking), self-indulgent (lacking empathy for others) and intemperate (lacking verbal restraint with name calling).

To ascertain *meaning* from the craving-heart realm is a function of ego that delights in reasoning, rationalizing, intellectualizing and otherwise to set up mechanisms and structures to create hierarchy and division among others. In this realm, we grant deference to ego; which delights in comparisons, contrasts and competition. Whereas Joe was fuse and/or disconnected from others due to the distortions of an indifferent-heart, *meaning* remains skewed, but skewed differently in the craving-heart realm with more competitive notions. Let's see how someone like Cheryl will project, "Who am I" in the craving-heart realm.

Cheryl is a 32, single, African-American woman that has been diagnosed with anxiety and panic disorder. She isolates herself and avoids social interactions. She is intellectually astute, in that she has a "command of the King's English" though she hasn't ventured very far in post-secondary educational pursuits. She avoids social interactions under the pretext that within the geographical rural community where she resides, she views others as "dumber than a box of rocks." She embraces esoteric views and intellectual "snobbery" that reinforces the above stated opinion about others. This form of intellectualizing justifies her pulling away from others and speaking critically of them. Yet in the process of dismissing others for their "intellectual inferiority" she is terribly lonely, forging relationships with therapists as her intellectual equal and "friend."

I often tell clients that "anxiety" is the manifestation of our fears and there is an infinite amount of things, people and situations that we can fear. There is "ablutophobia" (the fear of bathing, washing or cleaning one's self); "bogyphobia" (fear of bogies or the bogeyman); "claustrophobia" (the fear of being closed in); "epistemphobia" (fear of knowledge); "Hippopotomonstrosesquippedaliophobia" (fear of long words); "sociophobia" (fear of social situations or even the thought of being looked at) and rounding up a seemingly inexhaustible list is "zoophobia" (fear of animals). We can be afraid of being afraid; which can give rise to panic. Cheryl's fears are projected upon others ("they are dumber than a box of rocks"), with great insecurities that she'll be found out. After all, she hasn't achieved much of anything with her intellectual prowess; other than to separate herself from others.

There doesn't have to be anything about us that is "pathological" to reside in the craving-heart realm, but the ugliness of our being is creating artificial demarcations and hierarchies of separation from one another. In many ways, Cheryl's anxiety is adaptive. It keeps her at distance from those she doesn't want to be around and it provides her with a necessary disorder to maintain relationships with therapists. The anxiety and fear that has been diagnosed in Cheryl as a, "mental disorder," is a common spiritual level for many of us. It is hard not to separate and categorize things in the physical world to augment our intellectual understandings. In doing so, we create conditions to analyze, evaluate, compare, contrast and to judge. This is an important part of our spiritual development in moving from the indifferent-heart realm to the craving-heart realm, but as we continue to grow, we see less separation between ourselves and others.

When we are considering *meaning* at the pure-heart realm, we gain greater appreciation for who we are and greater clarity of why we are here. Ironically, I have seen people in therapy that have tremendously loving spirits and true representatives of the "pure-heart realm." It was initially perplexing to me, in that these individuals with a degree of spiritual differentiation that appeared to eclipse my level of spiritual evolution and yet they were receiving guidance, direction and therapy from me. They were spiritually astute, invested in their communities and exemplars in their fields. Why then, would they seek out me (or someone like me) to help them in their emotional, psychological and/ or spiritual journeys? How are they losing sight of "Who they are?"

Stages of spiritual development are not static! Though we are inclining toward spiritual advancement and reunification with the Ultimate, spiritual development is not only a linear process of progression. That is, we can expand beyond our original development but it doesn't mean we won't have relapses and regression. During our physical development we expand beyond childhood and adolescence into adulthood but there is still the "child" and "adolescent" within us that resurfaces at times. Similarly, in our spiritual development, we don't eradicate the indifferent-heart realm or the craving-heart ream once we've entered the pure-heart realm. There are things that are not as materialistically appealing once we advance in our spiritual maturity, but we cannot relinquish vigilance and practice if we are to remain spiritually fit. Therefore, therapy for someone residing in the pure-heart realm is akin to an extraordinary athlete, like tennis great, Serena Williams, still opting to use a coach for further development.

I attest that the only reason we (humans) are here (on Earth) is to have healthy relationships. Joe had unhealthy relationships with his family.

Cheryl had unhealthy relationship with others in her community. Both had unhealthy relationships with themselves and considering the degree of their dysfunction, they both had impaired relationships with God. Both Joe and Cheryl experience the world from the outer layers of the Ugli fruit but failed to see the inherent nature of who we are; thus, neither is fully able to embrace God's commandment relating to love. *"You shall love the Lord your God with all your heart, with all your soul and with all your mind. This is the first and great commandment."* And the second is similar to the first: *"You shall love your neighbor as yourself."* (Matthew 22:37-39-NKJV) The second commandment points to the next aspect of our spiritual essence—Purpose.

Having answered the questions of "Who am I" (the offspring of the All-mighty God, made in His image) and the meaning of our existence (Why are we here—to form healthy relationships), we are able to examine purpose. Purpose, as related to spirit, delves into the "what" questions. What are we here to do? What path shall we take? What type of relationships should we form? What type of character do we exemplify? What standards do we adhere to? What job do we work at? What church do we attend?

From a spiritual perspective, relating to purpose, we are called to serve others. God created humanity but He also serves humanity. God rained manna from the sky to feed the multitudes in their exodus from Egypt (Exodus 16:4-NKJV). He protected Shadrach, Meshach and Abed-nego from the fiery furnace (Daniel 3:19-26-NKJV). While in his incarnation as Christ, God instructed us, *"If I then, your Lord and Teacher, have washed your feet, you also ought to wash one another's feet. For I have given you an example, that you should do as I have done to you"* (John 13:14-15-NKJV). It is a reciprocal relationship with God serving humanity and humanity serving God but it is also a recursive relationship as we are called to "do onto others" without expecting a direct benefit of service (gifts) returned for what we've provided.

Within my role as a therapist (psychologist/clinical social worker), I am fulfilling my purpose to serve but service is manifested in many forms and fashion. Federal and state government provides service by protecting the nation from foreign or domestic threats…by providing K-12, free public education…constructing interstate highways and the like. People serve in a number of different types of vocations, such as: education, ministry, nursing, food industry, hospitality, libraries, childcare and other professions. Generalist social workers serve as brokers, mediators, enablers, facilitators, conveners, etc. We serve in our families as chauffeurs, cooks, laborers, mentors, companions, lovers, tutors, exemplars and in many other capacities. As you can see, service is an important part (purpose) of our human/spiritual experience and the specific/unique service we provide addresses the "what" questions. In establishing *who* we are, *why* we are here and *what* it is that we are here to do, the other component of spirit is *direction*.

"Direction," as it relates to spirit, deals with the "*where*" and "*when*" questions. I have worked (and continue to do so) providing service within the mental health field. I've worked in academia. I've also worked in food service and retail, earning barely above minimum wage. Regardless of the varied jobs/professions, a common factor I've found in each of the above is that the employers had vision statements, mission statements and goals. A mission statement may relate more closely with "what questions" (i.e., "What does the University, agency and store do?"), but a "vision" is an idea of "where" one is going and "goals" help us determine "when" one is going to get there. If Joe or Cheryl could develop a vision…a big picture outlook for their direction (where they want to go) and when they will start (and I would vote for now), they could have what they want (happier lives). It's ok for Joe to envision himself the leader of his family but he must lead by example and resist his ego temptation to dictate. If Cheryl can envision herself as a child of the Most High God and that she has parity with all others, she can allow herself to be vulnerable; thereby, authentically connecting with others.

In generating direction beyond our human inclinations, spirituality is no exception, as God has a vision for humankind and we all have a spiritual vision of ourselves that is contingent upon our level of spiritual differentiation. If we perceive ourselves with the same limitations and biases we have when we first glanced at the Ugli fruit, we are likely to dismiss ourselves completely without sampling the substance on the inside. Our vision is distorted, and out of that distortion come our maladaptive, dysfunctional and abnormal behaviors. Out of our vision (direction) for godly ideals, we are more inclined to seek the spiritual fruits that will enhance our wellbeing and that of others. We can have expansive views, as exemplified by a Visionary God who brought light to darkness and substance to void; or, we can endorse a myopic vision that promotes depression within ourselves and separation from others.

God has guided my steps and has graced me with a number of different service opportunities. I was blessed with the opportunity to have worked in a service providing agency in the heart of the inner city in St. Paul, Minnesota. Within that agency, we provided a number of in-house and outreach services to clients in need. During some of those outreach efforts it troubled me when our Male Awareness group would visit an adolescent male youth detention center in St. Paul, Minnesota, or when I would visit an urban classroom to mentor youth with challenging classroom behaviors (e.g., poor attendance, defiance toward authority, struggling academic performance, etc.), to witness the lack of vision these young people had. It is not that these youngsters didn't have any vision—they did. Only their vision was distorted by dilapidated and crime infested neighborhoods, stark economic disparities, low academic/vocational aspirations, fragmented and abusive families and a host of sociological maladies that middle and upper class Americans would find hard to conceive. In fact, it might be difficult for some readers to comprehend that some adolescents and young adults aspire to get into jails, detention centers and prisons to establish "street credibility."

These young people may envision themselves becoming the next great rapper or in the starting line up on some professional NBA team. If not this, they may see themselves trapped in an endless cycle of inter-generational poverty, underemployed in menial jobs or producing a number of children with dubious parentage who cycle in and out of governmental systems. This is the vision that is experience through the spiritual lens of an indifferent-heart. When our vision is distorted, we lose our focus upon the Ultimate (God) and the Fruit of the Spirit (which are the attributes of God). When we cannot see beyond the limitations of our lived experiences, we don't strive for anything different. Abraham had difficulty seeing or imagining that he would be the progenitor of a great nation that flows through his linage when he was childless and over 90 years old. His thoughts were limited and his vision was skewed but God had him come from inside of his tent to view the stars in heaven to show him that his descendants will be as numerous as the stars. (Genesis 15:5-NKJV)

Whether one resides in the inner city or rural community…black or white… young or old when they lack a vision or direction, they are literally stuck. There is no movement and oftentimes even those entering into therapy will endorse their depression…helplessness… hopelessness…and despair. I've virtually fought with clients (verbally speaking) who were adept in their intransigence with refusal to change. I believe it was psychologist, Carl Whitaker, who suggested that we need "therapeutic dynamite" to blow people out of their interactive patterns and intransigence. Their "stuckness," which they will complain is woeful and miserable, will not foster a desire for movement; indeed, their misery becomes adaptable and the client fights against attempts to change him or her.

I met with a woman, let's call her Judy. Judy was a delightful, middle-aged, Caucasian woman. She was married for 30+ years with grown children and with a loving and patient husband that yielded to Judy's persistent complaints. Judy had been in therapy for years and with multiple therapists wrestling with the same complaint. She felt that her husband had a greater emotional connection with his sisters (and they with him) and she was alienated and ignored. Her perceptions were borne out in her realities as his family members were fed up with her persistent complaints and indeed started to isolate and disconnect from her over time. Judy saw existing in her husband's family that which was missing in her own family of origin; with greater distance and fragmentation once her mother died.

Judy was referred to me (perhaps deliberately so as I don't engage clients in long term therapy) with persistent depression and anxiety. She also had a substance abuse history; which resulted in an arrest that she was deeply ashamed of. She thought that everyone knew about her ordeal and in a small, rural community, she was probably right. Nevertheless; she tried putting forth a façade that people didn't know and she wouldn't have any conversation about her ordeal to others and it ate away at her. In my view, Judy got a lot of her relationship and dependency needs met through her involvement with therapists and it appeared that previous therapists obliged her needs. I had no intention in fostering her dependency and informed Judy that we would engage in solution-focused, psychoeducational and spiritual-based therapy.

I educated Judy on the spiritual continuum from indifferent-heart to pure-heat realm. I challenged her to reframe cognitions, perceptions and word choices that endorsed a "victim-stance." We identified her responsibilities; along with concrete steps she could take to change self-defeating behaviors and her strained interpersonal relationships. Judy erroneously perceived what her husband's family thought about her; thus, when she quit isolating and approached them with a spirit of kindness, they reciprocated with generosity of spirit. She had to embrace the truth that her family of origin did not have the same degree of closeness that her husband's family has and that it was OK. I challenged her not to carry with her a shameful past of substance abuse and arrest as her "victim" story, but change it to a testimony of "triumph" (hero's story).

Judy had spiritual inclinations and was a Christian, thus, in my therapeutic capacity, I felt that I could talk directly about religious/spiritual matters and I reminded her when Adam and Eve were experiencing shame that they covered themselves up in a futile attempt to hide, which was similar to what she was doing. Shame and guilt demands punishment and as long as she held on to these negative attributes, she remained symptomatic (anxious/depressed); while isolating, disconnecting and erroneously judging others. The essence of God and spiritual advancement is the antithesis of spiritual fetters like shame and guilt. It is transparent! Once she embraced her truth that she erred in judgment and went down an ill-considered path; thus, using her story as testimony that she is on the pathway to recovery, her shame and guilt faded away.

Judy was like one of those "cream" clients. You know...like the "worried-well." They are high functioning, delightful, personable, and consistent with their appointments with a guaranteed payment source. I can see why other therapists kept her for so long. As Judy was making great gains, she was delighted about her therapy experience and wanted to continue with therapy for ongoing support. I dissuaded her from continuing and discharged her from therapy. I suspect that she'll resurface on my schedule or that of another therapist because one doesn't break a history of dependency needs overnight but I've implanted within Judy important, "seeds" of change which she must attend to produce her harvest.

The last spiritual aspect (and not the least in importance) is "connection." If, as I attest, the meaning of our existence is to have healthy relationships and our purpose is to serve and the way of which we are serving is reflected in the Fruit of the Spirit, then the "connection" part of our spirit returns us to our original question of "who?" If "who" we are, are children of the Most High God, then not only do we have a connection with God, we have a connection or fellowship with likeminded individuals. I have had pets that I couldn't have had any greater affinity for! Nevertheless, the Bible instructs us to have dominion over animals (Genesis 1:28-NKJV) and to love one another (which is the greatest act of service--indeed, we are called upon to "love" our enemies). This clearly distinguishes the "who" we are to serve. We may protect animals, use animals for service, eat animals to survive but our true "service" is toward humanity.

The meaning of who we are will be demonstrated by whom we chose to align ourselves with. Apostle Paul instructs, *"Do not be unequally yoked together with unbelievers. For what fellowship has righteousness with lawlessness? And what communion has light with darkness?"* (II Corinthians 6:14-15-NKJV) This will take a bit of spiritual wisdom to discern, as some will use Paul's instructions to justify bigoted views (i.e. no interracial or interfaith marriages) and a negative alliance can lead us into destruction. However, a Christian can be misaligned or unequally yoked with another Christian. A neo-Nazi, conservative Christian would be unequally yoked with a New Age, liberal minded Christian. A Christian with a literal interpretation of the Bible will not mesh well with a Christian who views the Bible figuratively. Someone lower on the spiritual differentiation continuum (indifferent-heart realm) will find little in common with the person that has arrived at the higher end of the continuum (pure-heart realm). It is important to fortify ourselves in the company of like-minded individuals that are heading in the direction of God (and not stuck at lower levels of differentiation). Likeminded others can comfort us, support us, mentor us; thereby, strengthening our edification and understanding upon this journey we've decided to take.

As a therapist, I have heard and I understand the dread in the voices of those who have to experience this physical journey alone. Who wants to live alone…eat alone…go to the movies alone…or even endure difficulties and life challenges alone? As a former professor, I've been to many graduations and it is sad to see that at the height of the students' achievement, there are always some students who are alone. In my clinical work, I know clients who feign their mental illness in order to maintain a relationship with their therapist or service provider in order not to be alone. Some mothers have given birth to over eight children with connection to none of them, in futile efforts in not being alone. They know that as long as they are "ill" or are living "dysfunctional lives," someone being paid to assist them will always be in their lives. One way or another, they are not alone.

In some ways, the journey that we are on can appear to be a solitary journey. Whether we are born into this world individually or we are a part of octuplets, we still have an individual journey to pursue. We have our own minds; our own unique interpretations of even similar experiences; unique gifts, skills and abilities; unique inclinations and aspirations; unique reactions to obstacles and challenges; unique interactions with people along the way and our own unique relationship with God. As powerful as the pull of ego that convinces us that we are alone or in competition with others; we can't do this journey alone and we are never truly alone. When we are not clear about who we are, our loneliness can couple us with undesirable people, undesirable substances and generate undesirable behaviors. If no one else is present, God is with us in our isolation, desperation, alienation, confusion, despair and any challenge or difficulty we have.

I referenced Judy above as someone with dependency needs and my therapeutic response was to break up her therapist dependent needs to foster greater independence. When clients are hurting and entering into a therapeutic process, our initial approach is to foster dependency. We are striving for rapport and developing a "safe holding place" for our clients in order for them to share with us their burdens. We stress confidentiality so that our clients can truly open up and unpack the complexities and shame of their stories to a non-judgmental, affirming and validating therapist. We offer them an unfettered opportunity to reveal the intricacies of their lives that they may or may have not ever told before. Why Judy and others wouldn't want to engage in the therapeutic process indefinitely? In some ways, therapists are like confessionals for priests or representatives of the Most High that receive wounded souls in a conversational embrace.

No matter what a client has done, therapists (though not all therapists can) receive the client without judgment and affirming his or her humanity with dignity and respect. Of course, atrocious acts are atrocious acts but spiritually advanced therapists can separate an atrocious act from the core of spiritual goodness that we all possess. We are intricately and inseparably connected; yet, each of us has an individualized responsibility for our journeys here. In paradoxical fashion, we do have a responsibility for our individual journeys but the essence of spirit that connotes connection means that we also have a responsibility to serve others along the way. I am edified by every connection I make. I am cognizant of the seeds that I am obliged to sow; however, I am not always aware (especially in the moment) of the seeds being sown in my life. I am not always appreciative of the "taxing client" at the moment of our connection and struggle, but then I am reminded that they reveal aspects of myself that I may be oblivious to. If I stay attuned, they will mirror back disconcerting aspects of myself that I must continue to work on.

In the mental health field of service, therapeutic approaches and techniques are innumerable. Not unlike pharmaceutical interventions the next great thing comes in with enthusiastic fanfare and/or aplomb and then fades away as we embark upon the next great thing. What we have learned in this mental health field of psychology and social work is that many of our therapeutic approaches have no greater efficacy than the relational component of therapy. We are not likely to tap dance or twirl during our therapeutic session with the clients but if we did and the client had faith in our therapeutic proficiency, we are likely to produce the same efficacious outcome as any therapeutic intervention.

Why is this the case? It is because connection is important in developing a therapeutic alliance for healing to occur. Relationships are about connections and connection is another aspect of our spiritual selves. And, before we get too puffed up, none of us (regardless of title) provides healing to another person. We are merely instruments from which God's Healing can flow. I have often marveled at the notion of clients who travel from Nebraska or South Dakota to receive therapy from me in a small Southwest Minnesota community. I wish I could say that there was something special about me that people will travel 50...75...100's of miles to receive therapy but it is not about me. My colleagues can boast of their own client connections that certainly supersedes mine. Their willingness to commute great distances is two-fold. 1). Clients are attempting to ensure confidentiality by not seeking therapy in their communities. 2). There is an attachment bond that some clients make with certain therapists that they are willing to commute great distances to continue that therapeutic relationship.

Both situations point to the importance of connection but again, we need to be careful about the types of connections we make. Psalms (1:1-NKJV) points to the importance of relationships, *"Blessed is the man who walks not in the counsel of the ungodly. Nor stands in the path of sinners, nor sit in the company of mockers; but his delight is in the law of the Lord, and in His law he meditates day and night."* I am a "seed sower," "way-shower," or "path-pointer" redirecting lost souls back to God and as a therapist, I have no capacity beyond that. I'm instructed to show people what lies beneath their outer surface. At the supermarket, there are all kinds of fruit that one might describe as "pretty." Perhaps, "pretty" is not the right word for fruit but they are esthetically pleasing, symmetrically shape, and brilliant array of colors with subtle; yet, fragrant scents. These are the ones we will likely pick. How can you walk by a polished red-delicious, Washington apple? Or a bunch of perfectly ripe bananas absent of any bruises or blemishes?

The spirit is that inner stuff…that juicy stuff…that hidden stuff that is beneath the surface of the Ugli fruit. The spirit truly is the essence of who we are and the embodiment of each of the process questions of "who, what, when, where and why" but the "how" is represented in the 2nd part of our triune self—our mental aspect of self. The "how" (as represented in the mind) develops a strategic plan to carry out the will of the spirit. A lower level of spiritual differentiation will construct a life plan that is filled with distortions, self-indulgences and an indifferent-heart. Our perceived "ugliness" and "unworthiness" is replicated in our understanding, life choices, endeavors and the company that we associate with. We are trapped in the ignorance of our own lack of understanding but we really don't care.

Scott is a tall, good looking, intelligent, young Caucasian man who grew up in a rural, Southwest Minnesota community. Ironically, his positive attributes, which should have been "protective factors" was exacerbating his distortion; therefore, his mental illness. This young man was feeling great emptiness and pain and arbitrarily began shredding his arms with deep and long lacerations. He was rushed to the emergency department and subsequently to the behavioral health unit (BHU), with family and professionals hearing the young man's anguish, to safeguard him from himself. "How" we understand the information we receive and "how" we comport ourselves is aligned with our level of spiritual differentiation and has little to do with how intelligent we claim to be.

Scott is an intelligent young man but it was his intelligence, coupled with his adolescent mentality that was confounding him. He viewed himself brighter than his contemporaries and he would cherry pick quotations from the Bible that seemed to be incredulous responses from a Loving God; such as, God reportedly becoming emotionally reactive and wanting to destroy the people of Israel. *"And the Lord said to Moses, "I have seen this people, and indeed it is a stiff-necked people! Now, therefore, let Me alone, that My wrath may burn hot against them and I may consume them…"* (Exodus 32:9-10-NKJV). How does a loving God display wrath and tyranny to a selected group of people on this Earth; while choosing to ignore the rest of creation who didn't happen to be descendants of Abraham?

Scott is not alone in his quandaries. Others have made similar arguments in an attempt to discredit the Bible; thereby, attempting to invalidate the essence of a Loving God. If we step away from theological constructs for just a moment (which is hard to do as I will use a theological concept of "faith" as I continue). Nevertheless, with theology aside, most would agree that our understanding of our world (including ourselves) is "socially constructed." There is not an "objective reality" (even if we use science as our measuring stick, as the "objective realities" of science is provisional). Socially, we construct, deconstruct and reconstruct narratives all the time. We try to drain from the "Ocean of Knowledge" a thimbleful with an arrogant claim that we now know it all! We take bits and pieces of our socially constructed knowledge and share it with others for self-puffery and their edification.

So, what we tend to do in understanding something that we don't know is to reference something that we think we do know. That is, if a child has never heard about dinosaurs, we might reference some type of reptile that the child is familiar with and reference that it is bigger than the elephant the child may also be familiar with. If the child still doesn't understand what we are talking about, we change the references again to create understanding within the ken of the child. Thus, we have "faith" in the child's capacity to understand what we are trying to convey based the other things that we've previously "socially constructed" (i.e., this is what a reptile is and this is what an elephant is; thus, this is what a dinosaur looks like). Indeed, for the rest of us that have never seen these creatures before, we too, must have "faith" that such creatures existed over 65 million years ago and roamed the planet.

When we, as humans, strive to understand the Absolute and Ultimate Essence of God, it will always be limited by our social conceptualizations. That is why we attribute streets paved with gold (a materialistic construct) with an ethereal heaven. Even if Scott was operating from the pure-heart realm of his spiritual development, his view of the world (and himself) would be constrained by the limitations of his human development. His spirit is inseparably intertwined with his mental capacity and human abilities. Nevertheless, he now strives for facts and hard evidence that can provide fodder for debate. Scott has not progressed far enough in his spiritual understandings to resist self-harm and his knowledge is skewed based upon his level of spiritual development.

In the craving-heart realm, people boast of their separateness and distinctiveness; thus, reinforcing their continued separation from others. This is a realm with a hierarchical understanding and exchange with others. Scott, (as I have done in my lower level of spiritual development) looks for fallacies in the Bible to invalidate it in order to ascend to a lofty place of intellectual superiority (arrogance) that he just knows more than others. He is not seeking to understand spiritual ideas to incorporate into his life; rather, he is seeking an intellectual club to whack someone over the head with during a course of debate. In doing so, he diminishes another's spiritual pursuits and does nothing for Scott's own advancement. What he doesn't know is that our socially constructed perceptions shift with our level of spiritual differentiation.

Scott teeters between the indifferent-heart realm (as anyone who truly understood him/herself and understood God would not engage within self-mutilating behaviors) and the craving-heart realm (the need to place himself above others). Likewise, his understanding of a socially constructed artifact (the Bible) is also skewed by his level of spiritual differentiation and creates his "strategy" (the "how") for living, which is borne out in his physical endeavors. Scott's intellect (associated with ego) soars; but he can't figure out a way to stop injuring himself. Indeed, when Scott cuts himself, he does so with deep and long lacerations. His arm(s) is/are totally shredded; yet, Scott often appears proud of his accomplishments. While others "freak out" about what he has done, he remains cool and calm. In the physical essence of who and what we are, the "where" questions relating to Scott's physical being shows up in the self-mutilation of his arms over legs, chest, face, or back and his intellectualizing may be attributed to his "why's."

Unlike Scott, I like to think that I am operating out of the pure-heart realm but I do know that there are elements of the other two realms that appear when I am not vigilant. When I examine a "socially constructed artifact" (The Bible), I don't have to deny it or dismiss it. I don't have to devalue it, debate it, argue it or elevate it. I view it as a tool that assists me in generating greater levels of spiritual advancement. My work at spiritual advancement reminds me and assists me in not creating separation between myself and others. I've never engaged in self- injurious behaviors (SIB) as exhibited through Scott's behaviors (severe cutting) but I've engaged in self-destructive behaviors (e.g., drinking, fighting, etc.) that derived from my lower level of spiritual differentiation. I have engaged people in nonsensical debates, imposing opinions that I like to attest as "facts" that derive from another's socially constructed reality that shifts when new data arrives. I can't see myself "superior" to Scott when I am humbled by the notion, "There, but for the grace of God, go I." Life events and experiences can shape us and I can see how a people's experience of 400 years of slavery can conceptualize God through the lens of fear and wrath. I can see how our degree of spiritual understanding creates our experiences upon this Earth. Therefore, I can see myself in a therapeutic setting, pointing out a pathway to peaceful coexist between one's self and the world that the client dismisses.

At the top of the chapter, I've implied what spiritual adaptation resembles in the pure-heart realm. I have described the essence of spirituality that entails "meaning, purpose, direction and connection." In the indifferent-heart realm, we don't have a clear awareness of our spiritual selves, even if we claim ourselves as being "spiritual." Ask the persons about their understanding of what it means to be spiritual and they don't have a clue. Watch the persons and their behaviors will clearly indicate that they've not progressed far along the spiritual continuum (as evidenced by Joe and Cheryl's stories). In the craving-heart realm, we see the progression from ignorance and narrow self-focus with a greater degree of self-awareness. This degree of spirituality is exhibit by Judy and Scott; with Judy viewing herself with dependency needs and Scott conveying the notion of superiority. However, I mentioned earlier that it was odd for me to see people I would attest residing in the pure-heart realm seeking therapy. I thought it best to give a brief vignette of one of these types of clients who've entered into therapy.

Advancement into the pure-heart realm is not a realm of "perfection." Indeed, notions of "perfection" typically reside in the indifferent-heart realm. The pure-heart realm is a realm of enlightenment; which, I define as having keen knowledge of self plus action steps aligned with this new awareness of oneself. One has spiritually evolved from selfishness to self-awareness to genuine selflessness. The pure-heart realm is a place of personal integrity, where we pull together the disparate pieces of ourselves into an integrated whole. It is a place of optimism vs. pessimism. One has reverence of God and unwavering faith in all aspects of spirituality vs. the material world. This person is humble and simplistic in his or her lifestyle. This type of person has great caring and compassion for others; perhaps to the detriment of him/herself.

This was the case of Peggy. Peggy is a 43 year old, married, Caucasian mother of one adult son. Peggy is slender with cropped blonde hair and greenish-blue eyes. She is attractively dressed with noticeable attention to her grooming but there is nothing garish about her. Indeed, Peggy has a demure persona and would rather blend into the background verses drawing any attention to herself. Peggy is surrounded by people in her family (including her son) with mental health issues and/or physical health issues. Peggy is invested, involved and always on the go. She works fulltime in a service providing field, continues her involvement with her adult son (who has serious, persistent mental illness), a devoted wife and homemaker, with significant involvement with her church and community.

When Peggy presented for therapy, she would have this cyclical bout of depression that she has endured for years that was tied in with her menses. Heretofore, she has marshalled through with her physical complaints that was taking an increasingly psychological toll on her. She reported symptoms of irritability, lethargy, hyper-somnolence, increased confrontations with her husband and other symptoms that led me to a diagnosis of premenstrual dysphoric disorder. I redirected Peggy back to her medical doctor for pharmaceutical support but we also examined her over-investment in the lives of others. She was determined to do "God's Work" but being so greatly other-focused was taxing her psychological and spiritual resources. I reminded Peggy that All-Mighty God rested from creation on the seventh day and instructs us to do likewise and Jesus had to break away from people in order to replenish himself to adequately serve others. Arriving into the pure-heart realm doesn't mean that we abandon ourselves in service of others. It means that we've reclaimed ourselves, in the fullness of our being, and then extend ourselves in service of others.

Peggy was taking on too much! Many of my fellow colleagues take on too much in the service of our clients. And, many others take on too much in the service of their agencies, families, communities and their churches. God expects us to serve but not to take over the responsibilities of others. Peggy is a great servant of God but she needed to be reminded that she needs to be served also.

Throughout our lives there are many things that have shaped our development and create false notions about who we've become. There are certainly loving, kind and wonderful events that need to be recognized, remembered and honored; however, it is likely the unpleasant and traumatic events that shape us in undesirable ways. If we are to purposefully grow on our spiritual path or heal from a traumatic past, we have to engage in the process of self-discovery, mindfulness and action. The following exercise will assist you in this process. As you re-examine your story, identify major events in your life and various developmental stages. Describe interactions and challenging/tragic episodes that you believe have shaped the person you have become. Use the graphic as a template for your journey but record those memories and reflections in a journal. Journaling is a wonderful therapeutic process of externalizing (thus, deconstructing) the totality of your previously lived histories with subsequent action steps to care for the wounded soul within.

There is no hurry, so detail with greater elaboration and specificity in your journal about your earlier life events, interactions, and/or traumatic episodes. Use the process questions to help you find clarity and then deconstruct the narrative (i.e., "Your Story"). Ask "what" questions, such as: What was the event? What caused it to happen? What changed in me following the event?, What was I like before the event?, etc. Examine the "who" questions, such as: Who was directly involved? Who had tacit involvement? Who reinforced the "secret keeping" around the event? Who was victimized? Who was villainous? Who was heroic?, etc. The "when" questions to examine may include: When did the event occur? When does it feel unsafe or scary for me? When do I lose control of myself? When does the event/episode seemingly repeat itself? Examine "where" questions: Where does the psychological trauma reside in my body? Where am I likely to experience flooding thoughts of remembrance? Where can I find refuge from my pain? The "why" questions can be: Why has this event happened? Why am I assessing guilt, shame and blame about the event? Why have I chosen to identify with the disturbing images from my past rather than observing them and letting them go, etc.? Lastly, (but in no particular order) we have "how" questions: How has this event knocked me off track? How has it consumed me for all of these years? How am I keeping the memory of this unpleasant event alive? How am I experiencing this event spiritually, mentally, emotionally and physically? How can I make new meaning out of what has occurred?

Ripening the Fruit -

The Story of Me!

There are significant life events (both good and bad); along with significant people in our lives (absent or present/good or bad) that initially scripts out a narrative about who we are and who we will become. Psychological, physiological, emotional, financial, and spiritual traumas leave an indelible mark in the "narrative" of defining ourselves that is difficult to overcome. But you CAN overcome this initial, poorly constructed script and rewrite a completely new life "narrative!" Begin by an earnest assessment of your own story at various developmental levels (e.g., 0-7, 8-14, 15-21, etc.). Recognize the impact of the traumas and how they have harmed you but start to challenge the core beliefs generated by these false scripts. That is, you must confront and continue to challenge "unlovable schemas," "unworthy schemas," "incompetent schemas," "powerless schemas" and the like.

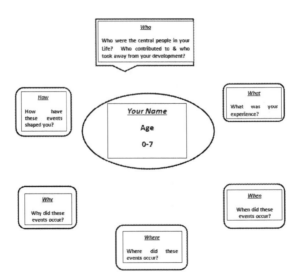

III

Renewing Your Mind

*This I say, therefore, and testify in the Lord, that you should
no longer walk as the rest of the Gentiles walk, in the futility
of their mind, having their understanding darkened, being
alienated from the life of God, because of the ignorance that
is in them, because of the blindness of their heart; who, being
past feeling, have given themselves over to lewdness, to work
all uncleanness with greediness. But you have not so learned
Christ, if indeed you have heard him and have been taught
by Him, as the truth is in Jesus: that you put off, concerning
your former conduct, the old man which grows corrupt
according to the deceitful lusts, and be renewed in the spirit
of your mind and that you put on the new man which was
created according to God, in true righteousness and holiness.*
(Ephesians 4: 17-24-NKJV)

In the field of psychology ("psyche" = mind; "ology" is "the study of"), the practitioners in this field seek to treat and serve those with mental health illnesses, concerns or issues. The medical model of "disease eradication" adds a theoretical framework for our work in this field; however, we must keep in mind that there is a relational component to mental health issues in that mental illness impairs functioning in one's ability to peacefully coexist within oneself and in the world of others (i.e., within families, in communities or within occupations, etc.). As our focus shifts, we adopt various views about etiologies, theoretical constructs and treatment modalities. When we start to look at "relational components" we are really talking about "spirituality." Some clinicians will winch (indeed, some have denied the existence of God), at the nebulous nature of introducing spiritual ideas to clinical practice but I am willing to concede that there can be physiological/biological/emotional/psychological components that can impact mental health. Nevertheless, we can't forget the importance of spirituality on the path to wellbeing. In referencing the Biblical passage above, a spiritual transformation from a lower self to a higher self requires spiritual understandings for a transformation of one's mind.

When we examine the above from a purely mental health perspective, whether it is depression, anger outbursts and/or factors leading to a divorce, it is the "renewing of the mind" that will make all the difference. Let's look at depression. Depression has three negative attributions that create and sustains it. That is, one must perceive negative attributes toward his/herself (e.g., "I'm a loser…unworthy…unattractive…etc.); to others or the world they live in (e.g., "The world is full of evil…people are out to get me…others are keeping me from what I'm entitled to); and to the future (e.g., "It is no use trying, I'm just going to fail anyway"). Brain injuries or some physical impairment to the brain (e.g., use of intoxicants of any form) alters the brain and shapes behaviors; however, our spirit (the ultimate essence of what we are) impacts brain development, functioning and how we think and behave.

Long before we had a psychological profession (or even a medical profession), people had to deal with "maladaptive" ways of "being" or "thinking" in this world. Two thousand years ago we did not have this acquired language that has derived out of these various "scientific" professions to talk about what people were experiencing in the past; however, we can see from the Bible passage that the Apostle Paul is letting us know that from a lower level of spiritual development we can have "*futility of the mind, dark understandings and alienation from others.*" This is depression!

Gladys is a petite (just barely five feet tall), raven hair, middle-aged, married, Caucasian mother of four grown children. Over the years, she has come to see me on several different occasions with the same complaint; a devitalized marriage. She was a demure woman with a flat affect and depressive mood that clearly pointed to major depressive disorder, recurrent episodes. I have also given her a delusional disorder based upon statements made that were consistent with persecutory delusions. She made unsubstantiated allegations of her husband "gas lighting" her by having things disappear and they would reappear with her husband asserting these objects were always there. He'd misappropriate checks and squander her finances. She felt harassed, maligned and that her husband was doing things deliberately to the house to torment her. Having met Gladys' husband, I started to wrestle with the accuracy of the delusional disorder diagnosis I have given Gladys when his character and behavior affirmed for me the accuracy of some of Gladys' allegations that was far from delusional; nevertheless, Gladys' delusions were more global and impacted her ability to work and to fellowship in her church (with thoughts about the pastor and congregation also was out to get her in some way).

Delusional or not, Gladys' perceptions of negative attributes including "*futility of mind, dark understandings and alienation from others*" kept her trapped in an unyielding bout of depression. Gladys had trouble in viewing herself as a "woman of worth" and a "child of God" and gave herself over to the insidious nature of what can occur in small, isolating communities. That is, from social system's theory, we know that closed systems bring about entropy (e.g., death, disorder, dysfunction, decline, etc.) and an open system (negative entropy) brings growth, development and renewal. At the time of this writing, Gladys has filed a petition for the dissolution of her marriage for the umpteenth time and I am not convinced that she won't withdraw this petition prior to its disposition. The "futility of mind" is manifesting in the futility of her behaviors with her petition and withdrawals in the legal system; along with her repetitive entering into and exiting therapy.

As a therapist, I know that unhealthy relationships can make one appear "crazy" and having met Gladys' husband, I could see him engaging in "crazy making" behaviors. At the same time, I also realize that relationship coupling is not often a random occurrence or haphazardly configured. People are coming together (consciously or unconsciously) to work through issues relative to themselves. Though, their mate selection is purposeful, it is not necessarily about the other person as to why we are in relationships. No matter how a relationship may look to others on the "outside" they are often adaptive to those who reside within the relationship. Indeed, there is a concept called, "social exchange theory"; whereas, those in a relationship conduct a "cost/benefit" analysis based upon criterion endemic to each of them to determine if the relationship originates, continues or ends. Assuming one or both choose to end the relationship; it doesn't mean that either or both have worked through the issues within themselves by which they've intuitively selected the other person. If we haven't worked through those issues, we select similar partners that will replicate the same type of relationship mess we've so desperately wanted to leave from.

In some ways, I want to advocate for all of those who love Gladys and are sick and tired of her complaining about her relationship status but Gladys hasn't fully examined her own spirituality (meaning, purpose, directions and connection) and the process questions of "who, what, when, where, why and how" that is connected to her spirituality. Let's, for the sake of discussion here and it is definitely not true, assert that we can all conclude that Gladys' husband is a "jerk." That doesn't free Gladys from her own critical examination and development of self. She is not a "victim" here but in order for her to play out the narrative scripted in her own mind that she is a victim, she needs an antagonist to play the villain. This antagonist is her husband; however, it is not just her husband. There were "villains" at her job that "forced" her out of her job. There were "villains" in her church that "forced" her out of church. There are "villains" in her family that "forced" her alienation from her family.

When there has not been any clear abuse or betrayal in the couple's system, I am not a big proponent of couple's separating to work on their relationship. I get it when it does happen and sometimes it may need to happen but I don't typically endorse this as a strategy for those who want to save their relationship. Having said this, I did propose to Gladys that she extricate herself from her marriage for a week or two to gain some clarity about her decision (one way or another) and to stand firm on that decision once she has made it. My intention for Gladys was for her to do a little "emotional spring cleaning" where she can "open up the windows" and let in some "fresh air." We must have clarity of mind if we are to renew the mind in a meaningful direction.

I like for clients to be mindful, strategic, proactive, and deliberate with their lives. It is the strategies they devise and the implementation of those strategies that lead to personal empowerment. Of course, within partnership relationships, there are others to consider and I wanted Gladys to talk with her husband about her need to get away (only for a short time) to gain some perspective in how she could move forward with greater mental and relationship ease. Gladys didn't proactively or rationally devise a strategic plan or talked with her husband about it. Even if Gladys' husband did not endorse her plan, she'd have the feeling of empowerment in following through with her plan and her husband would have been respected enough to at least know of her plan.

Gladys reactively decided to leave one day, and only for a day. She had never talked with her husband about what we've discussed in session about the plan. I gently chided her for this decision. Interestingly, when she implemented her plan, everything was going great between her and her husband. Gladys had gone out with her husband, having fun, shopping, eating dinner, enjoying the company of her husband. When they returned home, he went back out on his own and this incensed Gladys so much that she decided then and there to leave. She stayed at a local motel and when her husband returned, he frantically tried to find her. He called her phone repetitively and she refused to answer her phone until a day later, when she decided to return home. In gently chiding Gladys, this was neither what I wanted to happen nor what we talked about. Her actions were impulsive and manipulative. Whatever notions one might have about Gladys' husband, he didn't deserve coming home and not knowing the whereabouts of his wife; especially after the great day they both thought that they had with one another. Her actions were not constructive and they did not add to her ability to arrive at a decision that would be definitive.

Spirituality is a focus upon a truth paradigm. Galatians (6:7-NKJV) reveals, *"Do not be deceived, God is not mocked; for whatever a man sows, that he will also reap."* The directional compass for spiritual and psychological wellbeing will always point to God. As spiritual beings, made in the image of God, having a worldly experience, our health and wellbeing will always be in alignment with the Source. We need to understand the "nature" of

God and continue to replicate it in our lives. We can see throughout nature the replenishing, renewal and the revitalization of life. God sets before us clear choices for our healthy renewal process but He insists that we come aboard as Moses instructs, *"I call heaven and earth as witnesses today against you, that I have set before you life and death, blessing and cursing; therefore choose life, that both you and your descendants may live; that you may love the Lord your God, that you may obey His voice, and that you may cling to Him, for He is your life and the length of your days; and that you may dwell in the land which the Lord swore to your fathers, to Abraham, Isaac, and Jacob, to give them."* (Deuteronomy 30: 19-20-NKJV)

I don't know what Gladys will ultimately decide to do about her relationship. She was in therapy for many years prior to meeting with me for this very same issue. I would love to report here that a renewing of her mind has occurred and something different is happening in her life but she may return a week from now…a year from now…5 years from now with no significant movement.

The intransigence that is observed in the case of Gladys is not unique to Gladys. She has bought into the misbelief that she is powerless and a "victim." Unfortunately, too many people endorse the notion of "victimhood." Gladys fights with the notion of mental health issues but our "humanness" draws us to the limitations of "flesh." We wrestle with food, substances, sex, thrill seeking, danger, smoking, obsessive ideas and habitual behaviors that continues to draw us in; thereby, diverting our spiritual path. Some will argue, as Solomon has, that the pursuit of all things is vanity. Good, bad, righteousness or evil is all "grasping for the wind." Solomon writes, in Ecclesiastics (1: 12-18-NKJV), *"I, the Preacher, was king over Israel in Jerusalem. And I set my heart to seek and search out by wisdom concerning all that is done under heaven; this burdensome task God has given to the sons of man, by which they may be exercised. I have seen all the works that are done under the sun; and indeed, all is vanity and grasping for the wind. What is crooked cannot be made straight, and what is lacking cannot be numbered. I communed with my heart, saying, "Look, I have attained greatness, and have gained more wisdom than all who were before me in Jerusalem. My heart has understood great wisdom and knowledge." And I set my heart to know wisdom and to know madness and folly. I perceived that this also is grasping for the wind. For in much wisdom is much grief, and he who increases knowledge increases sorrow."*

Wiser people than I will have to ascertain why it is that the "wisest man in the world" (reportedly) wrestled with this degree of despair but it is a despair that confronts a lot of people. If it is all meaningless, why abandon the cravings of the "flesh" in pursuit of the "spirit?" Apostle Paul echoed similar notions reported by Solomon in Romans, *"For I know that nothing good dwells within me, that is, in my flesh. I can will what is right, but I cannot do it."* Gladys will surely attest that it is "all grasping for the wind" because her life hasn't seen any fundamental changes and she has been going to therapy for years! Why try to do anything if the end result is "futility" or "vanity?" Why get married? Why get a divorce? Why choose to have children? Why choose not to have children? Why educate ourselves or pursue higher echelon roles in society? These "whys" confounded Solomon and Gladys. The "whys" could spark movement for some but the rumination of "whys" often keep us stuck (i.e. "constant analysis creates paralysis").

What these great men and Gladys may not have construed in the midst of their despair is that although, fashioned in "flesh" to exhibit "human form," we are made in the image of God; thus, whatever it is that is comprised of God, we contain. Certainly, we enjoy the essence of each "fruit of the spirit" (i.e., love, joy, goodness, peace, patience, kindness, gentleness, faith, and self-control) but God is far more expansive than these nine specifically identified "fruit." Notice that the fruit of the spirit is not about intellectualizing or rationalizing or trying to discern the "whys" of this world. In addition to the aforementioned "fruit of spirit" God is also Truth; as well as The Creator. Likewise, we (as children of God) are constantly striving for "truth" (which I am going to equate with "integrity") and we have the power of "creativity."

What makes this knowledge important is that when we are inclining toward truth (integrity), we cannot have the negative attributes of depression; while conversely, an expanding vision gives rise to creativity.

49

Out of nothingness (the great void), God envisioned the universe, along with this Earth and the inhabitants of Earth. So out of nothing, something comes into being. As spiritual beings in human form we can create out of the "nothingness" of our ever-changing situations with the imagination to create the "substance" of things that were previously difficult to conceive of. We take it for granted now but it really is a marvel to conceive of live events occurring a continent or two away is unfolding on our TV screens in the comfort of our living rooms. Who could have imaged the Internet or Skyping 2-3 decades ago? The concentration on "self" with the hankering for satisfying the "flesh" takes our eyes off of God; which, reinforces our disempowerment and stymies our creativity.

When we are depressed, we feel as though we have little or no options. We are not tapping into our creativity. Gladys was trapped; not by her circumstances but by how she thought about her circumstances. The futility of Gladys' mind convinces her that she is a victim of her circumstances. The life she lives, the ideas she accepts and the stagnation of a closed system keeps her "breathing in toxic fumes" that continue to make her sick. *"Therefore we do not lose heart. Even though our outward man is perishing, yet the inward man is being renewed day by day. For our light affliction, which is but for a moment, is working for us a far more exceeding and eternal weight of glory, while we do not look at the things which are seen, but at the things which are not seen. For the things which are seen are temporary, but the things which are not seen are eternal."* (2 Corinthians 4:16-18-NKJV)

The next question now becomes, "What is the work of mental health professions who are receiving into therapy the Gladys' of the world?" Gladys' mental health disorder is profound (delusional disorder) but there is no real pharmaceutical approach to manage a delusion. When delusions are profound, talk therapy doesn't dispel a delusion. Though her issue remains, Gladys keeps showing up for something. She wants to reside in an affirming, validating, forgiving, loving presence of the Most High God. She had hope to find this "affirming, validating, forgiving and loving" experience in the confines of her marriage (as we all do) but our partners are limited. Therapy, pastoral counseling or friendship is another replica of the Ultimate in a limited form. Renewing our spirit by tapping into the Essence of God is the ideal but therapists/service providers are physical representatives (or surrogates) of God's Brilliant Light that momentarily comforts those in darkness.

Many of us (therapists/service providers) must constantly reassess what our responsibilities are for the client that comes before us. We are passionate, compassionate and empathic service providers in a life's vocation to assist others in finding their way out of their own misery. We are "path-pointers" and "way-showers" dedicated to healing and service. However, it is not our "duty" (per se) to rescue clients from the lives that they are choosing to live. Redirecting Gladys back to examining her life in line with her values, principles and grand ideas may be all that we can do...indeed, it may be all of what God expects us to do (despite the plethora of our therapeutic interventions). Gladys is obliged to renew her mind in order to experience a life free of darkness and futility. If she is not ready to change her life circumstances or to change how she is thinking about her life circumstances and if we are working harder for Gladys than she is working for herself, it will be us (as healing agents) who are "grasping for the wind" in hopes to produce change.

God, the Creator of the Universe, designs creation and grants us the gift of our physical being in order to experience the creation. Purely spiritual beings could not experience this physical world of creation or tap into the array of human emotions that we are granted for this experience without our physical essence. This opportunity for human experience is an example of God's Love for us. God asserts that He has something "special" (creation) and He wants "special" entities to enjoy it. In God's desire for us to make the best of this life's journey, God provided us with a human exemplar (Jesus) to model the way for us. After God provided the "creation" and the "model" He granted us the benefit of the Holy Spirit to "comfort" us throughout the rest of our journeys. Everything that we need, we have. What is missing is our responsibility and efforts. Therapists can't carry the clients and God is not going to "carry us through" our life experiences (per se). To be clear, we will never be abandoned by God but we have to do our work as well.

If we are trying to succeed in this world, we must set up our environments that are conducive for our successes. We need to change our cognitions and embrace the notion of "I can" vs. "I can't." Both Solomon and Paul know that the limitations of our flesh will circumvent our efforts; thus, we build into our environments opportunities for our success. An addict, having successfully completed treatment, is not served well by returning to his/her former environment that has seduced him/her into substance abuse in the first place. We've seen children, with a litany of mental health diagnoses head off to structured, residential treatment programs, learning skills that all but extinguish acting out behaviors, only to return home to an unchanged, chaotic environment, triggering behaviors worse than before. Likewise, dieters won't maintain their miraculous weight loss when their cabinets and refrigerators are filled with the same calorie rich foods that created their weight gain in the first place. Clients, wrestling with their own mental health issues will not find relief when they retain their former mind frame, while remaining in the same environment, to deal with their daily troubles.

Gladys is not pursuing the "lust of the flesh." She is not inclining for an adulterous relationship or imbibing in intoxicants that would clearly divert her path from God, but from a psychological perspective, she is still indulging in the flesh. Her feelings of unworthiness, helplessness and despair has become the narrative that she has help to write about herself and she continues to endorse each time she refuses to take some action. *"For those who live according to the flesh set their minds on the things of the flesh, but those who live according to the Spirit, the things of the Spirit. For to be carnally minded is death, but to be spiritually minded is life and peace. Because the carnal mind is enmity against God; for it is not subject to the law of God, nor indeed can be. So then, those who are in the flesh cannot please God."* (Romans 8:5-8-NKJV)

Gladys is not exercising her "self-control"; thus, giving herself over to the vagaries of her husband whose investment in her and/or their relationship is dubious at best. She has given herself over to therapists for years so that she can abdicate her responsibility to affect control/change in her own life. Her diagnoses, in some ways, keep her stagnant because she can blame her mental health condition for her inability to establish some clear direction and movement in her life. Not unlike the person who succumbs to his or her addiction, Gladys has given in to the disempowerment and despair of her disorders. Gladys appears to be a "gentle" and "kind" soul when she presents for therapy but has harshness and criticism of both herself and her husband that slips out of her from time to time while she is in therapy but may reveal itself more frequently in the private confines of her home environment. She has also unplugged from her employment and church with similar harsh views and criticisms.

Gladys has not lost her rhetoric about God, because if you asked her, she'd readily acknowledge the existence of God, but she has little faith in God. With little faith in God, we tend to rely on our own notions about ourselves and our experiences with the world but what we already know about Gladys is that her notions about herself and the world are distorted. The "measure of faith" that God has bestowed upon all of us can be developed within each of us; therefore, Gladys can plant, produce and harvest each and every fruit of the spirit. She can manifest "joy," "peace," "patience," "goodness" and the like whether she chooses to extricate herself from a dissatisfying relationship or if she elects to remain in it. Even though the etiology of mental illness may confound theorists, researchers and clinicians, if mental health was present in Gladys and changed to mental illness; mental illness can then change to mental health.

To Gladys, or anyone of us who no longer wants to "walk like the gentiles," we are empowered to "renew our minds" and proceed on this journey as a new man or woman. Renewing the mind will take a conscientious effort on the part of each individual to pursue higher level principles and a godly nature. If Gladys can rebuild herself from the person who touts to know God to the type of person who has a relationship with God, she'll no longer need the revolving door of therapy only to remain in her indecisiveness and her misery. There is the "fruit of patience" that we all must keep in mind when we are making a transition, but this doesn't mean we are to remain forever stuck. Gladys hasn't set up a vision for what a healthy lifestyle looks like for her; while systematically taking steps to achieve it.

Rather, she stews in misery, thinking that it is the fault of others and her life circumstances.

With things related to spirit and God, transformation can happen instantly. That is, without expectation or notice, instantly we can move from being unknown to celebrity status. We can instantly come into enormous wealth. We can instantly jump ahead of all the other "seemingly" more qualified individuals pursuing a job acquiring a job that we don't even believe that we were qualified to do. Instantly, a prognosis of impending death due to some malignant health condition can miraculously be eradicated from your body. Within an instant, one can wake up and have the courage to extricate one's self from an abusive, devitalizing relationship, while previously feeling trapped in for years. God is not a respecter of time and He can have a transformation happen instantly but the reason "patience" is a fruit of the spirit, God allows for the passage of time for most things to ripen.

Oftentimes, clients want their therapeutic experience to create instantaneous change within them and as a brief therapist, I may be inadvertently promoting "instantaneous change." However, I caution clients about instantaneous expectations with the following analogy. If someone's lifestyle has caused him or her to accumulate 600lbs before "waking up" and wanting to do something about the enormous weight gain, he or she cannot go to the gym for a week with the expectation that an ideal weight will result. Nor is therapy a "quick fix" in this regard. The renewal (changing) of one's mind can be instantaneous as well as the role of therapy can help to facilitate this but the effort to achieve sustaining change is in the hands of the client. Sustaining change takes perseverance and "patience." Therefore, "patience' is a valued "fruit of the spirit." I've planted numerous "seeds" in Gladys' "field of consciousness" and I have no idea what has taken root. I am often amazed, when hearing feedback from people later, of the seeds I've dispensed that permeated their "soil" and has developed into a fully fruit bearing plant later on.

What becomes disempowering for many of us is the perceived enormity of things. Break ups, in our minds, are huge! It doesn't matter if one is

13 years old and are experiencing what others would dismiss as merely "puppy love" or 90 years old and broke up with someone in the assisted living residence. Losses are perceived as catastrophic; whether one losses a favorite broach or an expected opportunity. We personalize things, magnify things and make them so insurmountable that it can only produce our misery. When the "molehills" of our life experiences are represented as "mountains" in our minds, we will feel defeated but what we forget is that whatever we are confronting in life is an artifact of creation adding to our human experience and transitory in nature.

"All conditioned things rise, fall and fade into oblivion." If there is a transitory nature of all things, our misery comes into being by trying to hang onto to what is inherently impermanent as if what we are attempting to grasp is permanent. In this case, Solomon was indeed right about our efforts are like "vanities" and the "grasping for the wind." We cannot hang onto our youth, our vitality, our wealth or our expectation about how a relationship MUST be and then impose those notions upon someone else. Spend some time getting to know yourself (and your relationship with God). The clearer you are about whom you are and your relationship with God, the more incline you are to make life decisions that are aligned with the Will of God that grants you peace. The following exercise will help with the renewal of your mind by first reclaiming yourself.

Ripening the Fruit-Mindfulness

Mindfulness is the awareness that keeps us present. It is not "hyper-vigilance" or "scanning" for the reoccurrence of past events that are laden with powerlessness and defeat. Nor is it projecting ahead with anticipatory fears of impending doom. It is consciously embracing the peacefulness and powerfulness of the present moment. ("This is the day God has made-rejoice!") It is a daily process of reclaiming your "true" self (which is free of the blemishes and distortions created by the mind). Ask yourself, "If I actually am in the present moment, unencumbered by the past and fearless of my future, what would I do this very moment?" Will I venture outdoors? Perhaps go to the grocery store? Will I say, "Hello," to my neighbor? Will I reconnect with an old acquaintance or family member? Will I forgive the transgressions of others and own my limitations for simply being human? Will I embrace that spark of creativity that I've tamped down over the years (or that has been minimized in me by others)?

Mindfulness is also "meta-awareness." That is, you are "aware of your awareness." It is not denying what may come up for you in the present moment but the awareness that for whatever comes up (e.g., fear, loneliness, lust, hatred, anger, irritation, panic, jealous, resentments, etc.); it is not you! You are not your thoughts. You are not your emotions. You are not your past. And you are not the accumulation of negative things that may have happened to you. Therefore, you can become the witness to the fear arising within you and not become that fear. You can become aware of the hatred or lust arising within you without becoming hateful or lustful.

After you've gain insight into your past; while deconstructing the false power that has held you stuck with your mindfulness and present awareness, start generating action steps for changing your direction. What is your plan...your agenda...your method for creating a healthier you? If past events, negative interactions with others and traumatic episodes have shaped you in the way that you no longer desire, what are the new action steps that you will do to become the man or woman that you want to be? Implement a strategy for reclamation of you that you'll carry out daily.

Address each with every facet of your being (e.g., spiritual, mental and physical).

Today, I will do the following to enhance myself spiritually:

_____

_____

_____

_____

Today, I will do the following to enhance myself mentally:

_____

_____

_____

_____

Today, I will do the following to enhance myself physically:

_____

_____

_____

_____

IV

Ripening and Rotting

The Lord is my shepherd;
I shall not want.
He makes me to lie down in green pastures.
He leads me beside the still waters.
He restores my soul;
He leads me in the paths of righteousness
For His name's sake.
Yeas, though I walk through the valley of the shadow of death,
I will fear no evil;
For you are with me;
Your rod and Your staff, they comfort me.
(Psalm 23: 1-4-NKJV)

I've been paying attention to many of the television ministries and I must say that many of them are extraordinary, relevant and necessary. Should you doubt the popularity of these ministries, watch the camera pan the audience of stadiums filled with spiritual-hungry people yearning for a deeper relationship with God. Among the pearls of wisdom, compassion and understanding that is offered by these ministers appears to be a sprinkling of fear and condemnation. Spiritual seekers are being cautioned about their conduct that may lead them to a fiery abyss of infinite suffering and pain. Contemporary ministers may be a little conflicted about their fear and condemnation message butted against the ultimate message that "God is Love," but they continue to promote this message. This conflicting message is hard to reconcile with those who recognize the Bible as their only credible source; thus, the various quotes from the Bible to "fear the Lord" is often softened or reframed to have a "reverential fear of the Lord." A "reverential fear" connotes a degree of "respect" or "love" but these are not the words used in the Bible. With this euphemistic reframe notwithstanding, we are still left with the notion of "condemnation" if we don't have this "reverential fear" of God.

When fruit ripens, we consume it. When it rots, we discard it. Likewise, we may think of ourselves as "rotting fruit" to be discarded by God when we are not pleasing Him but the truth is, God disposes of NO ONE! There is no "condemnation notions" in the "mind" and "heart" of God. "Now wait just a minute, Al," the reader might say. "Have you not read the Bible with very clear condemnation stories of those who did not fear God?" "Have you forgotten the severe retribution from God, when He and Moses returned to the camp with the Israeli's worshiping the golden calf?" The reader might go on to offer a direct quote from the Bible that bolsters his/her position, *"And the Lord Said to Moses, 'I have seen this people, and indeed it is a stiff-necked people! Now therefore, let Me alone, that My wrath may burn hot against them and I may consume them.'"* (Exodus, 32: 9-10-NKJV) Surely, this can be touted as "discarding of rotting fruit."

To this point, I have little in the way of an argument for the reader. When people are locked into their notions about God that are supported by citations that they claim to be irrefutable and credible, there is no argument that others can make to move them. Nevertheless, this distortion (and dare I say, "perversion") of God creates incredible harm. How we see God is very important. If we see God as an "Autocratic Disciplinarian" then it stands without reason that our best bet is to fear God. We have notions of correction and punishment meted out by a Hyper-vigilant God, trying to catch us being bad. As our consciousness shifts, with our spiritual maturity, we view God as the "Archetype of Love" and then we strive for a relationship with God. "Fear" generates different lived experiences in life than does "love." Fear-based individuals will generate harm. Love-based individuals generate peace and healing. Allow me to present this harm in two separate cases.

Brenda is a 42 year old, twice divorced, Caucasian mother of four adult children that have disengaged from her. She carried the weight of a middle-aged, Midwestern, rural community woman who perhaps retained a few pounds from each of the four children she gave birth to, but it didn't distract from her beauty. She was attractive, loving, kind but also insecure. Brenda presented for therapy with classic anxious and depressive symptoms, which she purports to have had for years. These symptoms have been more vividly felt in the last ten years following her divorce from a man she described as having been physically, emotionally and sexually abusive toward her. She railed against the husband who treated her so badly in her 2nd marriage but ironically, it was him who divorced her and despite her characterizations of her ex-husband, she continued to grieve the loss of that relationship for every year following their divorce.

Brenda grew up in a community with a ubiquitous religious foundation that teetered between Catholicism and Lutheranism. Nevertheless, Brenda hated and denounced God, because, "God was shoved down my throat for years while I was growing up and he never showed up in my life." Brenda was raised in a "godly" home with her mother so immersed in Scripture that she wasn't able to see or protect Brenda from a physically and sexually abusing stepfather. Brenda was sexually abused from the ages of 9 to 13 and when Brenda tried to bring this secret to light, she was banished from the home as a liar and temptress. How does one wrap their "heads" and "arms" around a loving God when the "representatives of God" behaved so poorly?

Brenda was broken and her spirit continued to fragment as she endured multiple foster home placements. She married early to escape the misery of her childhood; while erroneously seeking solace in an untenable marriage, with a man who was likely as broken as she was. Of course, we all know that "hurting people hurt others" (and themselves) along with "broken people breaking things," and Brenda's relationships were no exception. In her marriages they both hurt and harmed one another to the point that neither could endure in the relationship. The marriage Brenda idealistically hoped for to save her from her childhood resulted in the same abuse and neglect that she was so familiar with. Even her two children born of this relationship (which she hoped to be the substance of healing, peace and joy for her), ended up being unwanted appendages that she was unable to care for and relegated to the foster care system.

Given that pathology is often repeated, Brenda tried it all over again without repairing the defective schema of her unworthiness; thus, selecting another "unworthy" partner, who also caused her much pain and ultimately "kicked her to the curb." Most of us have little use for rotting fruit and will readily dispose of it without much thought and Brenda's lived experiences resulted in her getting disposed of. Fortunately, Brenda wasn't an illegal substance abuser but her 2nd husband was a methamphetamine abuser and that contributed to the dysfunction and demise of the 2nd marriage. Brenda prided herself in not slipping down the road of illegal substances but she was medicating her anxiety and despair with alcohol and checked out from being a good care provider for the two additional children that she brought into this world. They, too, became the product of the child welfare system and all of the children felt disdain for and disconnected from their mother.

So, Brenda hates her life, hates her ex-husband, hates God and denies the existence of a God that would have granted her the life she has led. If she ceases to acknowledge God, she certainly doesn't have any "reverential fear" of God and would likely attest that she has lived a life of "condemnation." She can envision herself to be the "rotting fruit" that is discarded again…and again…and again. As God comes down from the "mountaintop" to "discover" Brenda who denies and has disdain for Him and she seeks comfort in the "golden calf" as represented by her failed marriages, disconnected children, and alcoholism, does God now, strike her down? Does He banish her to hell? Some would say, "Yes," as some religions would evidence her marriage and remarriage as a sin of adultery that carves out a pathway toward hell. For others, the only "unforgivable sin" is blasphemy of the Holy Spirit, and Brenda has certainly engaged in that. Thus, Brenda's fate is sealed!

Brenda distorts a view of God with the denial of His existence and the outcome of her future life experiences doesn't bode well unless she has a substantial change in her vision of God. We cannot go to the Source to be made whole if we deny the Source exists. Nevertheless, a faulty connection to the Source, with distorted views, produces its own degree of harm. Let's talk about Johnny. Johnny is a 35 year old, biracial man. He takes good care of himself with a regular gym routine and he fits the ideal image of what women would clamor for in a chosen partner (e.g. tall, dark and handsome). Johnny is a religious man and he reads his Bible faithfully. He endeavors (and some would say, rigidly) to bring religious values into his home. He has endorsed the hierarchy of things placing God at the top, with Johnny being the "head" of his household, followed by the subordinates of his wife and child.

Johnny feels that it is his duty (as the head of the household) to inculcate religious doctrine into his household with service and honor to God. Johnny is married to Melody and they have a two year old son, Jeremiah. As part of the family's daily ritual, they give praise and prayer at mealtime with mom and child signing off on dad's recitations with an "amen." Those of you with two year olds or have had two year old children understand (even intuitively for those without child development knowledge) that a child at this age is developing his/her autonomy and will tell a parent, "No" a lot. "Can you come sit by momma?" "No." "Can you give me a kiss?" "No." And on the day of Johnny's rage toward Jeremiah, Johnny expected a "signoff" of his recitation and Jeremiah said, "No."

As the religious leader of Johnny's household, Johnny first tried to cajole Jerimiah in the importance of him signing off appropriately and Jerimiah plied him with an obstinate, "No." Johnny changed his tactics to firmness and insistence but Jerimiah was equally firm…"No." Johnny lost his patience and wailed on the child's bottom. We have a two year old crying out at the top of his lungs, a mother terrified and a father tempered in the thought process that he was doing God's bidding. There was significant bruising on Jeremiah's buttocks when their childcare worker was changing his diaper the next day and she made a report to child protective services; resulting in Johnny coming to me for an anger management evaluation.

When Johnny presented for his assessment, he was aloof and arrogant. He was fortified in his belief that he had not abused his child and the Bible gives him permission to raise his child with corporal punishment. He may have been referencing biblical quotes like the following: *"Do not withhold correction from a child. For if you beat him with a rod, he will not die. You shall beat him with a rod, and deliver his soul from hell."* (Proverbs, 23:

13-14-NKJV). He also expressed that his son might have defied him with his actions but he certainly wasn't going to "disrespect God." The abuse of a child stirs all kinds of negative emotions within us about the abuser (or any perpetrator) but the advancement in our own spiritual acuity will forestall our viewing of Johnny through a lens of condemnation. Johnny, indeed all of us, will always act out the level of spiritual differentiation that we are at. Johnny looked "good" on the outside and was striving for "good" intentions but he wasn't aware of the "rotting" on the inside that was making him overcompensate with religiosity as a means for covering up his own internal shame.

Two year old Jerimiah and forty-two year old Brenda couldn't be more different in terms of race, age, gender, status of life and personal development; however, each are experiencing similar pathways in life that may leave them in the fear of God and/or in disengagement from God. Assuming each of these suffering souls died today, the prevailing religious doctrine would further banish them from God's loving embrace. However, religious doctrine and dogma is not God. They are constructs of humanity that aid us in understanding our spiritual journey and the Ultimate Essence of God but we can't conflate the two. Solomon, reportedly the wisest man that ever lived informs us that, "*Then the dust will return to the earth as it was. And the spirit will return to God who gave it.*" (Ecclesiastes 12:7-NKJV)

God is Love and love will always vanquish fear. They cannot coexist in the same space, just as flicking on a light vanquishes darkness from the room. The First Epistle of John reveals to us, "*…God is love, and he who abides in love abides in God, and God in him. Love has been perfected among us in this: that we may have boldness in the day of judgement: because as He is, so are we in this world. There is no fear in love; but perfect love casts out fear, because fear involves torment…*" (4:16-18-NKJV). Brenda had a clinical diagnosis of anxiety and depression but anxiety is often thought of as a "manifestation of our fears"; along with depression that is considered "anger turned inward." Each is an impediment to spiritual growth and development. Brenda thought critically of herself, others and the world. She worried about her capacity to navigate successfully in this world and hunkered in the darkness (and familiarity) of her own distorted schema. Her experience in her family of origin was mired in dysfunction and pathology, thus, this intergenerational curse had her play out this dysfunction and pathology in the relationships she has chosen and instilled in the next generation.

Contrary to those who preach "fear" and "condemnation," the Bible also reveals that *"…God has not given us a spirit of fear, but of power and of love and of a sound mind"* (II Timothy, 1:7-NKJV). Brenda feels powerless. She discounts her capacity to be loved and to give love. She is tormented by fear and depression. She numbs herself with alcohol and refuses to believe in a Loving God that could lead her out of her darkness. Thus, my therapeutic approach was not to focus on the Entity of God, but the Attributes of God (Fruit of the Spirit). Atheists, agnostics and to my knowledge (quite frankly, I've only met a few people endorsing the following and it is not a subject matter that I would study), demonic worshipers are in pursuit of the Fruit of the Spirit. The reader may quickly challenge me on this last statement and I will willfully stand corrected but with the few examples of people I've known having this distorted view (Satan worshipers) still desired peace of mind and a loving connection with others. If this is true, they still seek the Essence of God in a distorted fashion.

Brenda thought of herself as rotting vs. ripening; thus, not deserving or entitled to God's Love. As such, she couldn't conceptualize in her mind, due to her upbringing that an Entity that loves her existed. I had to assist Brenda in breaking her unhealthy attachment to the past, including an abusive ex-husband who divorced her and forged what appeared to be a healthier relationship with the new woman he married (i.e., he was freed from meth and established a home and lifestyle that appeared significantly better than when Brenda was with him). What a message that is transmitted to Brenda in that an abusive and drug addicted person discards her but rallies to recovery and well-being in the absence of her. Thus, her loss remains palpable to her all these years later in not knowing what and how to grieve.

In simplistic terms, "grief" is the process of redefining oneself in the space of the loss. Regardless if the loss is related to a severed limb, a job, a death or the dissolution of a marriage, one has to redefine oneself. Divorce is not simply a legal dissolution; it is also psychological, emotional, familial, communal, financial, spiritual, etc. The legal process continues to wreak havoc upon Brenda with the loss of the investment in resources she was attached to (i.e., home, auto, furniture, mementoes, etc.). She was severed from psychological and emotional identity of a partnership where she could speak of her "husband" and describe herself as a "wife." Despite the dysfunction in her family of origin and the toxicity that existed in her marriage, she lost her attachment to her husband's side of the family (and the kids that were a byproduct of her marriage). She remains divested from the community and the few friends that have seen the two of them as a couple. Financially, she fell upon economic hardships, despite receiving half of the meager resources, due to her depression making it difficult for her to maintain employment; whereas, her ex-husband got clean from his drug use and stabilized his life. She was grieving the loss of the relationship she wished she had; expressing anger and envy that her ex-husband was thriving so well. Her spiritual severance (which she disclaimed spiritual ideas long before meeting either of her two husbands) has pushed her further away from notions of God.

Brenda had to work on forgiveness; which was no easy feat. She hated her stepfather's abuse and his molestation of her; while her mother professed Christian ideas and sided with the perpetrator against her. She hated God for not showing up when she cried out. She hated her mate selection choices that resulted in two failed marriages. She hated the fact that she lost her children to the child welfare system. She hated the fact that she longed to be back in a relationship with a man who abused her so, and "kicked her to the curb." And, she hated herself with each succeeding breath and the dismal life she has heretofore led.

During the therapeutic process, I typically promote journaling and handwriting out daily affirmations. We often have a negative script in our minds that disconfirm our value and worth; thus, I seek to have clients rewrite positive mind scripts for themselves, about themselves. As sophisticate as the brain is, it can't make a distinction between positive and negative statements. If the brain "hears" the statement, "You are stupid," the brain "says" "Sign me up for that." If the brain "hears", "You are brilliant," the brain says, "Sign me up for that too." Brenda resisted affirmations. It felt futile to her to write out positive statements about herself on a daily basis that she didn't believe was true. My work shifted to simply fostering a "safe holding environment" to allow Brenda to tell her story. My therapeutic style generally opposes people wallowing in their misery and regurgitating their life story over and over again but Brenda wasn't prepared to move so quickly; therefore, I positioned myself to become a validating listener for her to express the muck in her life that has tormented her so.

The word, "therapy" means to "heal"; thus, "therapists" are "healers" but it is hard to restore people with a broken or fragmented schema to a full integral self (e.g., spiritual wellbeing, mental wellbeing and physical wellbeing) without the intervention of God. I would like to boast of some keen therapeutic accomplishment of mine but I am in the early stages of working with Brenda and her transition from an "indifferent-heart" to a "craving-heart," where therapy has a chance to take root (both concepts are explained in detail in my book, *Fruit of the Spirit: A Primer for Spiritual-minded Social Workers*) will truly be based in God's grace and mercy for Brenda to transition into the new realm. *"For the Lord God is a sun and shield; The Lord will give grace and glory; No good thing will He withhold from those who walk uprightly."* (Psalms 84:11-NKJV)

There are agnostics and atheists in this world who have not experience the trauma that Brenda has and have come to their belief systems with introspective, deliberative and earnest critical analysis to arrive at the conclusion that Brenda as drawn. They'll offer intellectual fodder, framed in an empirical science package (scientific methods) that no Deity exists. With observation and experimentation, they can conclude that there is an "objective reality" far superior to any faith-based model that indulges people's fantasies. The fallacy of this argument is trying to measure the Infinite and Ultimate with finite tools that will come from all of our human endeavors. Indeed, it takes a greater amount of faith (and perhaps incredulity) to believe that the universe was the result of an explosion of energy and matter smaller than the size of one's fist over 13.82 billion years ago. However, the credence given to the position of Brenda and other non-believers (no Loving God exists) can be justified by the treatment of Brenda and Jerimiah by those of us that purport to believe, yet are confusing rhetoric from the Bible illustrating the "wrath of God."

We socially construct categories and language in an attempt to understand and communicate to each other about our understanding. Though the "word" is powerful, it is limiting. When authors of text written thousands of years ago it has context, meaning, historical and cultural reference points of the times. Even if historical prophets were able to envision life in the 21st Century (e.g., Smart Phones, Internet, computers, etc.), what reference point could they make at that time to convey these visions received from our time? It makes sense that in a polytheistic society of people making multiple types of sacrifices to multiple types of gods that the notion and desire of sacrifice would come into play even with those worshiping a monotheistic God. Society evolves from animal sacrifice to the notion of a human (aborted) sacrifice with Abraham and Isaac to the ultimate sacrifice of Christ so that we don't have to bring death to any lifeform to grant honor and praise to God. (Although, it should remain clear that to pursue God and spiritual ideas will, indeed, sacrifice our lower self.)

For those adherents to a monotheistic God, represented in the Old Testament, it may have made sense to grant God such high esteem and reverence that mere mortal haphazardly entering into the presence of God was killed immediately. However, as we evolve in our spiritual maturity represented by the New Covenant, God is a less menacing and wrathful God. The truth is, an Immutable God of Love could never be "menacing" or "wrathful" at any time. There is no "fear" associated with a Loving God; therefore, no "condemnation" from God. It is our conceptualizations or limited understanding of God that is constantly changing based upon our social constructs and level of spiritual differentiation. "*Therefore, since we are the offspring of God, we ought not to think that the Divine Nature is like gold or silver or stone, something shaped by art and man's devising.*" (Acts 17:29-NKJV)

Brenda needs to know that the Creator is a God of Love! Her mother may have been immersed in religiosity and with her limited understanding, she disposed of her daughter. Her mother is no different than the Pharisees of Old, choosing to stone a woman for her perceived improprieties verses engaging her with the compassion exhibited by Jesus Christ. A loving God has no ego to bruise that he would banish Brenda to an eternity of Hell simply due to her denying Him out of her ignorance and pain. The God of Love does not vanquish agnostics or atheists because they've erroneously denied His existence. The God of Love wouldn't endorse Johnny's action of corporally punishing his 2 year old son, Jeremiah, in a misguided effort to show deference to Him. While at the same time, neither Johnny nor Jeremiah will be lost to God.

As I've stated previously, the essence of our spirituality has four distinct aspects; which are meaning, purpose, direction and connection. If I partition out "direction" in reference to the above discourse, it underscores the ideas of the "ripening and rotting" metaphor. In cybernetic or system's theory we have such terms as "entropy" (i.e., all systems are destined for death, destruction, disorder and decline) and "negative entropy" (i.e., movement toward growth, development, order and renewal); therefore, the direction we head will enliven us or deaden us. Similarly, we can think of Eastern concepts of "attachment" and "non-attachment" (hanging on to our misery or letting it go). Or we can examine gardening concepts or social/educational learning concepts of "attending" and "non-attending" (what we attend to enhance our learning and/or grow in our lives and what we do not attend to dies). Or we can even incorporate relational concepts of "contributing to" or "contaminating" relationships (solvency). At the end of the day, spirituality points to a bifurcated "direction" of "ascension" or "descending" and in this case, keeping with the fruit metaphor, we are either "ripening or rotting" (going toward God or away from Him).

Now some fruit ripens even after having been picked from its source (e.g., bananas, apples, honeydew melons, papayas, etc.); while some fruit, after having been picked from its source, is as ripe as it will ever be (e.g., cherries, lemons, oranges, pineapples and indeed the Ugli fruit). The important thing here is that it is the "source" (or our "Source") that gives either fruit and/or spiritual beings the capacity to grow into its or our fullness. Some fruit (unfortunately) will rot on the vine. The circumstances in Brenda's life may have had her plucked too soon from the vine or not adequately nourished from the vine of her biological parents but depending upon the type of fruit she is, she may still have time to ripen. The spiritual direction we chose in life will keep the rest of us "ripening on the vine" or "rotting within our skin."

Unfortunately, the circumstances in Brenda's life had her "choose" anxiety, dissatisfaction and despair. In some ways, this may sound like, "blaming the victim." Brenda didn't "choose" a pretentious mother and an abusing stepfather. She didn't "choose" to be expelled from her home. She didn't "choose" abusive or drug using husbands. Why then would she "choose" to ruminate in the dissatisfaction of her life that leads to despair? Interestingly, we are right back to the "direction" aspect of our spiritual essence. If we are not heading towards God, we are heading toward despair and some of us will even choose the condition of our lives to align with the degree of connectedness that we have with God (or lack thereof). You wouldn't think that people would opt for misery but the Bible reveals that our spiritual orientation can be like dogs returning to eat their own vomit. Solomon wrote, *"As a dog returns to his own vomit, so a fool repeats his folly."* (Proverbs, 26:11-NKJV)

Of course, Brenda is not a "dog" and she is not literally eating her own "vomit" and she is not a "fool." She has lived a life of trauma and despair but figuratively the Proverb is very apt for her life. She was seeking salvation from an untenable childhood experience to find her mother and stepfather rolled into one-the first husband she married. The two children they produced, neither were able to keep in their custody. Virtually the same story was played out in her 2nd marriage. Recall that despite the years of abuse she took at the hands of her 2nd husband, it was him that ended the marriage with her and ten years after the fact, Brenda is still grieving the loss of that relationship. Will she return to her own "vomit" (figuratively)? Yes. She has and she will continue to do so unless she has a spiritual rebirth and a cognitive shift to allow her to change the direction she has been heading from a life that is "rotting" to one that is "ripening."

An important thing for all of us to remember is that all fruit is perishable! Nature reveals for us the impermanent condition of all things. All things "arise into consciousness, fall from consciousness and fades away." In my youth, I couldn't imagine reaching the old…old age of 30. It was an eternity away and almost inconceivable! In fact, with fatalistic notions, I thought that I would die before I reached the ripe old age of 30. Having surpassed the age of 30 by a couple of decades, it is now hard for me to imagine how quickly life has shot by. Depending upon one's perspective (and stage of life) our life's journey isn't a marathon or a leisurely jog… it is a sprint. It could be a 100 year burst to the finish line but it is still quickly over. This is why we must be mindful and work quickly to arrive into and experience the fruits of the "pure-heart" realm. We are continuing to have a human experience (God's gift to us) but our experience is in relationship with God. We can cease to deny God (as may be the case in the "indifferent-heart" realm). We can quit fighting with God (as may be the case in the "craving-heart" realm). We walk in partnership with God, "hand in hand" knowing that we are His offspring, made in His very image (as in the case when we arrive at the "pure-heart" realm).

The arrival into the "pure-heart" realm doesn't immune us from having life experiences. Spiritual adherents will have checkered pasts (consider Mary the prostitute becoming one of Christ's most faithful servants or Jacob, the "Trickster," becoming "Israel," which is "One who wrestles with God and wins" or "the Prince of God"). The arrival in this realm doesn't keep us there (consider David's anointing that makes him king only to slip into an adulterous relationship with Bathsheba and Moses' disobedience kept him out of the Promised Land). The arrival in the "pure-heart" realm doesn't make us "perfect beings" (consider Judas, the "Betrayer of Christ" and Peter who renounced knowing Christ). The direction we are heading is a march toward God with human inclinations that will have us falter along the way. I've stumbled quite a bit upon my spiritual journey, with the Mercy and Grace of God lifting me back up. I've exemplified each realm on the spiritual continuum. Unlike Brenda, I've never disclaimed the existence of God. However, just like Brenda and the rotting of my own soul, I've acted just like Brenda ("There, but for the Grace of God, go I.").

There is a confounding tension that we must work out as we are experiencing this "human" gift from God. Often, we are caught up in the busyness of this world that can contribute to our anxiety and agitation. A human "being" is counter to the notion of being a human "doer" and the wise man, Solomon, shares a spiritual injunctive from God, *"Be still, and know that I am God; I will be exalted among the nations, I will be exalted in the earth"* (Psalms 46:10-NKJV). Conversely, "doing" provides human beings with the pleasant accoutrements of life. Writing out these words on a laptop computer sure beats trying to write them out by dipping a brush in ink and scrawling these words out on some type of parchment paper; however, our incessant "doing" has not advanced us any closer in our relationship with God, thus, we are stumbling around as we were 6,000 years ago. So, if a human "being" implies that we are to "be still" how do we reconcile this with our understanding of "spirit"; which is always in "flux?"

God didn't sit "still" when it came to the creation of the universe. Everything within the universe is in constant motion. God even instructs us (through Adam) to be "fruitful (productive) and multiple"; which implies movement. Indeed, God instructed Abraham to move without knowing where he was going. He directed Moses to lead a captive people through the wilderness for 40 years. They weren't told to set up camp and settle in; rather, they were kept moving. The Disciples of Christ were dispatched to various areas to spread the "Good News" of the Gospel. Unlike earlier Jews who felt an exclusive relationship with God, evangelists of today are spreading this Word throughout the world. Each and every individual spirit is heading back home to the full and loving embrace of God, so what is this notion about "human beings" being still?

Who would impose upon Brenda, and those like her, to "be still"; thus, remaining in their circumstances? Johnny, who feels justified in beating his son, would find support in the Bible commanding his wife to "be still" and defer to his authority if she thought that the abuse of their son, Jerimiah, was more than the mother and child could handle and opted to divorce Johnny. How many of you are inclined to stay still when you are being besieged by undesirable conditions of depression, abuse, drug addiction, poverty, unemployment and other such conditions?

The confounding tension is absolved when we do have an awareness and appreciation that all things are in flux, therefore, impermanent. None of us can govern outcomes and in our frantic efforts to do so, we lose our peace. Every experience we have culminates in the fleeting moment of what we have right now. Whether the experiences were our victimization or our triumphs, our poverty or our accumulation of wealth, our illness or our physical and mental wellbeing, our marriages or divorces, our life and indeed our deaths are all but fleeting moments. To "be still" is to have patience but it also implies that we take a weekly pause (Sabbath), if not a daily pause to extricate ourselves from the past, experience calm in the present moment and reset our bearings for the future.

To the reader, it is important that you understand the nature of impermanence! Once this becomes an integrated part of your knowledge and being, it truly changes your life. God is the only immutable Entity, Force or Energy within existence. That means that everything else, including you and I, are subject to change. Given that all things are subject to change, there is not a thing that we can hang onto or even should hang onto. If we can truly understand that we were birthed into being in an ever changing body, within and ever changing universe, we don't have to "grasp" for anything in a foolish attempt to possess or own it. Life is nothing more than a series of ever changing experiences; thus, the Biblical injunctive of, "be still," reminds us to sit, reflect and enjoy the moments. The other part of the injunctive, "know that I am God" can reassure us that the only Immutable Force has it all worked out.

If The Omniscient God has it all worked out, then why are we trying to micro-manage the work of God? If God has it all worked out, we don't have to hang onto vengeance due to perceived injustices. We don't have to embrace feelings of guilt and shame. We don't have to worry and be fearful of our experiences in a material world of fleeting moments that truly doesn't have any substance. As terrible as Brenda's upbringing and marriages were, what keeps those negative experiences alive is her unwillingness let those experiences go. There is nothing that holds power over us unless we allow it. Brenda can have a new start to her life. Indeed, every day is a new opportunity for a new beginning. Every day is an opportunity to reclaim herself as the rightful heir to the Kingdom of God.

Brenda hasn't lost anything but her connection with God. She didn't lose her childhood. Whether a traumatic childhood or pleasant childhood, this stage of life will always give way to the next stage in life that follows it. She didn't lose her marriages because each is a sociological construct that we create to describe the coupling of two people in our society or a number of people in other societies. She hasn't lost her house, property or auto when her marriages dissolved because they were always gifts that were on loan and we never own anything. She didn't lose her children; though they came through her, they were never hers and if you believe you have ownership over your own children, watch how quickly the State steps in when you are deemed unfit to care for the "State's children" (though the truth is, we are all children of God and not children of each other). Brenda will not lose her body or her mind, as neither one of them is permeable. Therefore, neither she nor we ought to grieve the loss of anything, as nothing in the material world is ours to own. Jesus instructs us, *"Do not lay up for yourselves treasures on earth, where moth and rust destroy and where thieves break in and steal; but lay up for yourselves treasures in heaven, where neither moth nor rust destroys and where thieves do not break in and steal. For where your treasure is, there your heart will be also."* (Matthew 6:19-21-NKJV)

In the exercise below, you'll have an opportunity to collect your series of moments, not to hoard or possess, but as a visual reminder that we are just experiencing a series of moments. The exercise may trigger nostalgia but I don't want you to get stuck there. The moment you have now is as great as any moment that you've once had. My personal recollection of various moments, both good and bad, reminds me of how precious life is and how fleeting it is. The "valley of the shadow of death" is ever present because every preceding moment causes the "death" of the past moment. I do not "fear evil" because it is as transient as the last moment and am choosing to reside in the pure-heart realm (with deliberate and purposeful relationship with God). Recalling the moments of the past reminds me of how Great God's Love is in allowing me to have this experience…Thank You, God!

Ripening the Fruit-Pleasant Memory Biographies

Make an autobiography of pleasant memories for every developmental stage of your life. Look for old photos, news articles, magazines, yearbooks, toys, popular songs from the times, or recipes of favorite foods. Of course, you can't place and Easy Bake Oven or a GI Joe action figure in a memory album but make photos of these items. Generate written stories about those old memories and place it next to the photos. Reproduce these albums and share them with family and friends. Trauma and negative experiences tend to anchor us to the past with unpleasant memories and we tend to forget our pleasant moments, blessings, gifts and joys that were happening all around us. There hasn't really been a time that I haven't worn glasses. I do recall from childhood a memory of injuring the surrounding area of my eye by jumping on an old, battered pogo stick that I found in the junk yard. With no previous pogo stick jumping skills and no safety rubber stopping around the rusting metal pogo stick frame, I slipped and came down hard. Since God protects "fools" and children, my eye wasn't poked out but it swollen up and oozed mucus for a while. Who knows if that was the actual causal event triggering my need for glasses but they've always been a part of my life. This was not a pleasant experience but I fondly remember the events of childhood that includes this experience. In recent years, I've escorted my mother to see her brother on a road trip before he died and as it happens when one visits family members that you haven't seen for years, they pull out old photos and reminisce about old memories. What I discovered (and I couldn't believe my uncle would have such a picture) was a scrawny little boy approximately eight years old with these huge pop bottle glasses. He looked like the old cartoon character of "Fearless Fly." It was a funny sight of me, triggering laughs from the family and a memory that has long since faded from my memory. Though the pogo stick itself is not necessarily a "positive" memory, it doesn't carry any traumatic weight for me and I am regaled with memories of childhood adventures in the old junk yard.

I have the old picture and this is the descriptive story about that experience. Collect your own album and stories to share with people who will really value getting to know you!

> *Sing praise to the Lord, you saints of His,*
> *And give thanks at the remembrance of His holy name.*
> *For His anger is but for a moment,*
> *His favor is for life;*
> *Weeping may endure for a night,*
> *But joy comes in the morning.*
> *(Palms 30:4-6-NKJV)*

V

Path Pointer

*To the pure, all things are pure, but to those who are
defiled and unbelieving, nothing is pure; but even their
mind and conscience are defile. They profess to know
God, but in works they deny him, being abominable,
disobedient and disqualified for every good work.
(Titus, 1:15-16-NKJV)*

As a servant of God and a practitioner of psychology and clinical social work, I strive to do two things: 1) To continually evolve on this spiritual pathway and 2) To become an exemplar for the things that I believe about God, as represented by my level of spiritual differentiation on my pathway. In doing so, I become a "path-pointer" more than a service provider but the act of therapy provides opportunities of healing that is a tremendous service. The reason I reference myself as a "path-pointer" is that I realize the effort required for spiritual advancement or therapeutic healing is in the hands of God and the individual. According to Galatians (6:3-5-NKJV), Paul wrote, *"For if anyone thinks himself to be something, when he is nothing, he deceives himself. But let each one examine his own work, and then he will have rejoicing in himself alone, and not in another. For each one shall bear his own load."* Each and every one of us has a responsibility to work toward our own advancement but there are a couple of forces in place that keep us stuck: inertia and faulty perceptions.

Sir Isaac Newton, a renowned physicist, postulated his 1st law of motion, "objects in motion remain in motion." Additionally, he noted that "objects at rest stay at rest." This is the effect of inertia. It can confound some of my "solution-focused" colleagues (which is also one of the various therapeutic modalities that I use) when we encounter clients who rail about their current life situations, yet refuses to do anything about it or fail to act upon the sagacious advise their accomplished therapist conveys to him or her. How frustrating it is to see impending doom ahead for the client that he or she could easily circumvent if the client chose to receive and implement the therapist's advice. I can hear the same frustrated cry coming from non-professional family members and friends that could argue the same point, "*If you just listen to what I'm telling you, you wouldn't have such negative outcomes!*"

All of us have a psychological, emotional and spiritual "set point." It is akin to a physiological set point that dieters encounter when we try to maintain our weight loss, only to balloon back to our original weight and beyond. I've referenced this notion a couple of ways in my previous work, "*The Fruit of the Spirit.*" I've described the "nature" of human beings that is relatively set and I used a statistical analogy, "regression toward the mean," to showcase how we settle back into our original nature unless we transcend our nature. Likewise, with the above concept of "inertia" we tend to get stuck in our thought process (whether positive or negative). In our spiritual progression to the "pure-heart realm" we see and experience the world differently than we see and experience the world from either of the other two realms (i.e., "indifferent-heart realm" and the "craving-heart realm").

When I examined the above passage from the Apostle Paul to Titus, Paul is referring to foods one might determine as clean or unclean and there are tremendous dietary regulations cited in the Old Testament. However, what jumped out to me from reading the above passage is our state of mind. If there is purity in our heads and hearts then the actions that flow has pure intentions. That doesn't mean that our pure intentions will always be received in the spirit of which it originated. Paul goes on to infer that despite an action we may take originates from the purity of our intentions, if it creates offense within others, we should back off of those actions in the presence of others it offends. I see this as civility and courtesy that the pure-heart displays even though he or she may not adhere to that particular value. Consider the actions of CBS News journalists,

Leslie Stahl and Lara Logan, donning a hajib while reporting from a predominately Muslim country. It is the courtesy I extend in respecting the humanity of clients who may present in therapy with behaviors I may construe to be abominable (e.g., sadomasochism sexual practices outside, or inside, the confines of a marital relationship).

When we have a lust for impure things that sully's the mind and taints the spirit we are operating out of the indifferent-heart realm where nothing is sacred and anything goes. As Paul points out that *"they claim to know God but their conscience and minds are defiled."* Interestingly, this is what I am finding in clients who claim to want the attributes of God (e.g., peace, love, joy, etc.) or a life experience that is different than they've created, but remain stuck in the indifferent-heart realm. Their inertia holds them there and the plethora of psychological interventions don't tend to budge them. If they show up for therapy (and many do), they will ignore your advice, criticize your advice and sabotage any plan or strategy put in place designed for movement in a direction they may "say" that they want to go.

A frustrated colleague of mine; which whom I provide supervision, remarked on the challenge of trying to move a client to a higher level of functioning after years of therapy from multiple therapists (including the current therapist) with little obvious change. This is not a concern that hasn't been expressed by other therapists and felt by me, but in my role of supervision, I understand that a factor contributing to burnout is perceived lack of efficacy in the work that one does, so I cited the importance of merely being presence with the client can have some therapeutic value. *"You will not need to fight in this battle. Position yourselves, stand still and see the salvation of the Lord, who is with you, O Judah and Jerusalem!' Do not fear or be dismayed; tomorrow go out against them, for the Lord is with you."* (2 Chronicles 20:17-NKJV)

Whether we are looking at Newton's Law of Motion, nature, a set point, regression of mean, or inertia, human beings have very little movement in their psychological, emotional and spiritual development while residing in the indifferent-heart realm. Whether one is a gambler, a smoker, a philanderer or addict, and that person is being nudged by family members, a threat of job termination, treatment or incarceration, there is just no real movement for the person residing in the indifferent-heart realm. This is when we merely "position ourselves, stand still and wait on the salvation of the Lord." This inertia that we can clearly see within our clients is also represented in our society when we see policy initiatives stymied in congress, American's educational populace lagging behind many lessor developed countries of the world. The lack of movement we see in clients seeking therapy who claim to want something different in their lives may also appear within ourselves when we, too, are stuck.

So there is a "gravitational" force called, "inertia" holding many of us in place but an equally compelling force is "faulty perceptions." Our mind is set in a default positon of negativity, inaction or the pursuit of wrongheaded action. When we can't see that we are better and ought to do better, we choose not to do better. "*They profess to know God but in works they deny God by being abominable, disobedient and disqualified for every good work.*" The word, "abominable" (moral revulsion) sounds a bit harsh but it is easy to profess God and choose to engage in behaviors that are the antitheist of God. In doing so, we are in disobedience to God; which makes us poor exemplars and a testament to where we reside on the spiritual continuum.

In my previous book, "*The Fruit of the Spirit*", I have identified characteristics of those residing in the "indifferent-heart realm." These individuals have no concept of God but I don't want to necessarily define them as "agnostics" or "atheists." I have seen incredible humanity and spirituality in some of those who profess not to know or disconfirm the existence of God but they behave in a way that makes them exemplars of the Fruit of the Spirit. On the other hand, I seen those who voice loudly and repetitively that they are aligned with God but like the Pharisees and Sadducees of old, they have pompous ideas but wouldn't associate with women, children or those they perceived to be on the fringes of society. Indeed, part of the reason Christ was killed was due to the angst aroused in these men when Christ associated with women, children and those considered to be on the fringes of society.

Those residing in the indifferent-heart realm tend to be manipulators, exploiters and deceivers. They misrepresent themselves with a goal to satisfy their selfish desires, but there is also something malicious about what they are doing. Because they are hedonistic and self-indulgent they tend to be "takers." They take your time, your sympathy, your compassion, your money, your hospitality, your car, your food, your dignity, your respect; indeed, they become like "black holes" that siphons your soul. They can be curt and insensitive, cruel and objectifying. Don't be swayed by emotionality and tears. Some may find it hard to emote; whereas, others are masterful in using feigned emotional displays to pull you in to get what they want. I'm aware of these takers yet, I too, get sucked in when they repeatedly go beyond the scheduled time allotted for the session or they threaten meltdowns, hospitalizations and suicidal attempts when you try to discharge them from therapy.

Whatever characteristics that show up within these individuals in possession of an indifferent-heart is not likely to change with your largess or kindness. In our propensity to rescue clients, along with our zeal to heal and serve, has very little impact in changing the way these people are in the world. A local woman exploits churches, social service agencies, neighbors, family and friends has become a pariah in the community but she just doesn't care! She is cunning and won't stop because she told me in therapy, "I always get what I want." Inertia tends to hold people in place regardless of one's level of spiritual differentiation but in the indifferent-heart realm, there is little desire on the part of the individual to grow beyond this level and therapy is ineffective. Remember, that the word, "therapy" means to "heal" and those residing in the indifferent-heart realm deny that they are emotionally, psychologically or spiritually sick. They are orchestrating their lives to get exactly what they want; thus, we (in the helping profession) become their "footstools." There is no doubt that they are complainers, opinionated and critical of others but they are "stuck" and really don't seem to mind being "stuck."

In actuality, the essence of our spirituality is always in flux but the nature of our humanness anchors us in our tendency to remain "stuck." To further elaborate on Newton's Law, he stated that "an object in motion stays in motion; unless impacted by an external force." Likewise, "an object at rest stays in rest unless impacted by an external force." Given that God is an Internal/External Force, we are empowered to move despite our propensity to stay still. However, we as therapists (or concerned others), are not empowered to "move" anyone else. This is the reason that as a "service provider" I fancy myself as a "path-pointer." As a therapist, I seek to heal the wounds in clients who present with anxious, depressive and psychotic symptoms but the prognosis for healing is largely in their hands. I point them in the direction of restoration by facilitating a safe environment to share their stories, enable them to manage and cope with their daily life stressors, educate them on their disorders, encourage their empowerment, identify solutions, clarifying directions, etc. Nevertheless, whatever I do in the effort to serve the client, he/she must be complicit in his/her recovery, development and growth.

The National Association of Social Worker's Code of Ethics guides clinicians in our understanding of our duties and limits in working with clients. We are informed that the client has the right to self-determination; which mimics God's relationship with humanity. God doesn't "make" people conform to his directives. He grants us an opportunity for a human experience with clear directives in how we can get the most out of this experience. *"Cease listening to instruction, my son, and you will stray from the words of knowledge."* (Proverbs 19:27-NKJV) This is hard for some people to understand and they will turn against God if their life doesn't proceed in line with their faulty expectations. And, it may be hard for us, professionals, to fully understand, when we think that "service" is "carrying" a client with the capacity to walk but with an unwillingness to do so.

Have you ever purchased a package of build it yourself furniture? Let's say that you wanted an inexpensive computer hutch for your home office. You pull out all of the pieces and parts but there are also instructions in the box. Perhaps you are fairly handy and can grasp how the parts easily assemble into a completed whole, so you disregard the instructions and launch right into building your project. Your completed project is "perfect" and even if you have some parts remaining, it didn't take away from your completed project. However, there are some of us that will launch ahead with an overly inflated belief in our ability and we disregard the instructions, resulting in us becoming highly frustrated because nothing is coming out as we have hoped. When clients "cease listening to instruction" from their therapist, they deliberately stray away from opportunities to be informed. Pastor Randy Morrison (Speak the Word Church International) would likely say that "failure is a lack of appropriate knowledge" but people in this realm will even discount your instruction that would facilitate greater knowledge within them. Of course, there are those who recognize that the assembly of cabinetry is not their expertise; thus, they studiously read and follow the instructions.

A young woman came to me for therapy because she was stuck in her grieving process. Her brother, just a year older than she, had committed suicide. His life was filled with what he thought to be dissatisfying life experiences and after a history of intense illegal substance use/abuse, he opted to overdose to escape the pain and dissatisfaction he was experiencing. The young woman had gone down her own path of self-destruction, mimicking her brother's life with her use of drugs. She had gone through chemical dependency treatment, refusing to grant any allegiance, authority or existence of God and vacillated in our sessions between denying God's existence and blaming God for not interceding in the life of her brother.

The grief work that I do involves a protocol that explicitly involves God, so with her animus toward God, I didn't use God (per se) but I used "spiritual nuances" to shift her in her thinking to arrive at some peace. That is, the essence of grief work is for the client to redefine his or herself in the space of the loss. Of course, "loss" is always subjective to the individual experiencing the loss in that it could be a loss of a job...the loss of one's reputation...or in the case of this young woman (whom I'll call, "Marti"), it was the loss of her brother. In redefining one's self in the space of the loss goes back to asking those existential questions associated with one's spiritual essence; such as, "Who am I now in the absence of my brother?" And, "What meaning am I to make of this loss?" I was able to discuss with Marti her spiritual essence (i.e., meaning, purpose, direction and connection), without using the words "spirituality" and "God." I also pointed her in the direction of the Fruit of the Spirit, which are attributes of God, without confronting her atheistic or agnostic stance.

Of course, it would be easier to note that each person is merely having experiences in life but these experiences don't have to be fraught with frustration if we follow Godly instructions. The value of spiritual beings inhabiting physical form is to have experiences (whether they be "good" or "bad" experiences). Clients are coming to therapists, feeling troubled by their experiences. Therapists are feeling frustrated by our capacity (or incapacity) to help clients with their experiences but we must remain clear about our roles. We are path-pointers or the "instruction sheet" in the box in which the client (or customer) can choose to use or discard. We cannot fuse ourselves with the clients' emotionality, decision making process or actions taken (or not taken). A fellow colleague of mine was literally a basket case after each of her intense, emotional sessions. She felt that joining with the client at his or her emotional level was of therapeutic benefit for the client. Perhaps there is value in the cathartic release of emotion but I didn't see much growth in doing so. Indeed, the clients remained emotionally entrenched, bringing up the same emotionally charged story year after year and the therapist appeared to need therapy after those intense, emotional sessions.

I am often curious about the inertia that keeps people stuck. The guy that does nothing but complains about his job that he has worked for 20+ years, what keeps him there? The husband that says nothing redeeming about the quality of his marital relationship, what keeps him there? The mother with six children, each subsequently taken and placed in foster care services, chooses to have yet another child, what keeps her there? Advice would have no impact on the behaviors of any of these people. The guy was likely complaining at year one about how terrible his job is. Who hasn't told him that he ought to quit and find a job that he likes? The husband likely found fault in his wife even before he married her. Surely, someone told him that if he was dissatisfied with his partner prior to marriage he ought not to marry her. The mother didn't have the temperament, inclination or desire to parent the first child that was taken from her; what hasn't she been told about not having more children that she has chosen not to listen to?

A narrative that has defined us for years could be that of our "victim's story." Christ told Nicodemus that if one is to enter into the Kingdom of God, one must be born again (John 3) and this concept is also important to understand and embrace for therapeutic change. The challenge for people wanting to make this shift is to be born into something new requires us to put to "death" what we were. It requires a change in our "faulty expectations." Do you recall the story in the Bible of the disabled man who went to the pool that was stirred by an angel and the person entering it would receive his/her miracle? (John 5) He went there for 38 years. He used his disability (his "victim's story") as a reason why he was unable to get into the pool prior to anyone else. When Jesus came along, He asked the man, *"Do you want to be made well?"* It seemed like an odd question to pose to a disabled man who was coming to the pool for 38 years, but it is a question that is indicative of many clients coming to therapy year after year, "Do you want to be made well?" If we've claimed the victim story as our story it is hard to let it go because we'll have to kill off what we are familiar with for an uncertain future, which we are totally responsible for.

Perhaps there are competing interests within each of these people that pulls equally hard at them and they remain stuck. Perhaps, pulling at the guy who complains about his job is a desire to pursue something else and a fear that if he does so, he will fail. Perhaps the pull with the husband is a desire for another relationship; along with a competing fear that he is not competent enough to secure another relationship. Perhaps the mother's inadequacy of parenting is mixed with the hope that she'll get the next one right. Whatever is happening in the minds of these individuals, we have to assess their level of spiritual differentiation and their nature to determine their capacity to hear advice and move in the direction of the advice. *("He who has ears to hear, let him hear!"* Matthew 11:15-NKJV)

Each one of these individuals clearly resides in the "indifferent-heart" realm. Each is focused upon self-interests without consideration in how their words or actions impact others. One pollutes the office environment with his constant criticism. *"Do all things without complaining and disputing, that you may become blameless and harmless, children of God without fault in the midst of a crooked and perverse generation, among whom you shine as lights in the world…"* (Philippians 2:14-15-NKJV). The other berates his wife and diminishes her worth. *"So husbands ought to love their own wives as their own bodies; he who loves his wife loves himself"* (Ephesians 5:28-NKJV). While the last one place the next generation at risk of insecure attachments and repeating the neglect that has occurred to them. We have heard that the "sins of the father is visited upon the son." We've also seen in psychology "intergenerational toxic shame," but Ezekiel informs us that, *The one who sins is the one who will die. The child will not share the guilt of the parent, nor will the parent share the guilt of the child. The righteousness of the righteous will be credited to them, and the wickedness of the wicked will be charged against them."* (Ezekiel 18:20-NIV)

The nature of an individual can be determined by the frequency and consistency of his/her behaviors. The nature of the complainer is that he complains. Switching jobs will not stop him from complaining; thus, the energy that we expend to try to get him to change jobs will be in vain. He doesn't want to change jobs because it serves his adaptive need to complain. The husband's berating nature serves him well. He intuitively knows that he strips away his wife's esteem, piece by piece, so that she'll never have the confidence to ever leave him. The mother has a nature of checking out from parental responsibilities when the role of parenting gets too tough, while at the same time, trying to create something that will love her unconditionally because she feels unworthy to be loved.

It is only through the Grace of God that individuals are reborn out of the indifferent-heart realm into the craving-heart realm where therapy will begin to have utility. It is in this realm that we can at least see our bad behaviors, develop insight in order to change faulty expectations and experience the motivation to change. In this realm, the therapist points out a direction that the client will more readily heed. When we are lost and don't know it, we don't seek help but in the craving-heart realm, we know that we are lost and willfully seek help. Of course, willfully seeking help in the craving-heart realm doesn't mean that the client will transfer the learning within the therapist's office into his or her own life. This is the realm that we may spend our time intellectualizing, rationalizing and debating with the "path-pointer" or we may already know what needs to be done but we are not doing what needs to be done.

When we enact upon the spiritual wisdom that we innately know to be true, we've arrived in the "pure-heart spiritual realm." This is the realm where we not only acknowledge and appreciated faith but we act on faith. This is a realm of spiritual enlightenment where we let go of the ignorance of the indifferent-heart realm, adopting the new awareness/ knowledge of the craving-heart realm and putting it into action while residing in the pure-heart realm. Enlightenment is simply "knowledge" plus the "action step." It is Newton's Law of Motion "objects at rest stay at rest unless impacted by an external force." The Wisdom of God gives us the Knowledge for what it is that we must do; along with a gentle nudge and an empowering ability to do the things we choose to do. *"But be doers of the word, and not hearers only, deceiving yourselves. For if anyone is a hearer of the word and not a doer, he is like a man observing his natural face in a mirror; for he observes himself, goes away, and immediately forgets what kind of man he was. But he who looks into the perfect law of liberty and continues in it, and is not a forgetful hearer but a doer of the work, this one will be blessed in what he does."* (James 1:22-25-NKJV)

I was sitting in service on a Sunday morning at Speak the Word Church International with Pastor Randy Morrison and he reminded the congregation that "faith" is a seed that must be grown within us. He attested that everyone has a measure of faith [likely referencing Romans (12:3-NKJV), *"For I say, through the grace given to me, to everyone who is among you, not to think of himself more highly than he ought to think, but to think soberly, as God has dealt to each one a measure of faith"*]. Our degree of faith reveals where we are at in our spiritual journey and the Pastor stated that challenges in our lives "reveals our faith or exposes our fears." Fear is powerful, palpable and pervasive. Fear is "powerful" in a disempowering type of way. It immobilizes us when we ought to be moving. It traps us in a cycle of despair and defeat. We are gripped by the fear and it shows up in all aspects of our lives. As we sharpen our "faith" it will cut through our fear.

I don't believe that any emotion can be (or should be) completely vanquished in this world. Our undesirable emotions (e.g., anger, lust, greed, doubt, fear, etc.) are attached to our lower selves and provide us with a fuller emotional repertoire to have meaningful opportunities from the experiences upon this earth. Thus, we ought to experience these emotions without becoming these emotions. Our empowerment goal is to conquer these emotions and not to foolishly think that we can vanquish these emotions. As we "build the muscle of faith" that resides in our higher selves (along with the other spiritual attributes of the higher self), we'll have the strength to push back against the impulses and cravings of the lower self; along with the motivation and capability to extricate ourselves from the morass of the lower self that tends to keep us stuck.

Our interaction with others, our exposure to incidents/events and the environment that surrounds us influences us greatly. Each has its own level of "gravitational force" that can reshape us and redirect us from our spiritual journey. Consider a client of mine by the name of Charlie. Charlie is a 52 year old, single, Caucasian man, sporting more weight than he should and though very cordial and personable, he isolates himself from the community. Perhaps he was never a paragon in the community but he certainly wasn't a scourge either. He worked hard and minded his own business but now Charlie isolates himself due to his shame. Once, not so long ago, he has been an "upstanding" and "law abiding" man (so the community thought) until Charlie was caught in a police sting.

Charlie ingested an inordinate amount of pornographic materials. Perhaps he is not unlike a lot of people in this rural community with limited avenues of entertainment that seems to be relegated to swilling beer, throwing darts and entertained by casino gambling. I've seen a lot of people in therapy with a wide variety of sexual expressions and the consumption of pornographic materials just seems like "par for the course." Charlie's consumption of porn greatly exceeded what may be considered the general use of porn in this community; however, the lion's share of it was child pornography.

Charlie has been ingesting these materials long before the Internet but the Internet became a fantastic boon for him (as well as his curse). From the safety of his own home, Charlie download and masturbated to all types of pornographic images until the day he clicked on a child specific porn site that allowed the police unlimited access to Charlie's computer. He was arrested, jailed, humiliated by the public scorn, shamed his family, sent to a sex offenders' group and vowed not to go down this road again.

Despite all that has happened to Charlie, he "went down that road again." In addition to the sex offender's group, it was thought that Charlie could benefit from individual therapy. I gave Charlie a diagnosis of Impulse Control Disorder and administered therapy to him in a fashion I would with anyone with an addiction or compulsive behavioral disorder. I began with an education on "urges," "triggers" and "cravings." I illustrated on the whiteboard in my office the Toxic Shame Model, emphasizing that his own negative perception of himself carves out gaping holes in himself which the compulsive behavior is an attempt to fill in to make him whole. Of course, no compulsive behavior has ever made anyone whole; thereby, creating Charlie's relapse in behavior and having to receive additional therapeutic support.

As pointed out, Charlie was introduced to pornographic materials when he was very young. The imagines imprint in his mind in such a way that he never sought an intimate/sexual relationship with another live person. His sexual arousal needs were met by the two-dimensional images in magazines and through the Internet. Throughout this book, I've attempted to underscore that people who venture down an ugly path or exemplify ugly behaviors are not ugly people and neither is Charlie. The ingestion of these materials since childhood makes his cravings seemingly insurmountable; thus, gravitational pull of this pornographic material lures him back in despite his severe consequences and his "desire to quit." In my book, *"Break the Chains-Free the Heart: A Spiritual Pathway through Healing, Transformation and Mental Health,"* I highlighted among my concepts of Al's "A's," the notion of "awareness" as an important concept in the process of change. One must have an awareness of the self-destructive behaviors they are engaging in and a "desire to quit."

I put "desire to quit" in quotation marks because I am not sure if Charlie (like many addicts) truly desires to quit. Pornography has defined Charlie's life for the last 40+ of his 52 years of life and to end that aspect of who he is will be the "death" of the Charlie his knows. We, therapists, are essentially asking Charlie to "exterminate" himself with the promise that a new self will be available once he has done so. And, should that "new self" materialize, it will forever be associated with his "old self." The gravitational forces for Charlie to remain the same are huge! Nevertheless, what appears to be "huge" in the physical realm is not necessarily so in the spiritual realm. God can stop people in their tracks (like Saul on the road to Damascus and Jonan running away from his assignment in Nineveh) and turn these people around.

Jesus stated, *"Then He said to them all, 'If anyone desires to come after Me, let him deny himself, and take up his cross daily, and follow Me. For whoever desires to save his life will lose it, but whoever loses his life for My sake will save it.'"* (Luke 9:23-25-NKJV) Charlie has a huge cross to carry! At present, the prognosis for Charlie appears grim. He espouses the socially desirable responses that he wants to quit but he doesn't truly "desire to quit." Part of spiritual transformation is transparency and Charlie keeps engaging within deception (whether lies of commission or lies of omission). If a word or phrase is not worded correctly, Charlie will not reveal the truth, even though we both know what it is I am asking of him, but he justifies his deception because the question wasn't asked a certain way. Addicts are master manipulators and obfuscator's of truth. His penchant for change was not necessarily connected to awareness of wrongdoing and genuine repentance but due to the fact that he was caught.

Again, Charlie is not a terrible human being. He remains a child of God whose life choices led him down a wrong path that he reinforced for years. "Little by little, drop by drop" Charlie has been filled with "evil" (I'm not using this word to convey any demonic spirits within him but to connote that Charlie's indulgence in a hedonistic lifestyle for years is a departure from God). "Little by little, drop by drop," I and others will deposit "seeds" that Charlie must willfully collect, sow, attend to, produce and harvest from his own garden. Even if I could, I wouldn't stand with Charlie for the next 50 years to see what the new seeds produce. I cannot want for Charlie's transformation greater than he does. Each and every day, Charlie must make a renewed commitment to "pick up his cross" and follow the way of Christ. It is no different than any addict that seeks out the strength of his higher power to recommit daily to his/her sobriety.

Sexually prurient behaviors, especially those involving children, create additional layers of shame; thus, Charlie's case is seemingly unique and seemingly extreme. The vast majority of the readers can never see themselves in Charlie's shoes; therefore, his story may appear meaningless to you. I've come to understand in my own life's journey that no one's story is meaningless and everyone's story only differs from us by degree. If all of us have sinned and fallen short of the Glory of God, what impulsive behavior have we engaged in that separated us from God and what compulsive behaviors keeps us separated from God? The following exercise can assist us in regaining our bearings and readjust our emotional set points in order to break free of whatever gravitational force that holds us.

Ripening the Fruit-One Minute Exercises

Whether it is a "gravitational force" or an "emotional set point," we can use inertia (or Newton's Law of Motion) to get moving in the direction that we desire. The effort that I will describe here is called, "One Minute Exercises." It is hard to change the patterns of who we are (or the person that we've been for years) but change is inevitable and we can orchestrate the change we desire. Remember that we are tri-fold beings; thus, we access our spirit, mental and physical aspect of ourselves to generate and maintain the change. Spirit encompasses "meaning, purpose, direction and connection." Use the mind to cogitate upon each aspect of spirit to prompt the change that we desire and then implement the "One Minute Exercises" to initiate the change.

The 1st thing to do (regarding meaning), figure out what it is that you want to do. Do you want to lose weight, quit smoking, enhance your education, establish a friendship network, change your attitude, etc.? The next step is to create a rationale (purpose) for what you want or what you intend to do. Align your rationale (purpose) with spiritual ideas vs. vanities. Direction is related to the goal you want to achieve and "connection" is the alliances you make that will purposefully assist you with your goal (and please remember God as your ultimate connection).

To get moving toward your goal, attend to it for one minute at the top of every waking hour. It is a momentary mindfulness or mental exercise at the top of every waking hour until you start to make substantial movement toward your goal ("objects in motion stay in motion"). As you are mentally attending to your direction (goal) for that minute, consider a behavioral step that you can do. For instance, as you are deliberately cogitating on your weight loss goal, implement a physical activity (squats, curls, pushups, jumping jacks, sit ups, etc.). Consider that one could probably do 60 squats or 60 pushups in 60 seconds if one was fit but start off with 5 or just 1. Given that there are typically 16 hours in a person's wake-state during the course of the day and if one worked up to 60 squats in a minute at the top of the hour that is 960 squats in a day. Now that's a lot of squats, curls, pushups, jumping jacks, sit ups, etc.; thus, there is no way you won't get fit!

If you picked up a pocket Bible of the New Testament (or an App for your iPhone), you can exercised your spirit by reading the "Word" for a minute at the top of the hour and in short order you can tackle the entire New Testament! Try this method with any change that you want to implement and you will push past any set point that exists.

VI

I Don't Want to Live; I Don't Want to Die

My brethren, count it all joy when you fall into various trials, knowing that the testing of your faith produces patience. But let patience have its perfect work, that you may be perfect and complete, lacking nothing. If any of you lacks wisdom, let him ask of God, who gives to all liberally and without reproach, and it will be given to him. But let him ask in faith, with no doubting, for he who doubts is like a wave of the sea driven and tossed by the wind. For let not that man suppose that he will receive anything from the Lord; he is a double-minded man, unstable in all his ways.
(James 1:2-8-NKJV)

When I was a youngster, I was working hard in a fast-food, burger establishment and bringing home what I thought to be "big" money for an adolescent who still lived at home and had no real financial obligations. I don't recall what my wages were at the time but I do know that they were less than two dollars an hour, as I can recall my excitement when the minimum wage reached two dollars an hour. With fading memory, I don't recall if that was my first paycheck from the burger place but I do recall that there were some establishments 40+ years ago that didn't process your first paycheck for a month with subsequent biweekly pay periods. With the impatience of adolescence, a month was an eternity and I couldn't wait to be paid.

Lots of fads come in and go out of style and I was caught up in the pocket watch fad at the time. I sported a huge silver chain, fastened to a belt loop that attached to my watch and dangling out of my pocket. Throughout the day, I'd fiddle with the chain or twirl it, knowing that the watch, itself, was securely snuggled in my front, right pocket. I likely was fiddling with the chain when I went after my check. I was proud of my paycheck. I know I had over a hundred dollars embossed along with my name on a rectangular piece of paper that I could exchange for money. It was exciting. I went to the local store to cash my check. The customer service lady counted out upon the counter the sum of my check. I had a wallet, but I didn't want other people to see me with all that money, so I grabbed the fistful of money off the counter and quickly shoved it into my pocket. I was puffed up...a pocket full of money, swinging my "kool-duty" pocket watch chain, as I strolled to my car. When I got to my car, I must have been a bit distracted and by habit of checking the time, I tugged on the chain of the pocket watch; which, unbeknownst to me, pulled the wad of money out of my pocket. I checked the time, climbed into my car and drove back to my place of work for a burger, malt and fries.

The store was just down the street from the burger place and when I reached into my pocket for my money, there was nothing there! It couldn't have been more than five minutes that transpired from the store to the burger place and it dawned upon me what I must have done. I rushed back to the store, to the very same parking space and there was no evidence of my money in the parking lot. I was upset but not devastated. I felt foolish for what I had done to lose my entire wages! Perhaps a day or so later, I told my mother about the foolishness of my actions and she implored me to go back to the store to see if someone turned the money in. I was incredulous and defiant, "Mom, that money is not going to be at the store!" I refused to even go back and check; undoubtedly, to preserve some dignity from my moment of foolishness. What I couldn't grasp in my adolescent mind and hedonistic self was that not everybody was like me. Had I found the money, it would have been an unexpected payday for me and since that was my way of thinking, I couldn't conceive that anyone else would actually turn in the money, so I never checked (thinking my mother to be truly naïve).

Now that I've advanced my mother in the age that she was when she urged me to go back to the store and inquire inside about my money, I realize now that it was quite possibly there. Over the years I have seen news stories of kids returning sums of money. I've seen elderly people that could use money, return found money. I even saw a story of a homeless man who returned a large sum of money that he found in a lost cash deposit bag. I've seen people literally sacrifice their lives in the service of others (and I am not talking about those in the military or police who sign up with the intention to be honorable servants, but just regular, everyday folk who stepped up with honor and sacrifice). There are far more people with greater spiritual development than I was exhibiting at the time who may have taken that found money right into the store just like my mother said, but we live and we learn in this life.

In living and learning, I've began to understand the nature of loss. Loss can be pretty powerful in its affect that can bring a lot of us to our knees. Since the nature of our physical existence (in the material world) is one of impermanence, loss is a constant…it is inevitable. When we attempt to grasp and hang onto something that is impermanent with the hopes that it is permanent, we indulge a delusion and create our own suffering. At the time of this writing, "Father Time" has kissed "goodbye" to the previous year and "Baby New Year" is ushering in a new one. The inevitable cycle of endings and new beginnings is clearly represented in our celebratory hopes for the New Year and if I attempt to hang onto last year because I had some great human experience or interaction, I'm suffering because I can't carry that experience forward. Perhaps my great human experience of last year was to visit the Taj Mahal in India or Disneyland in California and now I can only bemoan the fact that I am not at either place this year.

Similarly, if I have a great meal yesterday, it is only a fond memory of what it is today. Of course, we can attempt to replicate those experiences and there can be great joy in doing so but the experiences are not the same (remember the old adage that "one can never step in the same river twice"). As I sit here today, there is no form or substance, nourishment or taste from the meal I had yesterday. The memory is fresh, yet it, too, will fade over time and the experience of actually eating the meal from yesterday cannot be replicated in this very moment. So each event is an experience, followed by the absence of the experience, which constitutes a loss. Now these are sort of "benign losses" but what about the losses that we've had greater attachments to? What about the loss of a loved one, a relationship, a job, a limb or our health? What about losing our identity, our faith, our confidence, our value and worth? What happens when we lose our way and become less of a person than we are designed to be?

All loses creates a singular demand upon us in that we are to redefine ourselves in the space of the loss. We are grieving the absence of the experience that we once had and foolishly believed it was permanent. People curse God because we feel entitled to a permanent experience and when it is over we are miserably upset! In fact, we stomp our feet, cry hysterically, scream obscenities and throw ourselves to the ground in an emotion fit that seem more suitable for a child that hasn't learned emotional regulation than a fully grown adult, but adults, too, behave badly. God doesn't promise us permanency in anything material or worldly. In fact, the Bible reveals that the world was destroyed by flood in days gone by and it prophesies the destruction of the world by fire in the future. We also learn that tomorrow is not promised to anyone. *"Do not boast about tomorrow, for you do not know what a day may bring forth"* (Proverbs 27:1-NKJV). With these biblical injunctions notwithstanding, we still try to hang onto notions of permanency and then experience either disappointment or devastation when impermanency occurs.

My loss was disappointing at the time and insignificant now, but what about those who are experiencing greater losses? What about those who feel devastated by their loss and then experience conflicting thoughts of, "I don't want to live; I don't want to die." I am writing this chapter following the end of year and during the holiday season I have had a spate of emergency client appointments. They are all quite different; yet, all quite the same. I've met with 39 year old Sandy, a very attractive woman and wonderfully kindhearted. She lost her custodial rights to her children in favor of her ex-husband due to her involvement in illegal substance use/abuse. She has long since been clean and sober from her drug use but her controlling ex-husband was manipulatively using their kids to woo her back. His strategy works in the short run because as a mother, she longs to be in the presence of her children and has returned home several times.

Though the ex-husband's strategy was manipulative, you'd think that having Sandy back, he'd be so grateful that he'd treat her with the dignity and respect that she deserves but all of his pent up anger comes out with an overbearing presence and demeaning attitude that stifles her spirit and she flees again.

After another failed attempt at reconciliation, Sandy fled again and her ex-husband was vindictive and withheld the children from their mother during this holiday season. He feeds the children with negative perceptions about their mother that they didn't always take in; however, his parental alienation strategies are working because some of the children, who once missed their mother terribly, are directly expressing to the mother that they don't ever want to see her again. Of course, Sandy is devastated and she presented at our agency for an emergency session. Sandy expressed notions that she, "doesn't want to live anymore, but she really doesn't want to die." Her heart ached and it was magnified by the holiday season. This loss is palatable and in dramatic flair (as Sandy really doesn't want to die), she may inadvertently harm herself to the degree there is no return. I certainly don't mean to minimize the palatable loss that any mother is likely to feel with the loss of her children especially around the holiday season but Sandy emotionally regresses to the level of her youngest child, having an emotional fit that will likely produce her harm. I've met Sandy's ex-husband and he is not in touch with the spiritual essence of his higher self but that doesn't mean Sandy doesn't have work to do in regards to her own spiritual maturity.

Seventy-nine year old, Robert married his wife, Jill, 55 years ago. They've met in the 1ˢᵗ grade and had an ongoing love story ever since. She died earlier in the year and Robert is beside himself. He doesn't know which way to turn. There is "nothing left for me on this earth," he reasons, and he longs to be with his wife. Robert is a "god-fearing" man and believes if he kills himself, this would be the ultimate sin which he could not be forgiven; thus, he wouldn't be with his wife in the afterlife. So Robert has come up with an alternative. He has concluded that he can drink himself to death, but in such a way that he'd be able to ask for forgiveness before he actually died. He expressed his secret plan to me to get pancreatic cancer from his abusive drinking, which he knows to be incurable, thus, he'll have a window to gain God's forgiveness in order to be with his wife when he died. Robert has family and a community that loves him. They know of his love story, which in some ways makes it even harder for Robert to live. His loss is recent and profound. His grief is seemingly unbearable, but Robert showed up for therapy and told me his plan that he has told no one else; thus, he doesn't want to die.

Another emergency assessment this week was 35 year old, Rebecca. The holidays were particularly hard on her because they represent "family" and she doesn't have "family" to speak of. She is a Caucasian woman and I know this is unkind but accurate descriptor, "portly" in her physical presentation. She has an undeniably beautiful essence that is marred by her negative perceptions and low esteem. Rebecca met and married a Hispanic man, who had illegally entered the Country approximately eleven years ago. Given her physical presentation, Rebecca, neither then nor now, saw herself as desirable enough to lure or capture a man; however, under the circumstance of mutual need, the couple married and Rebecca was immediately impregnated but there was a dubious outcome. Her beloved was deported back to his Central American homeland ten years ago and Rebecca has been pining after the guy ever since. He remains married to Rebecca as they've been fighting a ten year battle for his return but he has gone on with his life, forging other relationships and having other children while Rebecca languishes with enduring hopes that she'll get him back into the Country one day. Nevertheless, this holiday season was hard on her and she expressed that "she doesn't want to live" but she "didn't want to die."

And there was Jade. She, too, is a Caucasian woman. She is 32 years old with four children in the social welfare system and pregnant with her fifth. Jade is belligerent and feisty. She has an abrasive persona that any therapist could see is a cover up for her deep vulnerabilities and insecurities. She punctuates each sentence with the crudeness of "F-bombs" and is poised for an attack. In the machinations of her mind resulting from faulty schema development, Jade has concluded that having another child with her meth addicted partner is going to result in a favorable outcome. She regaled me with a litany of his abusive tirades of the most demeaning and cruel things one person could say to another person; yet, she still stays fused in this unhealthy, toxic relationship with her meth abusing partner. To the question of why Jade would stay in such an untenable and devaluing relationship, Jade's response is that she is "butt ugly." I've not previously heard a woman refer to herself as being "butt ugly" but Jade has a "shock and awe" type personality and it is easy to see why she views and expresses the image of herself in such a way. Her pregnancy being foolishly conceived has not brought Jade any peace or joy during the holiday season; thus, she presented on my schedule as an emergency session with statements that she "doesn't want to live anymore." However, "she doesn't want to die."

When I am working with clients with a variety of different symptoms or disorders (e.g., anxiety, depression, phobias, psychosis, etc.) and a variety of different issues (e.g., broken hearts, work conflicts or terminations, pending/post incarceration, etc.) the common factor of it all is loss. Dr. Pauline Boss, in her similarly title book, examined the concept of "ambiguous loss." Ambiguous loss is confusing loss resulting in a physiological presence and psychological absence, or psychological presence with physiological absence. The former may represent itself in situations like Jade's. She has the physiological presence of her partner (in that he is still alive and resides with her) but he is psychologically unavailable for her (in that their relationship is devoid of a healthy, emotional connection). In fairness to Boss' work, she references the experience of caring for a dementia sufferer, whose physical presence is there but he or she is certainly not the person he/she once was. The latter can be represented in the cases of Robert and Rebecca. It is more profound in Robert's case because his wife is deceased; yet, he feels her presence with him on a daily basis. In Rebecca's case, her ambiguous loss is more nostalgic or fantasy based in that she has never psychologically let go of a relationship that never really was.

Therapists understand that a common factor for mental illness is impairment in functioning. That is, when we fail to function adequately in our leisure time, maintaining healthy relationships and the ability to work effectively in order to maintain employment, we can point to some degree of mental impairment. If we refine this further in relating to "relational impairments" we are really talking about the degree of spiritual differentiation that one has (indifferent-heart to the pure-heart realm). Our degree of spiritual development reveals our nature and our nature is exhibited in our behaviors. Though I endorse both ways in understanding either the human or spiritual condition, a common factor not fully explored is how all of these mental health conditions relate to loss. In each case above (including my own) it was the loss that triggered a reaction from each of us.

The loss of my wages created my disappointment and disrupted my swagger. The loss made me angry with mother in her desire to help me possibly retrieve the lost money due to my ignorance in how the world works. The loss of Sandy's connection with her children created her despair and the loss the children had with their mother fleeing the home hardened some of their hearts in order not to be devastated with her absence. The loss of Robert's wife created his disillusionment with and his attempt to deceive God. He initially lost sight of the value of his presence with his family and friends that remain. Rebecca lost her esteem, confidence and value of herself; thus, creating her antagonism, negativity and anger. Jade's loss of the vision of herself as one of God's children and referencing herself as "butt-ugly" creates a schism between herself and all others.

What have you lost along the way? Have you lost recognition or status? Have you lost income or your career? Have you lost housing or health? Have you lost coordination, rhythm, memory, concentration, balance or focus? Have you lost your relationship, your youth, your vision or your hearing? Have you lost your confidence, respect or your reputation? Have you lost drive, motivation, enthusiasm or creativity? Have you lost your dignity, your hope or faith in all that matters? Have you lost a limb, your keys or your place in line? Whatever your experience is, it will be associated with loss. Thus, our healing and health has to do with our capacity to handle the inevitable of our losses. Incidentally Elisabeth Kubler-Ross' stages of grief appear to fit each of these loses. She postulated that there can be denial or disbelief, anger, bargaining, depression and acceptance.

I moved fairly quickly through Kubler-Ross' stages of grief when I lost my wages. I couldn't believe what I had done, but my disbelief was only for a second. There was no way for me to deny what had occurred. I knew that it was due to me foolishly pulling my chained watch out of my pocket that caused my loss. I didn't bargain with God, my mother or my employer for some way to recoup my loss. My anger may have been reignited and projected upon my mother who tried to get me to go back and check within the store for my money but at the end of the day, I settled into acceptance fairly quickly. With acceptance coming so quickly, I didn't mope around in a state of depression. Many times throughout our lives we may have to settle into the notion that "it is what it is" and not allow the original object of our loss to generate a loss within ourselves.

Rebecca wrestled with the loss of a dream. She wants what everybody wants…to love and be loved. She denied the fact that she had sufficient and significant appeal, so she allowed herself to be exploited by an undocumented immigrant hoping to establish roots in the United States. Her family had their own issues, in that she married someone non-white. They may have likely rallied for her after the her baby was born, given that some people may put bigotry aside when it comes to the birth of "their grandchild" but her family couldn't accept Rebecca's ongoing allegiance to a person they thought was exploiting her. In her loss, Rebecca projected anger at her parents and withdrew from them as well. She bargained with her husband in her willingness to accept him back regardless of his philandering and creation of other children. However, in the still moments of her day and evening, she'd realize her predicament, descended into depression and sought therapeutic support.

Due to the emergency and with Rebecca's original therapist unavailable, I assessed Rebecca's propensity to commit suicide. She conveyed to intake that suicide was her intention but Rebecca didn't want to die. I explored the events in her life that was making her depressed and I pushed her hard to make some immediate and fundamental changes. I educated her on the integrity model and pointed out that her husband was living his life as he was waiting for the legal process to allow him to return. I urged her to reconnect with the family she has and embrace a new emphasis for the start of the New Year. She felt drawn in by her husband even though she knew that he wasn't good for her. I validated that her attachment to her husband was like a drug; therefore, we had to treat it like a "drug." He called daily under the pretext of wanting to have daily contact with his son but he rarely talked with his son. I urged her to set up her environment so that she is not susceptible to his influence. She spent money that she didn't have on the failing efforts from her immigration attorney to get him back into this Country and I urged her to allow those efforts to be between the attorney and her husband. I informed her that her weight had nothing to do with her value and if she truly believed that no one else loved or could love her, to become her own "loving parent" to care for the wounded soul within.

Rebecca left the session with a new lease on life. After all, she had a child that she adored and knew he needed his mother. She had no history of suicidal attempts. She wasn't consuming alcohol or illegal substances that would alter her perception and perhaps trigger an impulsive act on her part. Yes, the holidays and disconnection from those she loved triggered her despair; along with her statements to Intake that she was suicidal, Rebecca didn't want to die. I validated Rebecca's story (sometimes just listening can be enough) and provided her with some concrete action steps that she could implement to empower herself. I assured her that she was much more than how she narrowly perceived herself. I realize that my one session "pep" talk will not likely change the outcome of Rebecca's life but I planted a "seed" within her and it is her responsibility to allow it to take root, sprout and blossom into a fruit bearing plant.

The end goal of all treatment models, whether mental health or substance abuse, is the concept of "acceptance." It is the final stage in Kubler-Ross's stages of grief because when we accept life as it is, all grief surrounding loss dissipates. Now be careful with this. I don't want anyone to accept the futility of life or the invalidation of him/herself. Isiah writes, *"He gives strength to the weary and increases the power of the weak. Even youths grow tired and weary, and young men stumble and fall; but those who hope in the Lord will renew their strength. They will soar on wings like eagles; they will run and not grow weary, they will walk and not be faint"* (40:29-31-NIV). God creates the world and we can create our responses to the experiences that we have in this world. The famous Serenity Prayer conveys this sentiment: "God grant me the serenity to accept the things I cannot change; courage to change the things I can; and wisdom to know the difference." Wow, what a pithy; yet profound, and powerful statement! We are not trying to "tough it out" or endorse an equally ego-centric (macho) attitude to "just get over it." We are soliciting God's grace, compassion and support to help us through each loss.

Robert must *accept* his loss for healing to be achieved but he doesn't have to accept his despair associated with his loss. Robert had 55 years in a marriage that he describes as a "love story." Add the previous 18+ years to that time to establish this love story (remember he met Jill in the 1ˢᵗ grade); thus Robert and Jill have had a 70+ year blessing! Robert is lamenting his loss and forgetting his blessings. He can accept with gratitude the gift that he has received and accept the fact that he has a tremendous legacy to the generations that follow. Or, he can cheapen his experience with an inappropriate exit from this world. Ultimately, Robert chose to accept the former attitude to his experience of loss. He ceased drinking completely and began plugging into his family more fully. We didn't forget Jill, which is why I think people hang onto the grief for so long in fear of forgetting their loved one and a need to demonstrate how deeply they loved the departed. Robert, like many people, experiencing many different types of losses is conflicted about the appropriate amount of time to grieve. A young woman, mutually ending her relationship with her boyfriend, came to me as livid as one could be, due to the fact that he was in a new relationship only weeks after their relationship ended. She equated his lack of mourning about the relationship loss with false notions about how little he must have loved her while they were in the relationship together. Robert was equally conflicted and needed "permission" (per se) to plug back into his life. The length of one's grieving tells us nothing about the quality of the couple's relationship; however, we did set up ways for Robert to continue honoring Jill and their life together without him choosing despair.

Jade has to deal with acceptance as well. Jade can erroneously *accept* the fact that she is "butt ugly" and go through this world feeling as though she is filled up with "p… (I'll say 'spit' to keep my language clean) and vinegar" while continuing to accept men who use meth and treat her with disregard. Or, she can accept the fact that she is a child of the Most High

God and there is nothing "butt ugly" about her. She can accept the notion that even though she has the physical capabilities to produce a child that she can restrain herself from having a child until she can embrace her own worthiness in order to see what she produces as worthy. She can also accept responsibility for the care and wellbeing of the children that she has previously birthed into this world. In a materialistic world we look for symmetry to convey aesthetics, like the ideal "hourglass" figure of a woman being 36-24-36. Jade has masculine features and a girth that would never conform to the "hourglass figure," but she could soften some of her hard and aggressive features that would allow more people within her inner circle to see the beauty that she truly does possess.

A misnomer about the grieving process that I know will be a challenge for people to let go of is that grief takes a long time for healing to occur. A typical grieving process can be up to two years but some can be stuck in this process for years or even decades. Like Robert, they choose not to relinquish their anger, depression or sadness because they may feel that it is a betrayal or diminishes the love they had for the "object" that is lost. We reason that if our attachment was great then our grieving process must equally be great to reflect the degree of our attachment. It is equivalent to our notions of forgiveness. Clients present for couple's therapy, perhaps encumbered by the remembrance of an affair. The betrayed partner often holds fast to his or her refusal to grant forgiveness as a way to keep the betraying partner in check. They often feel that if they forgive too soon that the depth of the betrayal wasn't that great; thus, the betraying partner may minimize what (s)he has done and repeat the behavior.

Initially, Robert was afraid to let go of Jill or his grieving process that was "killing" him. His fears of betrayal were understandable. Likewise, a betrayed partner's fears are understandable but in this case, the inability to forgive keeps toxins in the relationship and creates an unhealthy power dynamic of an over-functioner attempting to control the actions of an under-functioner. If the offending partner hasn't grown in the aftermath of his/her transgression, the over-functioner is not going to be able to keep the transgression from happening again. We are all flawed individuals and each of us fall short of the glory of God but if you have to monitor and attempt to control the integrity of another person, that person has little integrity and you shouldn't be with him or her.

The Bible informs us that when we seek forgiveness from God, it is granted immediately. We don't have to "tap dance" or "grovel." We ask with a sincere heart and God grants forgiveness. Indeed, godly people are obliged to forgive as according to Matthew *"For if you forgive men their trespasses, your heavenly Father will also forgive you. But if you do not forgive men their trespasses, neither will your Father forgive your trespasses"* (6:14-15-RSV). Therefore, in my clinical work, I move clients rapidly (after the 4th or 5th session) to granting forgiveness to the transgressing partner because forgiveness is a choice. It is not a warm, fuzzy feeling that washes over the person and it is not the passage of time that grants forgiveness. It is a deliberate process that we engage in.

The same process is true for the resolution of grief. It doesn't have to take years to go through and we can choose acceptance after any stage in the grieving process or over any stage in the forgiveness process. You can go through denial or disbelief ("This can't be happening to me; I'm a faithful servant of God"), but you don't have to. You can go through anger ("I hate God for taking my loved one") or bargaining ("Oh, take me Lord, don't take my loved one"), but you don't have to. You can sink into sadness or depression ("I'll never be whole again and wish I was dead"), but this is not mandatory either. You can go to acceptance with any loss a lot quicker when you start off embracing the truth about this universe (all things are in flux) and the nature of impermanence. The present moment has an immediacy of experiences that quickly fade with the subsequent moment.

As James wrote, *"My brethren, count it all joy when you fall into various trials, knowing that the testing of your faith produces patience."* The loss of my money was a trial. Rebecca losing her husband is a trail. Sandy and Jada losing their children is a trial. Robert losing his wife is a trial. James instructs us to have "joy" in the trial. In order to do that, we must shift our thought process. My loss reminded me of the value of non-attachment in a world of impermanence. James implies that these trials are beneficial in developing spiritual fruit. I've yet to count my specific loss as "joy" but

I am living a "joyful" life. Initially, I didn't take from my loss the lesson of "patience" that James alluded to in the above passage, but I did have to have patience to wait on the next check to arrive. If my faith was assailed, it may have been represented in not trusting in my mother's advice to go and ask about my lost money. Otherwise, I am not certain if this particular incident tested my faith, thereby, honing my patience but I do know that with that loss and all of my subsequent losses, I've lacked nothing.

The losses in life may feel like a betrayal to our lower selves that has a tendency to possess, hoard or control resources (e.g., money, time, people, etc.); however, the antidote to betrayal is forgiveness. God grants us life in physical form but there is an "expiration date" on all things in the physical universe. God instructs us to be "fruitful and multiply" and that we'll have to "labor" upon this earth, but He doesn't promise any of us a life devoid of losses. The wisdom that I have arrived at over the years is that our losses don't have to steal our joy. They merely remind us of the gift of our existence and the fleeting moments of life. Take ahold of life and command joy! Instead of the bleak vision of "I don't want to live; I don't want to die," boldly exclaim, "I WANT TO LIVE!" "THANK YOU GOD FOR THIS LIFE!"

Ripening the Fruit-Forgiveness

Take a moment each day for reflection and praise to God with gratitude for each breath you are taking. There is no doubt in my mind that previous losses and impending losses in your life shape you greatly but they don't have to take away your joy and appreciation for living. Life, with all trials, challenges and losses is still worthy living. Reflect on the concepts of impermanence, forgiveness and joy. Look for opportunities to give something away and opportunities to grant forgiveness; both actions will increase your joy.

Look through your cupboard for food items that you know you are not likely to consume but would have value for someone else. Collect it and give it away. (If the spirit moves you, give away food items that you love and know that you're likely to consume). Go through your closet and sort out clothing that is too big…too small or unworn in a year and donate it to charity. It is stuff that you don't need that will serve others well that you let go of in order to remind you of impermanence. Examine your soul for a kind word that you can give or a gesture of kindness (that could be as simple as holding the door for someone entering or exiting a building). Small and random acts of kindness feed the soul of both the giver and receiver.

As it relates to forgiveness, the Lord's Prayer asks God to "forgive our transgression as we forgive those who transgress against us." Forgive the person that walked by and didn't acknowledge your presence. Forgive the person who cut you off in traffic. Forgive the boss who passed over you for promotion. Forgive the drycleaner for ruining your outfit. Forgive your children for making noise while you were trying to sleep. Forgive your spouse for burning the toast. Forgive your neighbor for damaging your mailbox. Forgive the pastor for not living up to your high ideals. Forgive your parents for not plugging into your life like that of your friends. Forgive the cable company for increasing your monthly rates. Forgive your family for gossiping behind your back. Forgive your friend for letting you down. Forgive yourself for all of the above and the various transgressions you'll do on a daily basis.

Jesus instructed Peter to forgive his brother (sister) "seventy times seven" times. That's a lot of forgiveness! If you can find only seven opportunities to forgive people on a daily basis, you'll be far ahead of the curve.

VII

Worry Not

But seek first his kingdom and his righteousness, and all these things will be given to you as well. Therefore do not worry about tomorrow, for tomorrow will worry about itself. Each day has enough trouble of its own.
(Matthew 6: 33-34-NIV)

It was a very cold, but typical winter day in Minnesota when Stephanie presented for therapy. The outside temperature was below zero degrees Fahrenheit and the gust of wind penetrated one's clothing like an icy shiv; providing, little refuge from the cold. Stephanie expressed that she was referred to our mental health center by her primary care provider (PCP) with a diagnosis of depression. Among other brief screeners, we administered to her the Generalized Anxiety Disorder Scale (GAD-7) and it registered high at 18 points; thus, I deduced her presenting problems were more anxiety induced rather than depression and added this disorder to her diagnostic assessment. Interestingly, Stephanie's initial physical presentation revealed neither anxiety nor depression. She was personable, well groomed, delightful and grasped my hand at the moment of our introduction with a firm and meaningful handshake.

Stephanie dived into the litany of concerns she had, identifying a myriad of things she was worried about; which, confirmed my Generalized Anxiety Diagnosis. Her boyfriend, Ed, of six months, flew with a small contingent of "snow birds" to New Mexico for 3-4 months to await the arrival of spring prior to his return. Other obligations kept Stephanie from flying off to New Mexico with Ed but his departure provided her with a mixed blessing for the "worrier" to think. Ed had discussed the prospect of the two of them getting married and Stephanie was conflicted with the notion. She was widowed for the last 15 years and nostalgically held on to the memory of her deceased partner, describing him as the "love of my life." We tend to make icons out of those who have died; which, elevated Stephanie's ex-husband to a status that Ed could never meet.

Nevertheless, what struck me about this attractively groomed and positive presentation that belies her reported mood of anxiety and depression was her reaction when I asked her age. The truth is, her initial visit with Intake gathers all of her demographic, presenting problem and insurance information but I tend to be a bit redundant in my questioning during the assessment process because information can change drastically between the point of entry and the actual assessment. I suppose if one honor's societal conventions of a generation ago, people didn't tend to ask a woman's age and women certainly didn't offer this information up willingly. This appears to be changing in recent times as female celebrities are boasting about their advanced age but youthful appearances.

Stephanie was likely "old school" as she waffled...hemmed and hawed about her age. It was the only question she was stymied by and I found her reaction interesting. Ultimately she was able to tell me what I already knew that Stephanie was 65 years old. It was as if Stephanie could avoid saying her "dreaded age" out loud then the reality of her 65 years upon this earth wouldn't be true. There is a Geico commercial with the ageless (and in this case, annoying) Peter Pan commenting on a woman's age in that she "didn't look a day over 70" that came to mind when Stephanie was initially struggling with my question. Indeed, her age was just another one of the myriad of things that Stephanie worries about but it is her worry about all things beyond her control that robs her of her happiness.

Stephanie, like many people who worry, is trying to control the outcome of events. Worriers ascribe to themselves a power that they don't have and are not entitled to. They distort this power and think it to be an indication of the degree that they love or care about someone or something but that is patently false! Love and worry are mutually exclusive. They cannot exist in the same space. Our power comes from the acceptance of truth and the truth is; only God is in control! Stephanie's worrying about the loss of her husband, did not bring him back. Her worrying about her ability to love Ed in the same degree that she loved her deceased husband doesn't allow her to open up to the fullness of this new relationship. Stephanie's worry about me (or others) discovering her true age, does not make her younger.

Agitation and worry are fetters that bind us; thus, forestalling our development in our spiritual growth. Stephanie has a clinical diagnosis of anxiety; however, all of us can be agitated and worried to varying degrees that equally puts a halt in our own spiritual progression. We worry about our future. We worry about our past. We worry about our jobs…our communities…our homes and our families. We worry about our comings and goings…illness and health…living and dying. We worry about lack while in our state of poverty and then we worry about losing wealth in our state of affluence when our situation changes. We worry about being loved, and if so, we worry about our ability to return that love. We worry if we reside in a cold state and then worry about our decision if we decide to move to a warmer state. We worry if we'll ever have children and then worry about the children when we have them. We worry and worry and worry some more but our worry produces nothing!

Matthew advises us to consider the following about worrying: "*Therefore I tell you, do not worry about your life, what you will eat or drink; or about your body, what you will wear. Is not life more than food, and the body more than clothes? Look at the birds of the air; they do not sow or reap or store away in barns, and yet your heavenly Father feeds them. Are you not much more valuable than they? Can any one of you by worrying add a single hour to your life?*" (6:25-34-NKJV). Worriers think that their concerns are profound. Sure, this passage in Matthew makes sense for all others but "my worries are really, really important!"

I encourage my worriers to conduct an experiment in their lives as it relates to worry. You can't tell a person who is predisposed to worrying to stop their worrying. If I instruct the reader, for the next five minutes that I want you to under no circumstance to think about unicorns, how many times are you likely to think about unicorns in the next five minutes? Likewise, the nature of a worrier is to find things to worry about. So our experiment is a paradoxical intervention, to prescribe the symptom that the worrier is desperately trying to eliminate. Let's look at Stephanie and her age again. Stephanie has all kinds of erroneous notions about what is means to be 65, so her charge is to worry freely and deliberately about what it means to be exposed for being sixty-five? I want her to examine this from top to bottom. Is her worry centered on her losing her youth…her vitality…her health? Does it make her incompetent…unattractive…unfit? Purposefully immerse herself in every aspect of what it means to be exposed for her natural age of sixty-five.

I encouraged her to take the entire week between sessions to think about this topic and write about it in her journal at any moment that she is not preoccupied with another activity (i.e., work, laundry, meal preparation, etc.). As she gives herself permission to totally focus in on this worry, her mind can't think about other worries. The mind can't have two simultaneous thoughts at once; thus, with the permission and task to examine her age, it becomes exhausting and futile. The meaning, intensity of emotion and concern about being 65 diminishes. During the next phase of the experiment she will promote being 65 to family members, friends and strangers and write about what their reactions were to her revelation (as well as her reaction to their reactions). In some ways, Stephanie is experiencing "flooding" but not in a negative way one would experience if he/she was reliving a trauma. After all, we are talking about Stephanie worrying about something fairly innocuous as age but the more exposure to her concern that is brought into consciousness and spoken out loud the more Stephanie becomes desensitized to this worry.

When Stephanie started working on this assignment, it initially concerned her. Why wouldn't it? She's a worrier; however, in true paradoxical intervention form, Stephanie wasn't all over the map with her worries, she had a specific worry that she could now fully examine and get ahold of. As Stephanie was tackling the notion of her age, I began to reframe notions of anxiety from maladaptive to adaptive. I had heard a piece of "junk science" on a morning television show that worriers are smarter than the rest of the population because they are constantly thinking about something. Therefore, they are developing more neural pathways in the brain and this obsessive intellectual exercise makes them smarter. Who knows? I certainly don't know, but I used this information with Stephanie (and I also use it with other anxiety sufferers) to reframe their notions about anxiety/worrying from being "pathological" or "maladaptive" to the anxiety/worry being an "ally" or "friend."

Stephanie was able to research famous actresses over 60 (e.g., Goldie Hawn, Helen Mirren, Jane Seymour, Jacklyn Smith, Christie Brinkley, etc.) and discover that 60 truly is the "New Sexy!" Of course, some of these women had beauty regiments that included Botox, chin implants and taking the fat out of one's buttocks to inject it into specific areas of the face that generated a whole new set of worries for Stephanie but Stephanie seemed to be able to manage and cope with these new set of worries. What I found interesting about Stephanie was that age wasn't anything that she initially brought up as a concern that she worried about. It only became a focal point due to her reaction and reluctance to answer the basic intake question and it seemed to diminish the expressed concerns in these other areas as we didn't have to revisit each and every one of her concerns prior to her feeling well enough to be discharge from therapy.

Stephanie presented with overt fears, worries and concerns that resulted in a clinical diagnosis of Generalized Anxiety Disorder but I am mindful about the vast majority of us that have "closeted" fears, worries and concerns that we are wrestling with that even our most intimate partner doesn't know about because we haven't shared those fears, worries or concerns with him or her. We worry about job security, finances, retirement, our children, our family of origin, the neighbor's perception of us, gossip in the community, health concerns, terrorists' attacks, flying in a plane, our drinking water, food safety, fidelity, love, etc. All of our worries have a singular focus and that focus is upon ourselves. As we remain self-focused we disavow the magnificence of God, thus relying on our worry to control the outcome of events.

In the leading passage for this chapter, Jesus is clear about what we should focus upon to absolve ourselves of unnecessary worry. "*Seek first the kingdom of God and His righteousness and then all other things will be added to you.*" So what is the kingdom of God? Is it chaotic and unstable? Is it filled with strife and backbiting? Is it filled with gossip and innuendoes? Is it filled with entities jostling for position that replicates our status on earth with "haves" and the "have nots?" There is a different construct in place in the Kingdom of God. There are different emphases and different "laws" that operate in the Kingdom of God than we see operating in the material world. In the material world, there is always scarcity and lack; therefore, worry may even seem appropriate because as long as we are "worrying" about it (whatever it is), we may be motivated to seek it out or acquire it.

The Kingdom of God operates out of abundance; therefore, the counterintuitive spiritual injunctive, *"it is better to give than to receive,"* starts to make a lot more sense to us. The Kingdom of God is about a relationship. We figuratively are sitting in the lap of God, comforted by His full, loving embrace. The authors Jay Efran and Rob Fauber, in their article, "Spitting in the Client's Soup," created a "bogus treatment" that reportedly worked equally well as established treatments for overcoming fears and anxieties. So then the question becomes, "Is our therapeutic efficacy really about the 'therapeutic relationship' verses any particular method of intervention; along with the 'belief' that something constructive is happening within that 'therapeutic relationship?'"

Isn't this exactly what Christ revealed to us and recorded by Matthew over 2000 years ago that we can focus on the minutia in our lives and limitations, generating an ongoing need for worrying or we can focus on the Magnificence of God with an abundance of resources (namely Love); thus, our "belief" and "loving relationship" becomes therapeutic. Paul wrote that love bears all things; therefore, it is the source from which healing flows. Solomon wrote about the power or value of believing in this way, *"Do not deliver me to the will of my adversaries; For false witnesses have risen against me, and such as breathe out violence. I would have lost heart, unless I had believed that I would see the goodness of the LORD In the land of the living. Wait on the LORD; be of good courage, and He shall strengthen your heart. Wait, I say, on the LORD!"* (Psalms 27:12-14-NKJV)

From a psychological perspective, "the will of my adversaries" is our internal dialogue that we grant "aid and comfort" to that diminishes our peace. When I'm facilitating the anger management therapy group, which is often comprised of emotionally volatile, reactive and impulsive people, they witness within me a calm persona that is foreign to their general experiences. They've learned to yell, throw things, put others down and to have a fit when things are not going their way. As I am sharing with them new ways of being, inevitably someone will always ask, "Don't you get agitated about things…Don't you worry…Don't you get anger?" My answer is "YES!" Of course, I experience the array of human emotions as all people will. I don't want to not have a human emotional experience. What I don't want to have happen is that I am controlled by the human emotional experience.

I authentically share with my group members an incident that has occurred at my worksite to me that did created agitation, anger and worry initially for me. I was comfortably settled in what I erroneously believed to be "my" corner office. After all, it had my name prominently affixed on the door for everyone to see. I was settled in for about a year or more when without notice or consultation with me, I was relocated to share an office with another therapist who was established at the agency a lot longer than I had been at the time. My colleague also complied with the agency demands but didn't like another person invading "his" space either. As unhappy as he was, I too, became more agitated and angry about the move. I worried about the prospect of the agency willy-nilly assigning me to various office spaces without my consultation and knowledge. I sulked for a bit because I was under the misapprehension that I actually had an office at the agency. I indulged in the misconception that I possessed things that were not mine to possess (e.g., office space, computer, staplers, desk, etc.).

When I redirected my thoughts from myself and what I thought I was in possession of, I was able to remind myself that all things in this world are temporary gifts granted by God in a world of impermanence. As I seek first the "kingdom of God and His righteousness" I am not bothered as much about things that are outside of my control. Thus, the magnitude of my agitation, anger and worry is diminished (perhaps not eliminated) but there is less volatility of emotion than there would be if I wasn't focused upon God. Solomon writes, "*Commit your way to the Lord, Trust also in*

Him, and He shall bring it to pass. He shall bring forth your righteousness as the light, and your justice as the noonday. Rest in the Lord, and wait patiently for Him; Do not fret because of him who prospers in his way, because of the man who brings wicked schemes to pass. Cease from anger, and forsake wrath; Do not fret—it only causes harm." (Palms 37: 5-8-NKJV)

As I think about "fretting" (worrying) and the "harm" that it causes, I am reminded about several of the male clients on my caseload that produce harm in their lives due to their incessant worrying. Two of them are single men; one black and the other is white. The other is a Native American man who is a family man with a wife and three children. All of them are in their 40's and each of them has been afflicted (harmed) by their incessant worrying. The former was a hardworking, African American trucker who has delivered goods throughout this nation but generated fear, anxiety, and worry about his ability to drive semi-trucks any longer and was paralyzed in a panic attack on the side of the road. What once came natural to him in hauling goods from coast to coast became a terrifying ordeal for him. This panic and fear came on the heels of the notable Tracy Morgan's (a black comedian) auto accident; with Morgan being seriously injured and a friend of his died in the carnage. The accident resulted from a Walmart semi-truck driver (also African-American), falling asleep behind the wheel and crashing into Morgan's vehicle. I suspect that my client has overly identified with this incident and has had his own experience of falling asleep behind the wheel that did not result in an accident that was terrifying the client; thereby, causing his panic when he tries to resume driving. My client's fear/worry creates a lack of capacity to generate income; thereby, harming his lifestyle.

My single, Caucasian, male client is terrified by social interactions and relegates himself to the confines of his apartment complex. He isolates in his behaviors, avoids greetings and direct eye contact, setting up a habitual lack of interaction with others where he remains invisible. The client has no family or friends or the ability to work. This isolation harms his capacity to find joy in his life. He is contrasted with the Native American family man who does work and has limited interaction with his neighbors but he has performance anxieties at work that is limiting his potential and enough social anxiety that locks him in a pattern of worrying about what others may be thinking about him. His worrying generates harm that impacts his family. He doesn't go to family functions or show up to support his children's activities due to incessant worrying that people, who wouldn't think twice about him, are thinking about him.

Stephanie's "fretting" and worrying wasn't as disabling as it appears that these men's worry was but if it limits her joy it is still a product of harm. Her fears and worrying created hesitancy and doubt. It made her unsure of herself and insecure. Some theorists would likely surmise that Stephanie's anxieties are traced back to childhood and having the experiences of an abandoning parent, a neglectful parent, an overly involved parent, an overly indulging parent, an overly rigid or controlling parent. Others might attribute her anxieties to heredity or some other biological causes. Henry Emmons and Rachel Kranz, in their book, "*The Chemistry of Joy*," referenced chemical imbalance as a cause of anxious-depression. They wrote, "People with low levels of serotonin often feel fearful, inadequate, and nervous, always worried about the future and their own inability to measure up to life's demands. They tend to hold on too tightly and may become dependent in relationships."

Daniel Amen, in his book, "*Change your Brain Change your Life*," identifies biology, particularly brain functioning as the cause for mental health issues. Relative to anxiety, nervousness and panic disorders, he wrote, "Excessive basal ganglia activity resets the body's idle to a revved-up level and can make people feel anxious, nervous, tense, and pessimistic. Almost all of the patients we have treated with panic disorder whom we've scanned had heightened basal ganglia activity." We do know that pharmaceutical approaches (e.g. Xanax, Lorazepam, Klonopin, etc.) can have a rapid result in quelling the anxieties of some, but isn't this merely symptom suppression verses one dealing with his or her anxieties, worries and fears?

Our brains are a marvel of human biology! Certainly, sophisticated computers can make computations in what appears to be light speed but the complexity and potential of the human brain is enormous, barely explored and not matched by anything created thus far. I can see how we might marvel at this mechanism (brain) but there is something beyond the brain that uses this sophisticated mechanism. Caroline Leaf, in her book, "*Switch on your Brain*," responds to the homage that we, therapists, physicians, scientists, researchers and others attribute to the brain with, "We are not victims of our biology or circumstances. How we react to the events and circumstances of life can have an enormous impact on our mental and even physical health. As we think, we change the physical nature of our brain. As we consciously direct our thinking, we can wire out toxic patterns of thinking and replace them with healthy thoughts."

This is heartening because it reminds us that we can have all kinds of experiences and not be defined or predestined by the experience. That is, our experience of childhood, whether great or horrendous (e.g., abused, molested, taunted, etc.), doesn't need to define us (e.g., wimp, bully, jerk, etc.) or predestine us (e.g., failures, anxiousness, incompetency, etc.). Our lived circumstances of a broken home, unemployment, relationship break ups, incarceration, death of loved ones, etc., need not define or predict anything about us. And, as Leaf implies, our biology (including our brain) need not subject us to ongoing victimization and determination of our mental health.

It has been my observation that Stephanie and my other anxiety sufferers are focusing in on themselves with an attempt to control (or perceive they lack of control). As stated earlier, they are trying to control the outcome of events. The Apostle Peter suggests that our experience of grace and peace comes from the knowledge of God. He writes, "*But also for this very reason, giving all diligence, add to your faith virtue, to virtue knowledge, to knowledge self-control, to self-control perseverance, to perseverance godliness, to godliness brotherly kindness, and to brotherly kindness love. For if these things are yours and abound, you will be neither barren nor unfruitful in the knowledge of our Lord Jesus Christ. For he who lacks these things is shortsighted, even to blindness, and has forgotten that he was cleansed from his old sins.*" (2 Peter 1: 5-9-NKJV)

Wow! What a powerful statement. Let's parse it out a bit. To be "diligent" is to "purposefully attend" to something, and in this case, it is our faith.

"Faith" is not necessarily scientific or empirical but it certainly is powerful. Our belief system shapes our vision and determines how we are going to experience this world. If Stephanie believes no other man can compare favorably to the experience she has had with the husband she lost, she is absolutely right and her new suitor, Ed, has no chance. If she believes that being 65 makes her over the hill, she attempts to lie to herself in trying to project to the world that she is not 65 years old. As long as our trucker (above) believes that danger awaits him on the road, he is absolutely right (within his distorted thought process) and will rightly not return to trucking. Why would either the single guy or married guy above venture outside of the comfort of their own domiciles when each believes that the gossip's tongue is poised to criticize and eviscerate them?

Each of them (and all of us) is driven by our belief system (associated with our faith). David Sherwood, in an article entitled, "The Relationship Between Beliefs and Values in Social Work Practice: Worldviews Make a Difference," stated, "Everyone operates on the basis of some worldview or faith-based understanding of the universe and persons—examined, or unexamined, implicit or explicit, simplistic or sophisticated. One way or another, we develop functional assumptions which help us to sort through and make some sort of sense out of our experience." What resonates in the back of my mind in reading Sherwood's words is "adaptation." Whether the situation or circumstances are positive or negative, we tend to adapt ourselves to them. Just ask the person that lingers in an abusive situation for years, with a way out, but chooses not to get out of that situation.

Diligence adds to faith and faith adds to virtue. What is virtue? Virtue is a standard for behavior, or doing what is right (moral). Deviating from what we know to be right produces our anxieties. Shame triggers our avoidance and keeps us socially isolated from the neighbors or not involved in our children's social activities. Virtuous people don't operate out of shame but to establish what is virtuous takes a degree of discernment (or "knowledge"). Faulty knowledge coming in produces faulty output that can cause a reaction of fear but God hasn't given us a spirit of fear. Honing our knowledge takes a measure of self-control to determine what we "input" into our system that shapes our "worldview." I have been astonished by the input of people with anxiety that manifests in disturbing nightmares who watch "The Walking Dead" TV series and/or vampire movies. Peter tells us it is not only controlling what it is that we input but to persevere in doing so. Far too many clients (and far too many of each of us) give up after meager efforts. We want the body of Arnold Schwarzenegger in his prime, but we don't persevere in our gym commitment beyond the first week.

Peter tells us that our perseverance is in godliness and that godliness is exhibited in our acts of service and kindness (brotherly love and kindness) to others. Engaging in this process, our knowledge of Christ abounds (who is our exemplar for peace, tranquility, love, etc.) that vanquishes our anxieties, fears and worries. Allow me to add a caveat to what I just wrote regarding the word, "vanquish." I don't want the reader to misunderstand. We are on this earth (a gift from God) to have a human experience, which involves us tapping into our entire emotional array. God (with Christ's example) can grant us peace as we navigate the terrain of disquieting emotions that results from challenging, difficult and horrendous circumstances but our emotional array remains intact. Agitation, fears, hatred, worries, doubt, etc. will continue to reside in our lower selves but we have the ability and responsibility to attend to and develop our higher self to have a more bountiful experience upon our spiritual/physical journeys.

Ripening the Fruit-Conquering Fear

Anxiety is the manifestation of fear and worry. We can be (and sometimes people are) afraid of everything (i.e., Generalized Anxiety Disorder) and we'll churn this fear over and over again within our minds with excessive worry. Sometimes the fear is specific (e.g., reaction to a trauma or a stressor that exceeds our ability to cope at the time). Sometimes the fear is irrational; called "phobias" (e.g., fear of flying, cats, snakes, social settings, people, etc.). Sometimes the fear is obsessive and internalized (e.g., fear of contaminates, fear of succeeding fear or failing, fear of inadequacies being exposed, fear of rejection or not being accepted, etc.). The natural tendency, when confronted by our fears, is the "fight or flight" response. That is, we tend to do battle with the fear, with the fear getting the upper hand. Or, we run from the fear with avoidance. The alternative to confrontation or avoidance is to make peace with our fears. In doing so, we begin to work through our anxieties. Use the guide below to help you make peace with your fears and work through your anxieties.

- If you are anxious, deal squarely with your fear. That is, the somatic symptoms of anxiety can include insomnia, racing thoughts with tension in the head, tingling sensations, crawling skin sensations, rapid heart palpitation, shallow breathing, etc. These can be the focal point of your thoughts but what are your fears? Go beneath the surface as a fear of a social setting is really about fear of inadequacy or rejection. What do you know about yourself that makes you feel inadequate or feel that you'll be rejected? What don't you know about God that keeps you from reaching out to Him?
- Don't fight your symptoms. If you are awake at 2:00am, get up and get out of bed. If your thoughts are racing, let them race and take note as they may be telling you something about yourself. Therapists look for themes in dreams and themes in one's thought life to assist clients in gaining more insight into themselves.
- Don't use alcohol or drugs to cope with your symptoms. Alcohol is a depressant and marijuana actually induces anxiety.
- Incorporate physical fitness into your lifestyle. It will help distract your thinking while burning up restless energy.

- Use visualizations to move toward your fear while maintaining a relaxed state of mind (somatic quieting). For instance, a terrifying memory or trauma only retains its power when you hang onto the fear. Visualize the fear. Move toward the fear and befriend the fear while remaining physically relaxed.
- By befriending fear, ask yourself what it is that your fear wants you to know and how is your fear serving you? That is, does your fear give your permission to feign helplessness…to fulfill your role of dependency…to not try…to remain stuck…to not move forward in your life?
- Incorporate deep breathing exercises to manage your anxiety. Inhale through your nose, while in a relaxed state (and not in a heightened state of anxiety or panic), for 5 counts…hold your breath for 5 counts and then expel the breath through your mouth for 10 counts. Repeat for 5 to 10 times and then simply watch your breath for normal but deeper breathing.
- Monitor your diet. Avoid eating after 8pm. Do eat breakfast! Avoid stimulating beverages (e.g., coffee, pop, energy drinks, etc.).
- Do not watch the news, monster/vampire movies or ingest other types of scary/worrisome materials into your psyche.
- Use progressive muscle relaxation (deliberately tense and relax the muscles from your head to toes) and/or use earbuds/headphones of your favorite (but relaxing) music as you are drifting off to sleep.
- Give your worries over to God. *"And we know that all things work together for good to those who love God, to those who are the called according to His purpose."* (Romans 8:28-NKJV)

You have only one life to live! Have the courage to have some fun and to tackle your highest ambitions. Remember that "courage is not the absence of fear…courage is moving ahead despite your fear."

VIII

Temptation

Then Jesus was led up by the Spirit into the wilderness to be tempted by the devil. And when He had fasted forty days and forty nights, afterward He was hungry. Now when the tempter came to Him, he said, "If You are the Son of God, command that these stones become bread." But He answered and said, "It is written, 'Man shall not live by bread alone, but by every word that proceeds from the mouth of God.'" Then the devil took Him up into the holy city, set Him on the pinnacle of the temple, and said to Him, "If You are the Son of God, throw Yourself down. For it is written: 'He shall give His angels charge over you,' and, 'In their hands they shall bear you up, Lest you dash your foot against a stone.'" Jesus said to him, "It is written again, 'You shall not tempt the Lord your God.'" Again, the devil took Him up on an exceedingly high mountain, and showed Him all the kingdoms of the world and their glory. And he said to Him, "All these things I will give You if You will fall down and worship me." Then Jesus said to him, "Away with you, Satan! For it is written, 'You shall worship the Lord your God, and Him only you shall serve.'" Then the devil left Him, and behold, angels came and ministered to Him.
(**Matthew 4: 1-11-NKJV**)

I met Jody in the lobby of our clinical building in Marshall, MN and with my perfunctory greeting; I identified myself and asked, "How are you doing?" She replied, "I'm a mess." Well, she didn't look like a "mess." Jody has blonde hair and blue eyes. She was statuesque and strolled with an elegant confidence in her gait. Her hair was coiffed with long-wavy, blonde curves that extended to the shoulder blades of her back. She had on business attire and acknowledged that she would be returning to her place of work after our session. Her nails were manicured and her makeup was flawless. Taking a cursory look at her intake screening documents, I noticed that she had extreme scores for both anxiety and depression; though I quickly learned that Jody had a tendency to exaggerate things. When we settled into my office, I parroted back the statement that she made in the lobby, "So, you are a 'mess?' You don't appear to be a mess," I added. "Oh, but I am," she exclaimed. "I tend to put on a good front but I am crying all the time."

I inquired about what was causing her so much pain, and as her eyes welled up to begin telling me her story, she was at the same time seductively seeking male attention (Jody doesn't have any female friends due to her flirtatious behaviors, plus her feeling more comfortable in the presence of men). In short order, it dawned upon me that I've seen this presentation several times before (and have actually written about it before). Though I've written about this disorder occurring in both men and women, I am finding that my female clients with this disorder tend to present just like Jody. They have all been attractive but express feign notions that they are not good enough in order to seek reassurance from others that they are indeed desirable. They are superficial with their emotions and when you are initially drawn in by the vulnerability of their tears, you soon begin to recognize the exploitive nature of those tears. In psychological terms, we would classify this type of presentation as Histrionic Personality Disorder.

The Diagnostic Statistical Manual (DSM-5) is a manual that clinicians use to guide our clinical decision in making a diagnosis, states that Histrionic Personality Disorder is "[a] pervasive pattern of excessive emotionality and attention seeking, beginning by early adulthood and present in a variety of contexts, as indicated by five (or more) of the following:

1. Is uncomfortable in situations in which he or she is not the center of attention.
2. Interaction with others is often characterized by inappropriate sexually seductive or provocative behavior.
3. Displays rapidly shifting and shallow expression of emotions.
4. Consistently uses physical appearance to draw attention to self.

5. Has a style of speech that is excessively impressionistic and lacking in detail.
6. Shows self-dramatization, theatricality, and exaggerated expression of emotion.
7. Is suggestible (i.e., easily influenced by others or circumstances).
8. Considers relationships to be more intimate than they actually are."

The other similarity I have noticed by women with this disorder is that they actually are intelligent and well accomplished. I've found these traits in university professors, therapists, county attorneys, corporate business executives, etc. Each of these women, though I would not consider them "problem drinkers" per se, do seem to have a pattern of drinking that allows them to engage in behaviors that can be deemed as "problematic." It was just enough "social lubricant" for some to engage in over-the-top attention seeking behaviors that they were probably predisposed to do anyway. It is interesting that these women present very well in a therapeutic session or in their work environments but their interpersonal relationships are marred with difficulties. While in session, they appear docile and sweet but when you hear how they are behaving outside of the session, it is remarkable. That is, the "reserved" becomes "wild" (that's why I believe the one glass of wine gives them permission to behave in ways that they might find untenable prior to drinking the wine). They can appear to be the life of the party and everybody loves them but they don't seem to be able to find sustainable happiness or commitment within their intimate partner relationships.

Let me be clear. During the initial stages of their couple's relationship they will effusively express to the world how wonderful their selected partner is. These types of women will gush about her "wonderfully adoring partner." She may exclaim, "Oh, he has taken me out to the most wonderful place!" "You should see the most amazing gift he got me!" "He kissed me at the stroke of midnight and it was soooo amazing!" Her partner initially reigns as "King for the day," and then the thrill is gone; thus, the woman then seeks someone else to bring her that over-the-top thrill that has now waned in her current partner. Notice that the topic of conversation may be focused upon the occasion or upon her partner but the attention seeking is certainly upon her. Unlike the narcissist, who will definitely let you know that his/her self-focus excludes others ("Hey, it's all about me!"), histrionics can be indirect and deferential in getting the attention focused upon him or her.

Jody is a prime case of the above. She is 38 years old; married to a domineering and traditionalist thinking, luxury car salesman. He does well in his profession but commits long hours to his job. Jody is employed as well in one of the local businesses. Though she is not bringing home comparable income as her husband, she works exceedingly hard only to transition into other shift work once she returns home. While at home she manages four adorable but challenging children that dim her "emotional lights" and energy because they, too, are the attention seekers. In order for her to be the focal point of attention, Jody struck up what started as an emotional affair via the Internet that turned sexual. The affair was ultimately discovered and it has been my experience that the machismo expressed from men about what they'd do if they discovered their partner cheating on them ("kick her to the curb"), has not revealed itself to be true with the guys that show up for therapy. These "tough, stoic, non-emotional" guys are showing up in therapy sessions, sobbing and pleading for their partner not to leave them. And, this is when, the woman knows beyond doubt, "I got him!"

"She's got him" and Jody's husband is "tap dancing" hard to fix a 15 year old marriage that has fallen into neglect but the interesting thing is that Jody (and other women with this disorder that I've worked with) doesn't really want to reconcile her relationship. It is not so much about what her partner did or didn't do throughout the 15 year marriage. It is not about what he professes to do if the marriage moves forward. For Jody, the novelty of her marriage that she found in the early stages, which she thought she could reignite with each of her four children, has worn off. There are obligatory, societal, familial, financial and religious reasons for staying in her marriage, but now that Jody knows, "I got him," she does not give up the affair. She has the full attention of a desperate husband, trying to woo her back, along with the excitement of the affair; each satisfying her attention-seeking desires.

Jody expressed through a stream of some genuine and some faux tears that she was so confused that she doesn't know what to do. "But that is not true," I told her. "You knew what to do before you even came to me." "The question becomes, 'Are you going to do the things that you know are right to do?'" Interestingly, Jody didn't seem very concerned about the notion of her affair being exposed. Her husband knew about it (and undoubtedly the kids knew about it). Her pastor knew about it and her parents knew about it. They've all chimed in on what they thought was right for her to do but Jody railed against her father, in particular, because he has had an affair on her mother and now he wants to be moralistic toward her…"hypocrite," she announced. She was sensitive to the criticism that she was receiving from others but she was unmoved by what any of them said.

Jody's disorder, notwithstanding, we have a society of people behaving similarly as Jody. We are self-promoters and attention seekers. We have rapidly shifting emotions that doesn't reflect any deep thought or commitment to a set of behaviors (i.e., principles or standards). We project a façade of ourselves in dramatic displays (Have you seen shows like Jerry Springer or The Housewives of…*you name the city*?). We are seducers, provocateurs and tempters, and we are seduced, provoked and tempted. Titus wrote, "*Remind them to be subject to rulers and authorities, to obey, to be ready for every good work, to speak evil of no one, to be peaceable, gentle, showing all humility to all men. For we ourselves were also once foolish, disobedient, deceived, serving various lusts and pleasures, living in malice and envy, hateful and hating one another. But when the kindness and the love of God our Savior toward man appeared, not by works of righteousness which we have done, but according to His mercy He saved us, through the washing of regeneration and renewing of the Holy Spirit, whom He poured out on us abundantly through Jesus Christ our Savior, that having been justified by His grace we should become heirs according to the hope of eternal life.*" (Titus, 3:1-7-NKJV)

The Bible is replete with seducers, provocateurs and tempters; along with good people succumbing to the temptation. Of course, the first biblical account of this seduction and those seduced is when Satan beguiles Eve (who coops her partner, Adam) to defy God's command not to eat from the Tree of Knowledge (Genesis 1). Jacob (whose name implies, "Trickster", who tricked his brother out of his birthright), was later tricked by Laban when Jacob was told to work seven years for the hand of Rachel but then given her older sister, Leah, to marry. Jacob was so smitten by the beauty of Rachel that he worked for Laban another seven years for her hand as well (Genesis, 29). Biblical heroes like David, whether deliberately seduced or out of his own weakness, was tempted by the vision of Bathsheba as he watches her bathe nude from his rooftop and succumbs to his desire by seducing and impregnating this wife of a soldier (Uriah) in his command (2 Samuel, 11-NKJV).

I opened this chapter with a passage from the Bible about Jesus' temptation. I did so to illustrate that no matter what advancements we have made on the spiritual differentiation scale (indifferent-heart, craving-heart or pure-heart), we will encounter temptation. Jody wasn't resolute in her marriage; and, "Yes" she presented with the characteristics of a personality disorder but none of us are free of the constant bombardments of temptation that confront us on a daily basis. Those in substance abuse treatment facilities are educated on "urges, triggers and cravings" that can draw them back into seduction by their drug of choice and if we don't stay vigilant, we too will give in to whatever the "bright and shiny object" that allures us (e.g., power, fame, beauty, sex, prestige, celebrity, reputation, money, designer jeans, handbags, etc.). Jody's *urges* causes her to engage in an adulterous relationship with her paramour; which is *triggered* by her rationalization that her husband is not there for her in the ways that she would like and her *craving* is an insatiable need for attention.

As attractive as Jody is (and I know there must be, but I haven't found a male or female with this disorder who wasn't attractive), her spiritual development remains stymied between the indifferent-heart and craving-heart realm. She implies that she is not going to give up her paramour; which convey notions from the "indifferent-heart" realm, but she presented for therapy expressing that she was conflicted by her behaviors and decisions. The "craving-heart" realm is a realm of discernment where one can be conflicted about what to do and what path to take but I'm not sure this applies to Jody. She is reveling in all types of attention from several different sources and now she has a new source of attention from a therapist.

When we reside in the "indifferent-heart" realm, our higher-self diminishes. The higher-self is not eradicated because I've seen evidence of God consciousness exhibiting like "flickering lights" in the souls of those residing in this realm. A "bar" of temptation separates the higher-self from the lower-self in each of the realms that we occupy but it is the degree to which this separation occurs that allows us to be distinguished by the realms. That is, those residing in the indifferent-heart realm readily give in to temptation to fulfill hedonistic pursuits. There is little consideration and/or empathy for others while one resides in this realm, as exhibited by Jody but also as exhibited in our biblical hero, David's behaviors who actually set Uriah up to be killed in order to marry Uriah's wife, Bathsheba. Ignorance compliments indifference in the indifferent-heart realm. When we don't know who we are, we behave badly. There is no "push back" on our indulgences and little consideration for the rights or basic humanity for others. It is if we are on autopilot in pursuit of our indulgences and if someone gets in our way, we will plow right through them.

Movement into the "craving-heart" realm shifts the bar of temptation to reflect more of our higher-self than what is exhibited in the indifferent-heart realm. We care more about others, but we can remain conflicted. I listened intently through Jody's sobs and tears to hear if she had any empathy for her husband and any remorse about what she was engaging in. She stated that she was conflicted but the real intensity of her emotion came when confronted by the notion of giving up her paramour in order to salvage her marital relationship. Perhaps, by her presence in therapy, she was on the cusp of enlarging her higher-self but it would require that she push back on her bar of temptation. With the affair now exposed, it is not the attention that Jody would have chosen for herself. She is the subject of criticism and gossip from the community, family and former friends. No, it is not what she would have chosen but it is attention nevertheless and Jody is drinking it in. Being "honestly conflicted" does tend to place a person's spiritual development in the "craving-heart realm" but I don't think that Jody is really conflicted. Her paramour remains enticing and

Jody's husband continues to do "cartwheels of performance" in an effort to win her back. Why would she stop the affair now?

Don't be fooled into thinking that temptation is not present for those residing in the pure-heart realm. Paul struggled with his own self in his desire to do good at times. He was an apostle of Christ and had "literally seen the light" and sought to do good but succumbed to the vagaries of the self at times. So, too, does the greatest among us are tested by the temptations of this world. The passage at the top of this chapter doesn't say so, but as you read in your Bible, Jesus, was tested after his baptism and after the Holy Spirit descended upon him, with God's declaration that Jesus is His son with whom He is most pleased, and before he selected his disciplines to begin his ministry. This points out that at no point in our spiritual development when we will not be tested.

Perhaps some of you really didn't mind it but I'm venturing to guess that many of you did not relish taking a test in school. I know that I surely didn't like the process of cramming in information, trying desperately to retain it in order to spew it back in my answers to the test, only to forget whatever it was that I crammed for because the new test was coming. This was not fun at all. In my mature mind, I've come to understand the value of tests. There are tests in life like an academic test, a driver's license test, a professional license test, etc. that reveals what we know. However, there are many spiritual tests throughout our journey that reveals who we are. We can fail the test that determines what we "know," and we can fail the test that determines what we think we "are." What we are is exhibited in our character and our character is revealed with consistency over time. If, in a weak moment, Jody was swept away by the pursuits of her paramour, we could consider this an anomaly to her character. The fact that she continues the relationship after reflecting on it and even after the affair was exposed, is a pattern that reveals her character. She is not passing the test that would have her move forward on her spiritual journey.

We must be clear about the motive of some testing. There have been many times and examples throughout our history that tests were put in place to stymie our achievement or to prevent one from gaining access into some insider's protected group, organization or other segment within society. There have been tests designed to keep minorities and women from voting. There are tests to keep certain people from entering and excelling in the military; Tests to keep certain people out of certain communities; Tests in place to limit minority advancement in professions like firefighters and policer officers. There are tests that we use for mate selection and tests we put in place to stymie our own progress. Conversely, there are tests of human ingenuity and feats that are just plain remarkable! These tests are designed for enhancement and development of all of us, even if we are simply observers of these remarkable feats. We don't have to personally be rocketed to the moon or crucified on a cross to be the beneficiaries of those who've past those tests of achievements (or sacrifice). Spiritual tests help to strengthen our spiritual resolve; while exemplifying for others a model for their spiritual progression. Preparing for tests takes discernment, study and practice. Our spiritual development takes discernment, study and practice.

In the pure-heart realm, there is certainly a discernment to have propelled the individual in the direction of the pure-heart realm. There is a public declaration about whom we claim to be (e.g., minister, therapist, married, etc.) and the temptation arises in order to test our resolve. Jesus dealt decisively with Satan's temptation following an ordeal of great suffering (40 days of fasting). What might we give up if we were asked to fast for a morning or even after the meal we've just eaten? Our higher-self has enlarged to shrink the lower aspects of ourselves but the bar of temptation remains. What gives us strength and develops our higher-self is the capacity to say, "No" to the temptation that present itself. *"No temptation has overtaken you except such as is common to man; but God is faithful, who will not allow you to be tempted beyond what you are able, but with the temptation will also make the way of escape, that you may be able to bear it."* (1 Corinthians 10:13-NKJV) "Study" edifies us on or journey and "practice" builds up our capacity to pass the next test that comes our way.

By saying "No," to a temptation is like doing resistance training. If we show up at the gym for the first time and get underneath a weighted bar with two solid 45lb discs on each side, we might not even be able to bench press the total 135lbs for a single rep. Of course, everyone's fitness level is different and we have the latent muscle mass to bench press 225lbs or 315lbs but our muscles are not developed. Though we start out with smaller weights, we are pushing against the resistance of the bar (and weight) to develop greater muscle mass. In perseverance our bodies are transformed and our ability to lift more and more weight has been enhanced. The only thing we are doing to create this change is to "push against resistance." Similarly, our faith is enhanced by pushing against the resistance (which is our inability to say, "No" to temptation) and the more we push back against temptation, the more spiritually fit we become! It is that hard…it is that simple.

Jody needs to declare what type of woman she wants to be. Perhaps she chose wrong in the selection of the husband that she now has but when she grants herself permission to sleep with her paramour, she has devalued herself and anything else she holds dear. I happen to believe that all of our human interactions are temporary and we have purposeful intersection with others in our lives for the growth and development of the people involved. If Jody and her husband have ceased to grow in their mutual development then a declaration to move on may be right for them; however, Jody must finish what is "on her plate" before moving onto someone else. Given that I suspect Jody has a histrionic personality disorder, I believe that ending it with her husband would not be a healthy move for her and she will replicate her abandonment tendencies pursuing the "next shiny object" when she feels inadequate attention coming her way from the next guy, or the next. She needs to push back against her involvement with the paramour and push back on her craving and seeking inappropriate attention.

My hope for all the "Jody's" of the world (indeed, all of us) is that we advance in our spiritual development into the pure-heart realm. As noted by Viktor Frankl, in his book, *"Man's Search for Meaning,"* the pursuit of pleasure is not our ultimate aim. He wrote, "It is one of the basic tenets of logotherapy that man's main concern is not to gain pleasure or avoid pain but rather to see a meaning in his life." Frankl was a neurologist and psychiatrist who developed this form of therapy, Logotherapy ("logo" is a Greek word for "meaning" and "therapy" means to "heal") who derived this theoretical/therapeutic approach following his experience as a prisoner in the Nazi concentration camps. As meaning shifts while occupying each realm on the spiritual differentiation scale, temptation will always be a challenge that we'll have to confront.

Not unlike Jody, whom I don't believe has arrived in the pure-heart realm yet, we can see from the example of Jesus that we'll hunger for something. Jesus was letting us know by his example is that we can hunger for something that we hope will physically satiate us or for greater spiritual ideals. Bread was once called, "the staff of life." Bread, along with water, was the very basic nutrients one needed to survive physically but it is not only the physical needs we must care for. We are also nourished from "every word that proceeds out of the mouth of God." These are greater spiritual ideals like love, peace, joy, etc. that are represented in the Fruit of the Spirit. When Jody taps into "love," it is not for selfless pursuits; it is just the opposite. Sure, she is tempted by the affair. Who wouldn't be? We tend to love those people that love us back and if some guy conveys to Jody that she is the "best thing since sliced bread," why wouldn't she be attracted to him? However, love requires more discernment from all of us and that understanding changes contingent upon our level of spiritual progression.

The secondary meaning from the opening passage is for us not to pursue reckless endeavors. Satan tells Jesus to "…throw yourself down… and God will grant his angels…charge of you and in their hands will bear you up…" The truth is, with God's Mercy and Grace, He lifts us up again and again from the recklessness of our own choices and behaviors. How many failed treatments will an addict ultimately go through, exhibiting the recklessness of his or her behaviors prior to going into another treatment and God will lift him or her up yet again? How many incarcerations might a felon have to experience over and over again, but God lifts him/her up after each and every time? How many failed relationships do we encounter, hoping for something decisively different from the next relationship that is essentially the same, but God is still there! Jody is giving in to her temptation, thus, recklessly "throwing herself down" and God will still catch her but in her spiritual maturity, she'll cease to behave so recklessly.

The third meaning in the opening passage that spiritually enlightened beings will endorse in the pure-heart realm is not giving in to the indulgences of this material world. There are many "bright and shiny objects" out there that can distract us from our ultimate spiritual path and we must be careful not to allow fleeting material indulgences to divert us from our path. One of the fetters (binds) or weeds in our spiritual garden that stymies our spiritual development or reduces the yield of our spiritual harvest is the indulgence in sense desires. Information in the material world is received through our five senses (i.e., sight, hearing, smelling, tasting and touching). Each one of the senses can pull in sensations of tremendous delight: nudity, music, vanilla, barbeque and sex). A complimentary sense that is aligned with spirit is "intuition." Intuition is easily drowned out or ignored in favor of the things that appear to be more tangible for us. We can "intuit" (thus, be "in tune with") God or eat a cheeseburger. What are we most likely going to choose?

Our sensory experience is important. After all, God has given us this gift in order for us to experience the material world. The sensations that appeal to us during one point upon our spiritual journey will have negligible impact at a different level. In my youth, I've often saw the "object" of a woman (e.g., breast, flowing hair and a backside that stops you in your tracks, turns you around and makes you utter an audible sound to no one in particular..."Daaammnn!"). As I become more seasoned in my maturity, I still see the beauty of a woman (or person) that radiates from her or his inner being. I am transfixed by the eye that sees me and the smile that affirms me. I am lit up by the person who conveys the sense, "I know you have a story and I am honored to hear it!" I want to be touched with kindness and connection and with the person's presence who perceives me as a joy to be around. I want to drink in, hear, taste and smell the essence of the other person in way that I did not conceive of in my youth.

It may appear that I am framing this advanced level of spiritual development with the chronology of age but age and spiritual maturity does not necessarily coincide. Jody is getting older but her spiritual development is regressing. Personality may be static over time but the choice she is making is revealed in her degree of spiritual differentiation. The longing for an affair may have been ever present but her actions now convey the message that she chooses not to say, "No," to the temptation. Lack of vigilance and effort creates an insidious slip from our higher self into our lower self and the lower self is never satiated. The sense-desires of our lower self requires more and more from us and give us little in return. Whatever characteristic that Jody's paramour possesses and entices her to risk sacrificing her marriage will not hold her interest if she gives herself fully over to him. In limited fashion of furtive getaways and sexual raptures Jody's paramour is fully attentive to her. That will quickly cease if there were no obstacles for their togetherness and then it becomes the paramours "job" vs. "momentary passion" to meet Jody's attention seeking needs.

In our discerning mind, which is more developed in the craving-heart and pure-heart realms, resisting temptation also requires recognizing what we are exposing ourselves to. I recently met a gentleman in his fifties, Todd. He was referred to me while in treatment in a local chemical dependency treatment facility. Todd informed me that he lost control of his life in the past two years and as a result, he suffered great losses. He had immediately become addicted to methamphetamines following his first use and in the following two years, he lost his job, house, wife and his reputation in the community. What struck me, while conducting a drug history, is that this guy has never used any illegal substances up until his very first use of meth. I remarked to him that many people that I've seen in therapy had a trajectory of drug use experiences, starting in their adolescence (with marijuana), and progressively increasing to the harder drugs.

There may be some debate as to whether or not marijuana is a "gateway drug" but in my experience, I've yet to meet anyone (prior to Todd) that used harder drugs (e.g., heroin, cocaine, or methamphetamines) who hasn't used marijuana in their adolescence. Todd's history was an anomaly in that it wasn't his "temptations" that derailed him in life; it was his "exposures." In the case of this guy in his fifties, who never even thought about the appeal of drugs (it wasn't a part of his generation), he happened to be in the company of others who were smoking crystal meth and they encouraged him "just to try it once." He did and was hooked! Nothing mattered for him other than the drug; thus, he lost the things (wife, job, home, etc.) that didn't matter (after beginning his drug use) but should have. What Todd exposed himself to (the company he kept and the drug that he used), terribly impacted his life.

Exposure and temptation "walk hand in hand" with each other. Todd's exposure created a temptation for crystal meth that he didn't even know he had; whereas, Jody's attention seeking behaviors (temptation) exposed her propensity to engage in an affair. We can be exposed to many things that create temptations within us, or our temptation exposes us to undesirable things. It may be tempting to gossip to others in the office place about our supervisor, fellow colleagues, or those we serve (e.g., clients, consumers, patients, students, etc.) but if this is not our desire to engage in that type of behavior, don't expose ourselves to the group that is doing the gossiping. If we are not inclined to curse, don't expose ourselves to those who frequently use profanity. If we are trying to lose weight, we cannot expose ourselves to an environment that will trigger our temptation. *"Therefore gird up the loins of your mind, be sober, and rest your hope fully upon the grace that is to be brought to you at the revelation of Jesus Christ; as obedient children, not conforming yourselves to the former lusts, as in your ignorance; but as He who called you is holy, you also be holy in all your conduct, because it is written, 'Be holy, for I am holy.'"* (1 Peter 1:13-16-NKJV)

We are known by the "company we keep." We can couple this with another adage, "We are what we eat." Both adages imply that what we are exposing ourselves to is defining who we are. Both adages conveys perhaps a warning, but certainly a caution, that we ought to be mindful with regard to our associations, exposures and what we ingest into our being. Illegal substances appear to be an automatic "No-no," but we can see millions of people in our Country and throughout the world readily indulge in illegal substances. Whether tempted by or exposed to these illegal substances, ingesting them is likely to produce deleterious outcomes. However, being tempted by or exposed to seemingly innocuous things that are not in line with our spiritual development can have deleterious outcomes. Seducers, provocateurs and tempters (whether persons, substances and/or ideas) will always be present to divert our journey. We are empowered by God to resist this temptation. Once we have done so, we've passed the test at a certain level that informs us and others that we've mastered the level and we are ready to move on.

Jody has failed the test (both as a temptress and one being seduced) to continue residing in the indifferent-heart realm. Her refusal to say "No" to these indulgences keeps her trapped (and in this case) right where she wants to be. She wasn't seeking help from therapy to assist her in making changes or to support her in resisting the temptation of her paramour. If there is not a vision for a new direction and motivation for change, Jody will not buy into the therapeutic process; thus, no movement into the craving-heart realm can occur. If she was earnestly conflicted, a therapist can help in pointing out a way of salvation for her (even if she chose her paramour over her husband), but Jody is not ready to push back on the bar of temptation at this time.

The following exercise will help you identify the areas of temptation for you. It will also provide clues about your level of spiritual differentiation; along with opportunities to advance you forward.

Ripening the Fruit-Gratitude and Appreciation

All of us, during each phase of our spiritual development, will face temptations and exposures to things that impede our spiritual journey. We will succumb to the temptation in the indifferent-heart realm. We will analyze and debate our exposures and relationship with temptation in the craving-heart realm. We will recognize and resist the temptations in the pure-heart realm. Each time we empower ourselves by saying, "No," to the temptation it strengthens our spirit, enhances our faith and demonstrates to others the degree of our integrity. If we are indulging the self by giving in to our hedonistic inclinations, the antithesis of this is the focus on others. Thus, we need a paradigm shift from focusing upon our perceived lack to recognizing how fully blessed we are. In doing so, we will give of ourselves vs. continually indulging ourselves.

Identify and examine what it is that tempts you. Is it sex, status, power, approval, acclaim, relevance, drugs, beauty, cars, homes, jewelry…you name it. Consider how the urges, triggers and cravings come into being. Perhaps you are craving a doughnut after an emotional tiff because you are feeling misunderstood. So, is it the doughnuts you need or do you need to clear up the misunderstanding? It is easier to push back against a craving, trigger and urge from the temptation when you set your environment up in a way that does not allow you to succumb to the temptation. Many intense cravings have a short "shelf life" of around 20 minutes; thus, if you don't have the doughnuts in your home that you are readily exposed to, you are less likely to go after one when that craving is upon you.

Temptation works on the concept of "resource depletion." When we are feeling inadequate, deprived or that we are missing out, it is a result of "gaping holes" within us that longs for satiation. When we focus upon God, it is "resource abundance"; thus, tapping into God can fill us up and circumvent the erroneous belief that we are missing out. Write a letter to God, describing in great detail, (or with daily reminders in your journal) what you are grateful for. If we understood what it is that we have, we are less likely to lust after what we don't have.

Secondly, write a note of appreciation (or make an expression of appreciation) to someone during each and every day. This is a proactive assignment that helps build the "spiritual muscles" of your higher self. It is recursive in that it throws good will out in the world in which others benefit and pass on in their own small circle of intimates. In many ways, this exercise costs you very little but generates a lot.

Lastly, pay attention to what you expose yourself to. What we ingest spiritually, psychologically and physically will determine the level of our spiritual, psychological and physical wellbeing while we are present on this planet. Exposure to the "seeds" of godly ideas will produce the "fruit" of a "spiritual harvest." When we consume from the Source of Spiritual Abundance, it helps us to resist the temptations abound in a hedonistic world.

Circling the Mountain

For I know that nothing good dwells within me, that is, in my flesh. I can will what is right, but I cannot do it. For I do not do the good I want, but the evil I do not want is what I do. Now if I do what I do not want, it is no longer I that do it, but sin that dwells within me. So I find it to be a law that when I want to do what is good, evil lies close at hand. For I delight in the law of God in my inmost self, but I see in my members another law at war with the law of my mind, making me captive to the law of sin that dwells in my members. Wretched man that I am! Who will rescue me from this body of death? Thanks be to God through Jesus Christ our Lord! So then, with my mind I am a slave to the law of God, but with my flesh I am a slave to the law of sin.
(Romans 7:17-23-RSV)

I originally met Oscar approximately 4-5 years ago. He was being released from prison and residing in the local ISR (Intensive Supervised Residence) managed by the Department of Corrections (DOC). Despite his less than auspicious beginnings in life, Oscar is a dapper man with a decisively calming persona. He is approaching 50 with Hispanic origins. He is tall with the attractive characteristics of a Ricardo Montalban, who played the dashing Mr. Roarke in the television series, "Fantasy Island." Oscar would likely have women swooning over him if it wasn't for the fact that he is gay and expresses a dislike and distrust of woman.

Oscar has had a lot of losses and betrayals in his nearly 50 years of life. He learned during his adolescence that the people raising him were not his biological parents; rather, it was his biological uncle and his uncle's wife that he believed to be his father and mother. His mother, whom he thought was his aunt, was strung out on drugs and earned money to pay for her addiction through prostitution. Learning later that she gave him up for these prurient indulgencies/addictions didn't set well with Oscar and he struggled throughout his life to find out where he belonged and if anyone really cared about him. Each succeeding developmental level for Oscar was fraught with shame-inducing emotional, psychological, physiological and spiritual insults that shaped his schema along the way. His distrust for women grew exponentially due to his experience of being severely beaten by his uncle's wife, who had little patience in dealing with a child she knew wasn't hers.

Boys have an attachment to their primary male care providers (as do girls with their mothers) and Oscar was no exception. His father, a calm and passive man, was Oscar's refuge, especially when his mother's stereotypical Latin rage manifested toward him. Oscar, perhaps he should have been in school, arrived home unpredictably one day and caught his mother in a torrid sexual encounter with another man. The initial response of ego is for self-protection. It is more reactive than logical and Oscar's mother reacted harshly and inappropriately to Oscar's unexpected arrival at home. Oscar's mother was filled with embarrassment, shame and fears of the information getting back to her husband beat Oscar savagely with an iron cord and promised more of the same if he ever revealed to his father what he had seen.

Oscar didn't know to whom he could turn to. Imprinted in his mind was distrust for women and the knowledge that his father was rather ineffectual when it came to matters of the household or actually stopping his mother's over-the-top disciplinary techniques; thus, Oscar kept his mother's secret but gravitated to other adult males for comfort. It would be nice if I could report to the reader that Oscar secured a connection with positive male mentors. As we know, those type of positive external mentorship relationships (i.e. grandparent, teacher, concerned neighbor, scout master, etc.) can create resiliency in a child that has had the most challenging and difficult early beginnings, but this is not the case for Oscar.

Oscar found his relationship with these adult males to be exploitive and like a moth attracted to the light of a backyard bug zapper, Oscar would find these exploitive relationships and he somehow felt complicit in the molestations that occurred. From a history of abandonment, abuse, betrayals and sexual molestations, Oscar reflected the ugliness that he felt within by engaging in his own series of exploitive and acting out behaviors. Oscar was in and out of detention centers, substance abuse treatment facilities, prisons and mental health therapy. Since the age of 13 and continuing up through his 49th years of age are petty thefts, shoplifting, multiply grand theft auto larcenies, burglaries, assaults, check forgeries, giving false information to authorities, fleeing from authorities and perhaps other crimes he has neglected to acknowledge. To quell the "demons" rising up within him, he wrestles with alcohol, cannabis, cocaine and methamphetamines.

Anyone who has ever conducted a social history on Oscar would conclude that his life has been tragic. Life dealt him a precarious hand of cards that he was ill-prepared to play. Prior to his last session with me, Oscar was bemoaning the facts of his negative life history and the current facts that numerous people have turned him down for employment opportunities; thus, he concluded that he would never find a job. I challenged these notions of Oscar; informing him that there have been many others returning from prisons that I've encountered, coming from the same institution that he was in, with a more severe rap sheet than his, who have found employment. I didn't deny that his efforts to locate a job wouldn't be hard, as I haven't denied the difficulties of these efforts even for a displaced executive in a soft economy.

For weeks, I kept encouraging Oscar not to give up and to keep putting effort into securing employment, and to maintain his faith (as God would be faithful toward someone who maintains his/her faith). While in treatment, Oscar was showing up regularly for his weekly mental health appointments and suddenly he did not show for two of his previously scheduled appointments. In passing, one of the receptionists informed me that she hasn't checked the jail roster but presumed that the only reason Oscar would likely miss two appointments was that he was in jail. I was disappointed in the notion that Oscar may be back in jail. I wanted more for Oscar than what he has received at the hands of others while growing up and by what he has caused by his own hands. There were systems in place, with a lot of good people, rallying in behalf of Oscar and the thought of him going back to jail was disheartening; but it wasn't true. Unbeknownst to all of us was that Oscar found work!

When Oscar made and kept his next appointment, I learned that he did so because he called in sick to his employer in order to meet with me to process his decision to now quit his job. He complained of the fact that he was nearing 50 and the 10 hour shift of manual labor was hard on him. He was blessed with getting a free ride to the worksite (several miles away) but complained of the fact that the guy loudly played "annoying" country music on the way to work and back; thus, these "silly lyrics are in my head all night long." Though he is Hispanic/Latino by origin, Oscar doesn't speak Spanish and was troubled by the side conversations people were having at work in Spanish that he couldn't understand. Despite anything I said to counter his thinking, Oscar developed for himself a rationalization for quitting his job, and did so.

Oscar's situation was frustrating me. I get it that he has a terrible beginning for his life and I understand the concept of "learned helplessness." I didn't want to discredit or invalidate his experience but he was doing what people will do in therapy a lot; which is to tell their stories ad nauseam with little therapeutic advancement or relief. As a therapist, I'm trying to broaden his narrow perceptions and encourage him to move in a direction that is likely to benefit his life; however, Oscar has adopted his "victim" story and uses it to justify his notions of entitlement while abdicating his responsibilities. He stole because he felt entitled to what was not his. He lies to justify protecting himself. He laments his criminal past that obstructs his ability to find a job but then quits the job once he gets one. He doesn't recognize the blessings that comes his way and spends his therapy sessions, "murmuring" with little desire to change.

I reminded Oscar of the Exodus story in the Old Testament. I shared with him that for 400 years, the enslaved Israelites pleaded with God to change their life circumstances. They were three million in number, hauling out great wealth of gold and silver for recompense of their indentured service when God answered their prayers. Interestingly, it was under this hardship, while enslaved, when their census grew exponentially, so the wealth was not simply in the material wealth they took with them, it was in the people as well. These were the people with firsthand, direct knowledge of the power of God. They saw God's work, through Moses, with a series of plagues and miraculous events, in order to free the people. When Pharaoh, reneged on his promise to release the people, the Israelis saw the awesome power of God administered for their protection. While the Egyptian army was in pursuit to recapture them, God rained fire from the sky and then breached the Red Sea, permitting each and every one of the Israelites to cross and then engulfs the pursuers.

It is said, that the destination for the Israelis (The Promised Land) was only 11 days journey from where they started but took 40 years for them to arrive at (and only some were allowed to go in). God was with them in their journey granting clear instructions from his emissary, Moses. God took care of their physical needs, providing them manna and quail; yet, the people murmured daily with feelings of dissatisfaction, impatience and entitlement. God understood that His "chosen" people were significantly traumatized by captivity, oppression and the lash from their Egyptian overseers but He didn't excuse the Israelis of their current responsibilities. I asked Oscar to reflect on this story and apply it to his life.

Far too many of us lack gratefulness and lack expressed gratitude for the tremendous blessings that we receive on a daily basis! God's favor is bestowed upon us on a daily basis and we search endlessly for something to complain about. Oscar had a terrible life, but welcome to the club! God didn't promise "success only journeys" for any of us. This can be a tough world, with tough experiences and tough interactions with others along the way. Christ's journey was no "bed of roses" either. He was born from a teenage mother. There was a cloud of suspicions regarding Mary's pregnancy prior to her marrying Joseph. They had to take an arduous journey back to Nazareth to be counted in a census where the family of the "King of kings" was relegated to a stable. The Creator of the Universe could have created a Hyatt Regency Hotel with the top floor reserved for Jesus and his entourage, but Jesus's story conveys not only humble beginnings, but challenging times as well.

We know that Jesus and his family had to flee the persecution of Herod who ordered the slaughter of all male children under the age of three when those who sought to honor Christ did not return with details about where they found him. There is not a lot of information about Jesus during his childhood but I can image that being a son of a carpenter was no pleasant task, as all occupations tend to be hard work. What we also know that Jesus wasn't received well when he began his ministry and went home to those who previously knew him (*a prophet is not without honor except in his hometown and his family*). And, of course, his short tenure on this earth after he started his ministry was fraught with difficulties. Jesus came with a purpose of healing and reconciling humanity with God; yet, he was disaffirmed, dehumanized and killed by the very people he came to save. This is certainly an indignity many of us will not have to endure but God didn't promise even for Jesus that his journey would be a "success only journey."

So why is it that the least worthy of us often feels the greatest since of entitlement? Unlike Christ, Oscar wasn't working for anything beyond himself. He may have had similar disaffirming and dehumanizing stories that Christ has had but Christ didn't disavow his responsibilities or presented with an arrogant notion of entitlement. Oscar did. His calm persona (likely learned from his father) and his eloquent articulations (perhaps as a defense mechanism to discount his Hispanic/Latino heritage) have served him well in exploiting others and abdicating his responsibilities. I have diagnosed him with a mood disorder when he presented with a persistent attitude of "Oh woe is me" and "doom and gloom." Additionally, I gave him a diagnosis of Post-Traumatic Stress Disorder (PTSD) following the severe abuse at the hands of his "mother." I gave him a number of Substance Use/Abuse Disorders due to his repeated illegal substance use and failed treatments. I diagnosed him with Antisocial Personality Disorder (resulting from his propensity to engage in legal infractions, producing his incarcerations); along with dependent traits but later found these traits to be significant features to assign a separate Dependent Personality Disorder diagnosis. Oscar relished all of the diagnoses because they affirmed his "victim" status and confirms why he is not able to be a responsible citizen.

I try to impart to clients that diagnoses are merely "descriptive" in nature and not "predictive" of anything, but this is often perceived scantly as my interpretation flies in the face of all the information and perceptions they have had over the years that makes them think of their disorders as "predictive." In reality, diagnoses are a cluster of symptoms and behaviors that we have classified into categories that mental health professionals call "disorders." To disrupt Oscar's victim stories and promote his need to be more responsible in his behaviors was disconcerting to Oscar. If I challenge him too directly about his need to be more responsible in his life will likely cause him to bolt from therapy with me (albeit his dependency features will likely have him arrive at the office of another therapist). Though the risk of him bolting is ever-present I won't promote his "past" as "prologue" orientation to the world because therapy remains a stagnant endeavor if Oscar arrives to our weekly sessions and I simply indulge his victim stories.

Just like the Israelites fleeing their oppressive hardship in Egypt with the hopes of a promised new land, murmurs, complains and threatens to return to what they previously have known, Oscar is the same way. God had to wait 40 years for that generation with their "victim mentality" to die out before he could introduce them to something new but even at that only 2 of the 12 tribal representatives believed that they could conquer the land that God directed them to because it inhabited giants. We will always find ourselves defeated by the perception of "giants" in our future when we carry memories about a disquieting, disempowering and dehumanizing past. God doesn't absolve people of what they need to do because of their pasts. He stands with us but we must confront and defeat the "giants" in our world.

God empowers a murderer and stutterer (Moses) to lead his people out of bondage (though Moses ascended to second in power to Pharaoh's throne, he murdered an Egyptian and fled Egypt for 40 years). God empowers an elderly man and woman (Abraham and Sarah) to give birth to a new nation. God empowers a coward (Jonah) to return to Nineveh to warn them about their impending demise. God empowered Rahab the prostitute to protect the spies Joshua sent into the land that included Jericho (despite Rahab's questionable past, she was in the direct bloodline which Christ was born). God empowers the lame to walk, the blind to see and the deceased to rise again. God doesn't always use the best of humanity to do his bidding and he doesn't excuse anyone from their responsibilities because of their circumstances.

The Constitution of the United States grants it citizens the right to "life, liberty and the pursuit of happiness." Notice that "happiness" is not a Constitutional guarantee but we are granted the "life" and "freedom" in order to pursue this "happiness." Indeed, a lot of people are in pursuit of what they think makes them happy like racing cars, jumping out of planes, modeling outfits, becoming politicians or movie stars, joining professional sports teams and even playing the lottery for a million dollar (perhaps a billion dollar) payout. God grants us life and a certain amount of liberty but instead of happiness, He imposes a responsibility upon us to work. According to Genesis (2:15-NKJV), *"The Lord God took the man and put him in the Garden of Eden to work it and take care of it."* And also, 2 Thessalonians (3:10-NKJV) states, *"For even when we were with you, we gave you this rule: "The one who is unwilling to work shall not eat."* And, even if we choose to activate our faith, it takes work, *"But do you want to know, O foolish man, that faith without works is dead?"* (James 2:20-NKJV)

If we are to receive God's favor, it is a transaction that often requires obedience and this obedience is exemplified in our work. I want to be clear that God is God; thus, He can override this basic transaction with humans with His Mercy and Grace but a relationship generally involves mutual exchanges between both parties. When there is not a feeling of mutual exchange, contracts are broken and relationships end. To have a sense of esteem, value and worth, Oscar needs to work and he cannot be absolved of working. If not working to receive an income to sustain a livelihood, he needs to work at excavating his past, examine it thoroughly, arrive at a different conclusion about his worthiness as a child of God, and promote a new way of being as he marches forward. His life can change, indeed it will change, but he (along with God's help) can be the director of his life's journey. For now, he "circle's the mountain" telling all those who will listen his woeful story with little intention of changing the trajectory of his life.

Work requires work. Relationships require work. The development of ourselves requires work. As therapists, along with ministers, priests and a good friend, we are uniquely positioned to be the repository of people's stories. Though the enormity of stories from those in pain can overwhelm us, there is a privilege for us to be honored with, and care for someone's story. The totality of our stories constructs what we are. The interpretation of our stories creates our empowerment or our disempowerment. It is important to acknowledge the experiences of what has happened to us and what hasn't happened for us, but what is far more important is how we perceive or interpret what has happened to us and what hasn't happened for us. To change perceptions takes willingness and work. There is no "period" at the end of Oscar's story; however, he needs to work on writing new chapters in his life that doesn't have a disempowering theme.

Etched into my mind are the words from Pastor Randy Morrison (Speak the Word Church International, Golden Valley, MN) who says, "God never consults your past to predict your future." I believe that about God but far too often we are embracing the narratives of our own pasts to define what we are in the present moment and to stymie our futures. It is unconscionable to consider the egregious levels of physical, psychological, emotional and spiritual insults that people suffer at the hands of others but again, the greater importance is not so much about what happens to us but how our minds make sense out of what has happened. Viktor Frankl (a holocaust survivor), in his book, *"Man's Search for Meaning,"* asserts that "[m]an can preserve a vestige of spiritual freedom, of independence of mind, even in such terrible conditions of psychic and physical stress." He goes on to say about human freedom is "...to choose one's attitude in any given set of circumstances, to choose one's own way."

God wants us to have a life filled with experiences. In our limited understanding of spiritual matters, we may conclude that an "All Good God" would want nothing for us other than "all good experiences," but we cannot have a life of meaning without the prospect of suffering. The egregious acts of the world, stemming from ignorance or darkness provides a contrast for light to be seen and appreciated. *"And who is he who will harm you if you become followers of what is good? But even if you should suffer for righteousness' sake, you are blessed. And do not be afraid of their threats, nor be troubled."* (1 Peter 3:13-14-NKJV) The adversities of life are like sharpening stones, that hone us like sharp blades to cut through whatever difficulties that lie ahead.

As the holders of people's stories, we must be careful not to become adversely transformed by vicarious trauma. Thus, we must honor the stories we hear while not succumbing to the stories. We must be careful not to become diverted from our spiritual path as we bear witness to the atrocities of other people's lived experiences; additionally, become a beacon of light that leads others out of their darkness when they are ready to move. Don't assume that the storyteller, who arrives in therapy or on your doorstep as a friend is ready to move. When I am "circling my own mountain" with frustration and disappointment in the lack of movement on the part of my clients, I realize that I am becoming too enmeshed in my clients' lives; thereby, ceasing to focus upon my own spiritual development and regressing in my journey towards God.

Client enmeshment means that I am not fully endorsing my own spiritual development of "meaning, purpose, direction and connection." It means that I am forgetting about "whom" I am and "who" you are: both children of the Most High God. I start to lose focus upon "what" it is that we are here to do; which is to have human experiences and have healthy relationships. If my faith wanes, my vision of "where" I am going diminishes, placing emphasis on material things and flesh vs. spirit and God. "When" I am not moving forward, I've given myself over to futility and despair vs. the knowledge that *"all things work together for the good for those who love God, to those who are the called according to His purpose."* (Romans 8:28-NKJV) I falter once I can't find "how" to make a way when a way has already been made clear: *"Thomas said to Him, 'Lord, we do not know where You are going, and how can we know the way?' Jesus said to him, 'I am the way, the truth, and the life. No one comes to the Father except through Me.'"* (John 14: 5-6-NKJV)

As I reflected further on the opening passage, I wrestled a bit, as a therapist, with Paul's admonition about the "law of flesh" resulting in sin and the Law of God, resulting in our goodness of spirit that is connected to God but perhaps Paul is more prescient than I am able to fully grasp. "Law" implies something immutable, like the law of physics or the law of gravity. Indeed, even spiritual laws appear rather immutable. Jesus referenced the Ten Commandments by saying that he didn't come to change the law but to fulfill the law. Of course, when one compares this spiritual law with the litany of dietary rules, customs, practices and regulations that are revealed in the Book of Leviticus, we can be glad that they weren't immutable spiritual laws that were carved into stone. The New Testament appears to render these Ten Commandments (Laws) down to two (to love God and to love each other); it doesn't take anything away from the original ten. Thus, religiosity may change but spiritual laws remain immutable.

If the "law" is a "binding practice or custom, with submission to authority," I struggled with the notion of granting "flesh" or "sin" credence of authority. As Americans, we have to adhere to the laws of our Nation (federal laws) and of our individual States. Ignorance of the law is no excuse for the violation of the law and corrective action will be meted out whether one wittingly or unwittingly violates the law. These laws have a sovereign authority that enacts the laws and whether we like an individual law or not, we still grant credence to that authority. What about this notion of sin? Do we grant sin credence of authority; thereby, legitimizing sin?

Paul struggled with the law of flesh that was at war with the law of spirit and succumbs to the notion that he didn't have what it took to defeat the law of flesh. He had to give himself over to Christ and allow Christ to do the battle against this "gravitational" pull of "flesh." Likewise, in 12 step treatment models, one calls upon a "power" or "source" outside of his/herself (however he/she might see that "power" or "source") to help defeat the tenacious grip of addiction. Nevertheless, I still struggle with granting the "legitimacy" of the law with the "illegitimacy" of sin. Addiction, sin or the ways of the flesh has no legitimacy. An assailant may break into our house, administer harm to us and steal our things but his or her ability to do this doesn't grant him or her legitimacy. There is no governing power that grants legitimacy to these illegitimate actions. Even if one buys into the notion of a demonic force called, Satan, and we likened him to a great criminal syndicate boss, Satan still has no legitimacy; therefore, no "law" can be associated with Satan.

As a therapist, I see people granting "legitimacy" to "illegitimate" things all the time; while incredulously wondering why they are trapped in misery (*"the wages of sin is death"*). A motto that I share with clients is that "you can't make sense out of nonsense." Nevertheless, people spend a whole lot of time, energy and effort trying to make sense out of nonsense. They are "circling the mountain" when there is a more direct path to "paradise." They are inflicting upon themselves and others unnecessary pain and suffering circling the same mountain again and again. They seek to return to captivity while freedom is at hand. They renounce the bright light of day in favor of stumbling around in the dark. They cry out for the clarity of vision that is exemplified in a living God only to return to worshiping idols of self-destruction.

Approximately 15-20 years ago, I had a private practice called "Break the Chains" in St. Paul, MN and a woman, married to a wealthy surgeon, would travel over 90 miles to see me once a week about the status of her marriage. She felt trapped in a devitalized marriage for years and throughout their lengthy marriage her husband unabashedly continued an open affair with another woman and allegedly fathered her son. The wife was so wounded that her behaviors were caustic; thus, she spewed venom in her home and within her worksite when she did decide to take on a job or two (prior to being let go for having a cantankerous persona in the workplace). This woman was trying to make sense out of nonsense, "circling the mountain" for years hoping for a different outcome that was never to be forthcoming. Her emancipation came when she looked at her situation squarely and made proactive steps to extricate herself from the relationship. Healing could not occur each time she would return to a situation that she knew to be contaminating her soul.

Fast forwarding to my current practice in a rural community mental health center, these clients are similarly lost as the woman I've worked with

15-20 years ago and the people fleeing Egypt over 4000 years ago. They are trying to legitimize illegitimate ideas and I am not sure what words or therapeutic interventions will move them from their fixation upon their illegitimate ideas. In the 2016 political campaign season there has been nasty and vicious vitriol spewed at fellow candidates and about various groups of people. This vitriol has seeped into the psyche of everyday Americans; thus, this "hateful" attitude and caustic speech is coming out brazenly in therapy sessions. I don't remember a time, while in a therapy session, that people felt so free to say the most hateful things in session.

In the last week, I've had three white women, one white man and one black man say the most hateful things with zero sensitivity or concern that they were spewing their hateful rhetoric to a black male therapist. Two of the white women talked about their hatred for Mexicans. One had generalized hatred for undocumented workers and talked about how they were ruining the Country, using typical stereotypes that I've heard coming out of the mouth of presidential candidate Donald Trump. The other was recently attacked by someone she described as being Mexican and I understood the rawness of her emotion but not her insistence in painting all Spanish speaking people with the same hateful brush. Neither woman minced words when it came to their bigoted rhetoric.

The third white woman focused her disdain upon Somalians and people from the Middle East. She, in my presence, referred to them as "towel heads" and "sand n*word" and what incensed me most was that she kept calling me "dude." The white man railed about taking the country back from "those people" that has taken it over; while decrying the Obama Presidency. He too, was a proponent of Trump and he flared up at his wife for not supporting him. The couple had separated with hopes to reconcile and the wife told her husband that her mother said that it was great that they separated and she needed to be through with her "no good husband." The husband was incensed not only because she didn't defend him to her mother but also the fact that she even told him what her mother said. He told her in session, "The only reason you should have told me such a thing is as a way of explanation for why you struck your mother in the head with a shovel for saying that to you!"

Lastly, the black guy was railing against white people and particularly police officers, resulted from the national protest of "Black Lives Matter." He wasn't able to separate his vitriol from various incidents of police abuse of black people that should make everyone with a conscience uneasy, but he had generalized his hatred to all white people. What was apparent, that in all of these cases was an endorsement of bigotry, where each individual was trying to make their illegitimate positions, legitimate. This rancor was seething within each of them, adding to their depressive mood; yet, no one wanted to budge from their position. *"The wicked covet the catch of evil men, but the root of the righteous yields fruit. The wicked is ensnared by the transgression of his lips, but the righteous will come through trouble. A man will be satisfied with good by the fruit of his mouth, and the recompense of a man's hands will be rendered to him. The way of a fool is right in his own eyes, but he who heeds counsel is wise."* (Proverbs 12:12-15-NKJV)

What we have here are "idol worshipers" that derail their pursuit of God. The Israelites created a golden calf that was tangible, audacious and representative of their Egyptian past while enslaved. They went back to what was familiar at a cost of their own destruction and a delay of their own reward. The "gods" of Egypt were prolific (e.g., Anubis, god of the underworld; Babi, god of baboons; Hapi, god of the Nile; Ra, god of the sun; Shu, god of the air/wind; etc.). The material representations of these images are among the idols that God warned people about. However, there are other types of idols that we pay homage to that we need to be mindful of. Bigotry is an idol. Hatred is an idol. Self-indulgence, along with ignorance, is an idol. People forge idols out of arrogance, greed, fear, self-pity, etc. and give credence to these idols vs. God. God's Love and Knowledge is Expansive. "Idol worshipers" promote their self-interest, disconnect from others and delight in the limitation of their knowledge. They endorse ego defense mechanisms in all fashion that includes: blaming, projecting, denial, minimizing, rationalizing, intellectualizing, introjection, isolation, identification and the like.

If, as Paul clearly states that there is a "law of sin" (which I discount because "sin" has no authority over us), perhaps we should abandon all earthly efforts to be in league with the Will of God. However, we do have the capacity to resist sin and make choices in order not to go around and around in our own machinations or habitual behaviors. God told Cain, after having rejected his offering and inquiring about why he was upset that, *"If you do well, will you not be accepted? And if you do not do well, sin lies at the door. And its desire is for you, but you should rule over it."* (Genesis 4:7-NKJV) Yes, there is original sin, intergenerational sin, we are born into sin and we constantly exposed to sin but sin doesn't have to rule us and we don't have to wander in the wilderness for years due to a sin that we've committed.

Jesus is our salvation because He has sacrificed for us and is an exemplar for our daily living but we, too, are children of the Most High God thus an inheritor of God's Goodness that is represented in each Fruit of the Spirit. God doesn't embody the mistrust and shame that Oscar carries with him; nor does He embody the bigotry and hatred revealed in the clients above. Let's quit circling the mountain and reclaim our position as the rightful heirs of the Most High God.

Ripening the Fruit-Affirming Yourself

Every human being is a precious soul! You are a precious soul! As we experience the world, other people (sometimes well-meaning and sometimes with ill-intentions) contaminate the perceptions we have of ourselves. With this distorted vision we end up furthering the contamination with negative critiques that we make of ourselves. That is, having once been told by significant people in our lives that we are "worthless, stupid, ugly or don't matter," we then begin telling ourselves that we are "worthless, stupid, ugly or don't matter." Of course, if this is what we believe about ourselves, it becomes the life of which we live. Indeed, we select partners, vocations, behaviors, duties, tasks or interactions that confirm the worthlessness that we feel. We can rewrite these negative scripts and become aware of the precious souls that we already are. When you realize your true value, you will no longer subject yourself to misery, dehumanization, or violations (even if it is you who is doing the violating). Affirmations are opportunities that we have to re-write our negative scripts.

Your assignment: Select the most negative message that was originally shaped in your mind by others, but you've now adopted. Let's say that the script originally written by others and now adopted by you is, "I am incompetent." Thus, you have proceeded throughout life reinforcing this notion that you are incompetent (i.e., dropping out of school, pursuing the wrong relationships, going from job to job, etc.). Your affirmative statement would now be, "I am competent!" In a notebook, write this positive affirmation about yourself every day for 30 days. Be consistent because the effort is designed to re-write the negative script that you've re-enforced for years. Handwrite out (don't type) these affirmations daily in 1st person, 2nd, person and 3rd person. This is an example of how the affirmation might look like:

1st person: "I, ('John Smith' -- write your name) am a competent person."
      (Write this statement 10 times daily.)
2nd person: "You, ('John Smith' -- write your name) are a competent person." (Write this statement 10 times daily.)
3rd person: "('John Smith' -- write your name) is a competent person." (Write this statement 10 times daily.)

You'll have 30 entries per day for 30 days and as you are reshaping your thought process, ask yourself how a competent person behaves and then behave accordingly. That is, you might say, "When I was feeling incompetent, I selected partners that confirmed my incompetence. Now that I am redefining myself as a person of competence, 'Who are the people that I can select in my life that affirms my competence?'" Or, "At 16, I was feeling incompetent and dropped out of school. At 36, I can competently pursue earning a GED (and beyond!)" and then go about the process of earning this. At the end of 30 days, change the affirmative statement to another deeply held belief about yourself. Such as, if you feel "unlovable," write the scripts to be "lovable"…if you feel "unworthy," re-write your scripts to be "worthy." ***You are a precious soul!***

X

Emotions Can Deceive Us

Therefore, laying aside all malice, all deceit, hypocrisy, envy, and all evil speaking, as newborn babes, *desire* the pure milk of the word, that you may grow thereby, if indeed you have tasted that the Lord *is* gracious. (I Peter 2:1-NKJV)

What makes us decisively "human" is our capacity to tap into our affective (emotional) range. There is tremendous value in experiencing the world with the wide variety of emotions that we possess. Just like there are regions within the face of this Earth that has yet to be explored and most assuredly the complexity of our own human brains have yet to be fully explored, there is likely a wealth of unexplored human emotions that has yet to be uncovered or fully realized. Women tend to have greater insight into their emotional repertoire than men. We, men, do have some sensation or experiences with our "tender" emotions but will likely cover them up with more socially acceptable emotions. That is, we might not readily identify that we are "frightened, embarrassed, confused, unsure, inept, humiliated, etc." but we'll willfully acknowledge and tap into "anger, bravado, false confidence or pride."

Interestingly, in the triadic essence of our being, (spiritual, mental and physical), our "spiritual selves" are not aligned with any emotion other than love. Now this can become a bit confusing to the reader after you've examined the Bible and see declarative statements within the Old Testament of God being, "raging, wrathful and jealous." I don't want to dismiss other people's interpretation of their readings but I hope to augment your understanding. In our infancy or childhood minds, when we look at something and attempt to make a definitive interpretation of that event, it filters through the mind contingent upon our frame of reference. If a child, or an adult rather, has never seen a plane, the frame of reference in seeing it for the first time may be a giant silver bird. Observing combustible, jet propelled engines that have never been seen before there may be notions and stories of fire being exuded from the wings of this huge bird; along with terrifying sounds when the plane breaks the sound barrier. When we don't have new knowledge, we compare unfamiliar things to old knowledge (or what we are familiar with).

Our capacity for obtaining knowledge in human form may be <u>limitless</u> but the knowledge we acquired thus far is extremely <u>limited</u>. I underscore this, because with our earlier interactions and relationship with God, we tended to reduce God down to understandings that fit our limited frame of references. We've built symbolic animal (or human) replicas of what our notion of God was or is. Some are fantastic caricatures of winged beings with conjoined animals and human forms. So when we are trying to have an understanding and relationship with the Ultimate, we reduce that involvement down to the level in which we can understand. Consequently, we can understand a "jealous God" because we understand "jealousy." We can understand a "wrathful God" because we've engaged in wrath. We know what rage looks like when we don't get our way; whether it is when we are two years old and throwing a tantrum or forty-two years old and punching holes in the wall. Nevertheless, emotion (with the exception of Love) is not associated with our spiritual selves but it is keenly tied to our humanness.

To be clear, none of the other human emotions tie into the spiritual phenomenon of love either. One may assert that he or she was stalking another person because of their *love* for him/her but the emotion is insecurity, jealous, fear, mistrust or some other negatively skewed emotion. Likewise, when we yell at or spank a child because he or she has walked away from the play area and we claim to be doing the negative action out of *love* (as no parent wants their child abducted), the sentiment is understandable but the action is not *love*. That is, we are using our power differential (we are bigger than the kid), abuse (inflicting harm under the guise of discipline) and fear (to institute corrective action). Coercive actions can gain compliance whether it is from a parent toward a child, a man toward a woman, a master toward slave and our notion of God toward humanity; but it is not love on any account. When we are aligned with spirit (e.g. meaning, purpose, direction and connection) the emotions of humanness can disrupt our spiritual attainment. Our human emotions are fleeting, transient, deceiving and can outright lie to us. Our spirit is aligned with God and God can't lie! *"God is not a man, that He should lie, nor a son of man, that He should repent. Has He said, and will He not do?"* (Numbers 23:19-NKJV)

We can see by the above quoted that "God is not a man." Most certainly God is not a man; thus, He doesn't contain "human emotions" which deceive us because God cannot lie. However, God is indeed Love, as referenced by John, *"Beloved, let us love one another, for love is of God; and everyone who loves is born of God and knows God. He who does not love does not know God, for **God is love**."* (1 John 4: 7-9-NKJV) Love is qualitatively different than "emotion," so what is it? Gary Zukav, in his book, "*The Seat of The Soul*," associates love with power and action. He asserts that "[a]n authentically empowered person lives in love." He goes on to say, "Love is not a passive state. It is an active force. It is the force of the soul. Love does more than bring peace where there is conflict. It brings a different way of being in the world. It brings harmony and an active interest in the well-being of others. It brings concern and care. It brings light." All spiritually enlightened beings attest to the power of love that transcends an emotional feeling.

In the "*Fruit of the Spirit*," I've described "love" as form of "praxis." "Praxis" is "informed action." It is not a "feeling/emotion;" it is a call to action with purposeful discernment and that is why it separates itself from the traditional array of human emotions. Think about it, in the famous biblical quote of John 3:16 it states, *"For God so loved the world that he gave his one and only Son, that whoever believes in him shall not perish but have eternal life."* It doesn't say, "For God so loved the world that He felt oowee, gooey and gushy inside." God, out of discernment and concern for the world, sacrificed his only begotten son. So what does the Son say about love? *"If you love Me, keep My commandments. And I will pray the Father, and He will give you another Helper, that He may abide with you forever,"* (John 14: 14-16-NKJV). Thus, love is "obedience"...a deontology...a duty...an active force...personal empowerment...a call to action...praxis.

There are people that say, "I just love the world!" and they may express that they have good loving feelings inside of themselves for the world but their feelings are meaningless if not exhibited by healthy discernment and action. If you are a benevolent sort, your heart may swell enough for you to convey love to a segment of people in Bangladesh (and you will be extending yourself in a much more loving way than I have) by going to the country and serving a segment of people. Actions are contemplated upon, extolled and then received. However, in your limitations you can't commit the same service at the same time to a segment of people in Guatemala. Spirit (meaning, purpose, direction and connection) provides us with the mechanism to discern what the love means, what's it for, where's it heading and who is it for, when will it be administered and how will it be administered? Our mental capacity augments the "praxis" (informed action) to allow the love to be distributed from the limitations of our physical being.

Wally is a 42 year old, Somalian born American. He has a relatively large family network around him within this rural, SW Minnesota community. He is married with a couple of preadolescent children and from my perspective, he appears to be living the "American Dream." The family has a modest home and judging by his robust stature, he is eating well. He has worked stable jobs with modest income to help support the lifestyle that he has; however, the woman he has married, Fatima, has an extended family that has done exceedingly well in obtaining the American Dream. Wally has worked in the social service profession (including mental health and chemical health services) and has never earned a salary that has exceeded $50,000 annually. His wife's family has no one making less than six figure income per year! From a financial point of view, Wally's in-laws perceive him as a dismal failure and they want more for Fatima than what Wally is currently providing.

Wally's service is really quite noble but he has been pressured over the years by the demeaning comments and attitude from Fatima's family. He has also generated negative images of himself independent of what others have actually said about him. To compensate for feelings of inadequacy and unworthiness, Wally tried to do expedient things to enlarge his income in order to feel accepted by a family that appears to always put him down. When you are not on a good path, expedient behaviors will always lead to ruin and Wally was no exception. He developed a gambling habit that jeopardized his home, job, family and his own mental health. Wally, the service provider, compromised himself to the point where he had to solicit help from another service provider. I had diagnosed Wally with Major Depressive Disorder, Generalized Anxiety Disorder, Pathological Gambling Disorder and Partner Relationship Problems when I completed his diagnostic assessment; however, psychiatry saw a Bipolar Disorder component to his presenting symptoms and was medicating him accordingly.

Wally was cogent, compassionate, understood clinical language and readily embraced the diagnostic labels to help rationalize why he got off track and why he his ambition was such that he never aspired to excel to the career and financial achievements of Fatima's family. Wally had an abiding faith and we could discuss freely spiritual ideas in association with his mental health. He kept broaching the notion of "feelings" or "emotions" as a driving force for his experiences on this earth. In some ways, he was absolutely correct because to be human is to experience (indulge) our vast emotional repertoire but the "human" part of us is the antithesis of spirit. Wally's emotions kept deceiving him, creating visions of himself that he is less than what he is (a child of a Loving God). Wally was a good and religious man but he descended from his "spiritual mountaintop" to worship the idols of "perceived success, affluence and expediency."

One explicitly stated fruit of the spirit is joy. Of the nine explicitly state fruit, the pursuit of material wealth is not one of them. Like Wally and his in-laws, we tend to measure our relevance by the size of our financial portfolio but the Bible has given us a couple of warnings in this area. We are informed that the "love of money is the pursuit of evil" and *"No one can serve two masters; for either he will hate the one and love the other, or else he will be loyal to the one and despise the other. You cannot serve God and mammon"* (Matthew 6:24). Regarding money, Timothy writes: *"But those*

who desire to be rich fall into temptation and a snare, and into many foolish and harmful lusts which drown men in destruction and perdition. For the love of money is a root of all kinds of evil, for which some have strayed from the faith in their greediness, and pierced themselves through with many sorrows."
(I Timothy 6:9-11-NKJV)

After his financial, familial, vocational and mental collapse, Wally secured another job that was outside of his field of training and was paying him less than his previous job, so he worried about the implications of this with his in-laws. He worried about meeting the demands of his children who are eyewitnesses to the largess doled out to their cousins; with thoughts of them missing out in comparison. He worried about not being the man that his wife should have married. He worried about what people from the community were thinking about him as he walked through the stores. He worried when his depression eased and he was feeling relatively whole if his contentment would shift to boredom, which would trigger a chaotic impulse to resume gambling, resulting in guilt, shame and despair? Wally was tapping into an array of discursive emotions, causing chaos in his life.

The true "chaos" was the cascade of all these competing emotions that Wally was giving credence to. I challenged Wally to change his paradigm from the fleeting and deceptively false emotional feelings to being principled centered with the focus on his spiritual development. A capitalistic, industrialized, informational management and service country needs corporate executives to run the various aspects of our Country; however, Wally was not, is not and will likely never be a corporate executive. It is not within his "psychological DNA" to pursue such things. As it relates to spirit, he has to deduce what that now means; as it is never what happens or doesn't happen to us, it is how we make meaning out of what happens or doesn't happened to us. Wally's value is not contingent upon the size of his house or the amount of income he brings in each year or by the amount of toys his children can collect. His worth is contingent upon the clarity of his vision that is tied in with his spirit and connection to God.

Likewise, we have Jessica. Jessica, a 27 year old, married, Caucasian mother of three year old Tammy, and married for four years to 27 year old Matt, struggled with these issues too. Jessica was seething with self-recrimination, self-loathing, self-devaluation with years of despondency and depression. Her husband described her as "needy, emotionally volatile and angry." Jessica asserted (rather oblivious to her husband sitting right next to her in the room) that the only thing that is meaningful in her life is her daughter, Tammy and even she, Jessica, was meaningless. Jessica's mother, Matt's parents and the couple live within blocks of each other and are highly enmeshed in each other's lives. The couple was in agreement that Jessica's relationship with her own mother was toxic; however, Matt's mother, throughout their four year marriage has been telling Matt that he should have never married Jessica. Jessica's mother waits until Matt is away from the home to confront Jessica about the wisdom of ever marrying Matt and neither mother believes that Jessica is an appropriate mother for Tammy. Each, in their own way, undermines Jessica's parenting ability; thus, she feels like a lousy mother and a lousy wife.

Jessica passively absorbs her mother's criticism, disapproval and disappointment within her and then redirects her hostility toward Matt. She calls him repeatedly during the workday with perceived slights that she has concocted having talked with her mother and any statement he can make is indefensible. And, God help Matt if he doesn't take the berating when Jessica calls the minute she calls or she flares up even more, shows up at his work, threatens to leave him or harms herself in some way. I shared with the couple that Matt is feverishly trying to fill up Jessica's love tank with buckets of love but her tank is a sieve. Jessica is looking for the allusive "oowee, gooey, gushy" feeling of love that has yet to be forthcoming. Her raw emotions, filled with deceit, contaminate her soul. Along with abandonment and abuse during her formative years, Jessica doesn't have an appropriate frame of reference for what love is; thus, it is painful for her when whatever conjecture or feeling of love she has is not forthcoming or sustaining.

As with Wally, Jessica's emotions are wreaking havoc in her life. They are all over the place, they are not serving her well, indeed, they are causing her misery; yet, she yields to her emotions as a truth paradigm and they are literally lying to her constantly. She calls Matt at work and yells at him, "How can you love me?" No matter what Matt says, it is not received well because Jessica doesn't love herself. I am working with Jessica to help her put boundaries in place with her mother and in-laws. I am educating her on self-soothing techniques and calming strategies. I am assisting her with building competency in her abilities as a mother and wife. I am encouraging her to identify what it is that she thinks and feels while being able to assertively ask for what she needs from others. We are developing appropriate standards for comportment of behaviors; thus, not directing verbal hostilities toward her husband, when she really just needs a hug and reassurance. She has to rewrite the narratives of her distorted thought process because she is a child of God and there are no deficits within her. She has to lean on her spirit to defuse her emotional array to manageable emotions that serve her and her family.

We are spiritual beings but the gift that God grants us is having a "human" experience. In having the "human" experience, it is imperative that we use these human emotions to experience this material world. We can use these emotions to augment our experience in this world or we can we allow ourselves to be consumed and destroy by this gift God has granted to us. In parenting, Jessica won't tell her daughter, "No." She doesn't want to deny Tammy what she demands because if she does so, Tammy gets upset. When Tammy whines, cries and declares, "I hate you Mommy," (with her three year old emotional repertoire), Jessica gives in. We can see a mirroring effect due to Jessica's 27 year old emotional repertoire, likely stymied at the developmental level of Tammy's, (as you recall Jessica will "whine, rage and show up at Matts' work" when she is emotionally disturbed), is being modeled for Tammy. Emotion is driving Tammy's demand and emotion is fueling Jessica's response and neither's behaviors are governed by spirit.

Since Jessica is troubled by the notion that she is not a good mother, she must discern what it means to be a good mother and with her informed knowledge (praxis) implement that love in Tammy's life. Since Jessica doubts that she is a good wife, she must discern what it means to her to be a good wife; followed by daily action steps that comport with her notions of being a "good wife." And since Jessica has a poor image of herself, she must discern what it means to love herself? Remember, love is the antithesis of human emotions. It is innately spiritual and the essence of what God is (God is Love!). If she can connect herself to the Source of All-Sustaining Love, then she doesn't have to desperately seek it in the depleting resources from her husband, Matt. As she is replenished by God's Love, she'll then have adequate supply to bestow this love to her daughter, Tammy.

I'd like to examine this notion of love being an abiding spiritual principle verses being aligned with human emotion a little more deeply with a narrative from my own life story. Currently, I see myself consistently operating from one degree or another in the pure-heart realm on the spiritual differentiation scale. I would hope that any honest, neutral observer of my public and personal persona and the comportment of behaviors would find me fluctuating from a 70 to an 85 of the scale of 100. That's not to say that there wouldn't be any observations among the sample of observations where one couldn't say that a particular behavior or attitude is clearly indicative of the craving-heart realm or indifferent-heart realm. On the spiritual pathway, our goal is not "perfection" but evolving within our own integrity to our best actualized self on this physical plane. So when other people are trying to determine if there is integrity within our character, there should be a fairly consistent alignment in our thoughts, words and actions. *"For every tree is known by its own fruit."* (Luke 6:44-NKJV)

In my spiritual immaturity, I understood of concepts like "love" through the understandings of a child or young adult and thus understood how "appropriately" love was considered a human emotion. With this being the case, my physical pursuit was aligned with other people I knew to obtain, possess and hoard this notion of love. Love is the stuff of romance novels, movies, political conquests, wars and biblical references throughout time. We see demigods or angels consorting with humans [("*the sons of God saw the daughters of men, that they were beautiful; and they took wives for themselves of all whom they chose"*) Genesis 6:2-NKJV] stoking this passion of emotion we've associated with love. Love was revealed in the great stories of the ages: Romeo and Juliet, Humphrey Bogart and Lauren Bacall; along with Luke and Laura (of All My Children fame).

Obviously, there was something emotional about these great loves and for us who bear witness to these loves (whether real or fictional). When I was tapping into this concept of love as human emotions while in my lessor self, there was something undeniable about the "feeling." In borrowing from my mother and father in how love was demonstrated, my father's approach was stoic, rational and dutiful when it came to his display of love. Indeed, "loving action" from him could be meted out in the form of providing adequate provisions for the family or from the leather strap of a belt with his interpretation of love. (*"He who spares his rod hates his son, But he who loves him disciplines him promptly"* Proverbs, 13:24-NKJV). My mother was more effusive when it came to love. She just loved you when you were right…loved you when you were wrong…loved you when you colored outside the lines and loved you when you decided not to color at all. One adopts what he knows and some mixture of the two concepts I've took with me on my quest to find and receive love.

What has struck me while embracing this concept of love being a human emotion that I was never more fully in love than after the birth of my son, Jabari. You see, (previous to my son's birth) my quest for love was rather self-indulgent. I wanted someone to make me feel good about myself. It is often said that "we love the ones' that love us back" so love becomes a mutual exchange of "good feelings" between two or more people, while operating in our lessor self. With the birth of my son, Jabari, something transformative happened to me. It has never happened to me before and it has never happened to me since. I've had loving relationships with friends, family, neighbors and others. I've been in awe about these little precious souls that come into this world, like my nieces, nephews and even a stranger's newborn baby that you get a glimpse of at a supermarket. They are all precious but Jabari's birth was literally transformative for me. It was like an immediate rebirth on my part from a self-indulgent entity to one who was purely selfless in his behalf. There wasn't the notion of mutual exchange whereas if he loved me, I would love him back. The directional flow of love was one-sided and he had all of me!

To this day, it remains true. My love for him continues to operate from the pure-heart realm and I am enormously proud of him. He is MIT grad who has deviated from some of his earlier interests to work at an oil company (but I won't hold that against him), a world traveler and an accomplished musician. He had picked up the guitar that my mother had given to me years before his birth that remain pristine by its nonuse and he turned it into a thing of beauty. He has a passion to play (not necessarily to "perform" but he does perform) and seems totally enthralled with the guitar that I didn't do more with than strum it a couple of times. Jabari has a compassion and concern for people that I saw in him while he was young but is commensurate in his travels abroad. He was likely born a better person that I will ever be; thus, from a human emotion perspective, my heart remains full.

Now, I love my father, too. He has guided me in ways that he doesn't even know but when I evaluate my love for each of these men of the spiritual differentiation scale, which is not so much about what we are receiving; but what we are ready to give, some difference occurs. That is, my human "feeling" of love would be expressed equally for both but the practice of love can look very different contingent upon my level of spiritual differentiation. So if my son needed a kidney (as I am operating from the pure-heart realm) without hesitation I would sacrifice them both for his life to extend. Though I earnestly love my father, I can see my level of spiritual differentiation regressing with thoughts of giving up a kidney to my father. I can see myself slipping into the craving-heart realm where there is not an immediate bestowal of the lifesaving gift to my father without a bit more deliberation. "Well, Dad, you are kinda getting a little old there…do you really need a kidney?" "Maybe I can move a little closer to you and provide you with needed trips to dialysis." "Maybe we can test each of your offspring to see who has the most compatible kidney to give you and consider that one once the testing is completed." Or I can drop down to the indifferent-heart realm, "Well, Dad, I'm getting older too, and my kidneys aren't holding out so well." "The moment I consider letting one go, the other one is likely to fail me." "We'll have to find some other way to help you out."

Love is not only dispensed in grand gestures but can be dispensed in the little things that we do. There are microcosms of social interactions that happen all around us where we can find the three distinct spiritual differentiated realms operating and I certainly notice these various levels operating within our mental health center. I am cognizant and deliberate about my spiritual pursuits and I am humbled by the degree of spiritual evolution attained by those who may not have even given their spiritual development much thought. We have colleagues, staff and clients who have certainly evolved into the pure-heart spiritual realm and the comportment of their behaviors consistently demonstrates this. They genuinely are "other-focused" and dutiful in their service to others. They suspend their judgment regarding the intricate, bizarre or heinous stories the clients have lived and perpetrated upon others. There are some people working in maintenance, Intake, front desk, therapy, psychiatry and within administration at all levels whose souls are so pure that it fills my heart just to be in their presence.

Unfortunately, there are others, in the craving-heart realm, who are backbiters and complainers. They create separation and division; while viewing themselves as victims or have a sense of entitlement. They run "hot" and "cold;" thus, one day they are cheerfully in your face and the next day (or next moment) they don't care that you exist. They are in a service providing profession but will begrudge providing service. As their spirit dims, they slip into the "indifferent-heart realm" where their actions and attitudes are indicative of burnout. They'll see you approaching and will deliberately avert eye contact with you. If circumstances forces them into an awkward greeting they'll feel compelled to offer a stilted greeting with a sanguine, over-the-top salutation that is as disingenuous as the day is long. They are more likely to express emotions of condemnation verses anything remotely associated with love. I often find this interesting because one might assume that certain professions invite into it certain type of people from a specific realm but the truth is, one can have pastors and therapists operating out of the indifferent-heart realm; with construction workers and prison guards operating from the pure-heart realm. As you can see, "love" (as considered a human emotion) is fickle and disseminated differently as we functioning at various stages on the spiritual continuum.

A concept I like from psychology that pairs well with the spiritual essence of love but also recognize the uniquely human experience comes from

Sternberg. Robert Sternberg postulated that love has three distinct components that when coming into full alignment produces "Consummate Love." In Sternberg's Love Triangle he discusses "intimacy, passion and commitment." When consummate love is absent any one of each of these attributes, it is deficient. That is, there can be "no love" existing between couples; thus, they are not likely to be in a couple's relationship with no display of intimacy, passion or commitment. There can be "liking or friendship" existing between a couple, resulting in perhaps intimacy only. "Romantic-love" may encompass intimacy and passion; whereas, "fatuous-love and infatuated-love" is largely the result of passion only with either one or both parties feeling a connection. "Companionate love" consists of a desire for togetherness, thus honoring the commitment phase of the triangle; along with intimacy but devoid of passion. Lastly, couples can engage within "empty-love"; whereas they are committed to a long term investment in the relationship but the relationship is devoid of intimacy and passion. Of course within our human strivings, we seek Sternberg's ultimate ideal love, which is, "consummate-love." In many ways, this concept of love is as simple as all spiritual ideas tend to be; however, it seems to be a difficult challenge that is borne out in the statistics with over 50% divorce rate in this County and with many clients on my caseload having relationship difficulties central to their mental health issues.

I've often told clients that my definition of "intimacy" is the "sharing of souls"; thus, when we are feeling safe and secure we can share our strengths and vulnerabilities in mutual exchange with others. Intimacy occurs within a therapist's office (though it tends to be one-sided). It happens in a treatment group where one strips down his or her pretentiousness and bares personal testimony bravely in front of others. It happens in couple's relationships where our shaming, secretive pasts are revealed to another that we've trusted not to hurt us. Over the years, I have heard "intimacy" described by spiritual gurus like Iyanla Vanzant and Dr. Wayne Dyer as *"into me see,"* and I thought this is a perfect way to talk about intimacy. Our spiritual selves hunger to be seen but our human part covers us up in shame. To cover up and hide was a shame response from Adam and Eve when they disobeyed God. Shame makes us feel badly about whom we are; which triggers a defense mode, attack mode or cover up mode. Whereas, if we are feeling emotionally indicted for something, guilt demands that we be punished.

Absent shame, we want to be seen…we want to be validated…we want to matter to others in this world. With our humanness making us "egocentric" it is hard for us to fully grant that component of love (intimacy) for the benefit of others until we come to know ourselves. Christ's ministry didn't start at birth or during his childhood or even during his young adulthood. Though I have read apocryphal accounts where Jesus' childhood antics caused blessings and curses to others, we don't have such accounts in the standard Bible and his ministry didn't start until he was thirty years old. The Bible doesn't make us privy to the life of Jesus from his adolescence until he becomes 30 but we do know that he had to confront himself while fasting 40 days in the wilderness being tempted by Satan. Thus, "intimacy" or "awareness of self" took some time to develop and prepare Jesus for his ministry. It may take some time for us to develop enough intimacy within ourselves in order to be able to extend ourselves to sharing and willingness to discover the "intimacy" of another.

So, as we are seeking a safe place, a safe environment or a safe person to allow intimacy to develop, our first endeavor is to see ourselves clearly and rid ourselves of toxic emotions like shame or guilt that triggers our propensity to cover up and hide; along with making a faulty demand from ourselves that we be punished. I recall a client whom felt so guilty and ashamed about her involvement in a local drug bust that she couldn't face the community and ended up with a diagnosis of Panic Disorder with Agoraphobia. When she stepped outside of her apartment, she felt an indictment from the eyes of others; although, many didn't even know who she was or her circumstances. She lingered with this disorder despite her legitimately prescribed medication use or with her self-medicating attempts with illegal substances. When a shift in her thinking occurred (absolving her guilt and shame), she lost her fear and need to be punished; thus, she was able to reengage within the community. Interestingly, it wasn't a therapeutic intervention that produced a cognitive shift for her. It was by some guy stepping up by words and deeds to affirm, "I don't care what you have done. I don't care what you think other people think about you. I love you and I want to be with you!" Our intimacy with self and others comes out when we are feeling safe and secure; thereby, facilitating our passion. This guy's affirmation helped the client reignite her passion to plug into him, re-examine herself and plug back into the community. She is now panic free, medication free and therapy free.

Given our humanness or our physical being is sensory and longs for the physical connection, "passion" facilitates the necessity to connect with one another. It can be affection, hugs and sex that fulfill our skin-hunger but mutual passion helps us to remain stimulated by the other. Maybe the passionate togetherness is powering down a ski slope in Vale, Colorado. Maybe it is rallying at a Viking's game or sitting in an icehouse on a frozen lake during a Minnesota winter. Passion comes in all types of forms and fashion and the passion can also mean suffering (i.e., the Passion of Christ resulting from his crucifixion). Passion can reveal itself in the work that we service providers do. I've seen caring staff and service providers go beyond the "traditional call of duty" in meeting the emotional, psychological and physical needs of another. They've given up time, money, food, clothing, and space in their homes on behalf of others in need. They step up in providing the surrogacy of God's Love and familial connection that has been lost based upon the client's life circumstances.

When we show up in someone's life, both (s)he and we, will bring to the table our beauty and our flaws. There are aspects of our lower selves and theirs that flares up from time to time. These flare ups create disharmony. The disharmony creates rancor and distance. Sufficient disharmony will ultimately create separation. The commitment part of Sternberg's Triangle gets us to hang in there when things are tough. We are fallible. We'll make mistakes. We'll inadvertently injure one another. We overtly injure one another. Commitment honors the spiritual value of forgiveness ("*God forgive our transgressions as we forgive others that transgress against us*"). Commitment allows for stability in order to develop security and safety in the relationship. In doing so, there becomes a recursive feedback loop where the commitment allowing security and safety, facilitates trust in sharing one's soul; thereby, increasing the couple's passion in being with one another.

When the concept of love is aligned with spirit, we can get rid of the fickleness that results when we align it with human emotions. The *direction* of love is unwavering because in the pure-heart realm, "God is Love" and our destiny is to always return home to God. Within our spiritual capacity to ascertain "meaning," as spiritual beings having a human experience, the *meaning* of love is clearly represented in duty, obedience and praxis, as we know it is an action step to be fulfilled. Our *purpose* is to serve others and the "others" are in our sphere of "*connection;*" furthermore, fulfilling each aspect of spirit (i.e., meaning, purpose, direction and connection). In our couple's relationship, which the Sternberg model applies, Ephesians 5:32-NKJV instructs wives to submit themselves to their husbands (identifying the male as the head of the household). This may not fly very well in the 21st Century where I would even concur that the subordination of others is wrong but if each of us took upon ourselves a "servant's attitude" in relationship with our chosen partners, our relationships would produce far greater fruit. Jesus didn't lose his status by washing the feet of others and we will do well to follow His example.

People tend to see spiritual ideas as fairly abstract and ambiguous but they are really pragmatic and simple. With spirituality, you can essentially boil everything I've written in this chapter relating to love and spirituality down to "consideration." "Intimacy" (into me see) is about "consideration." Saying, "hello" to a stranger is about "consideration." Hearing the client's story is about "consideration." Saying, "please" and "thank you" is about "consideration." Holding the door for the person behind you is "consideration." Checking on an elderly parent or a resident in a nursing home without family is "consideration." It is not complicated, it is not intense, it is not undoable…it is simply "consideration." When we feel consideration is being extended to us, we know that we matter and if we matter, we know that we've been seen.

Wally matters! Fatima matters! Jessica…Matt…Tammy and you matter! Let's start becoming better ambassadors of God's directives for us to love one another. Sternberg's model and the spiritual essence of God's Love may be separated only by a small degree. Sternberg's model is focused upon a dyad in pursuit of "consummate love." As great and worthy this pursuit is, it is largely egocentric for the benefit of the "self." God's Love and direction for us to display love is often counterintuitive to those residing in the indifferent-heart and craving-heart realms. Our love expands to love our "enemies," to love those who don't love us back and to love those that we may feel are least desirous of our love. Jesus stated, "*Then the righteous will answer Him, saying, 'Lord, when did we see You hungry and feed You, or thirsty and give You drink? When did we see You a stranger and take You in, or naked and clothe You? Or when did we see You sick, or in prison, and come to You?' And the King will answer and say to them, 'Assuredly, I say to you, inasmuch as you did it to one of the least of these My brethren, you did it to Me.'*" (Matthew 25: 37-40-NKJV) So, Dad, perhaps you'll get that kidney after all.

Love is a spiritual ideal! Emotions titillate us and provide us with a "human experience." The titillation can deceive us and cause us to believe that we are less than what we are called to be. We are the sons and daughters of a Loving God that is beyond the pale of human emotions. Though our emotions make us fundamentally human, we are spiritual entities that extend us beyond the pale of humanness. Therefore, we, too, are beyond the limitations of our human emotions. Like Wally and Jessica, we can "feel" unloved or inadequate but neither "feeling" is true. When we break free of discursive and deceptive emotions we can have a more pleasant life journey by simply observing these emotions that come our way without being the emotion. Indeed, our ability to separate our spiritual selves (which embody love) from the egocentrism of human emotion, we can do as Peter states above; which is to lay "*...aside all malice, all deceit, hypocrisy, envy, and all evil speaking...*"

Ripening the Fruit-Micro Aggressions

Minorities, people with mental illness, those with substance abuse problems, victims of physical, sexual, verbal assaults, low wage earners, gays/lesbians, physically disabled, overweight people, overly thin people, those with obvious physical deformities, those with hidden or invisible "deformities" (e.g., eating disorders, peculiar sexual practices), elderly, infirmed, prisoners, ex-felons, gang members, excessively pierced and tattooed individuals and all of those others that deviate from the perceived status quo majority are often the victims of outright hostility but more insidiously they are victims of micro-aggressions and micro-insults. These are subtle, not so glaringly obvious attempts to discount the divinity of the person who stands before you (e.g., sighing, yawning, eye rolling, gaze avoidance, limp handshake, crushing handshake, snide comments and putdowns, etc.). In the pure-heart realm, all humanity is honored, validated, affirmed and appreciated.

In this exercise, I want you to become mindful of the micro-aggressive behaviors and micro-insults that you are exhibiting on a daily basis to people that you've determine do not exhibit the divinity of God based upon their presentation. No matter how magnanimous we think we've become, we'll find a pattern in our behaviors toward the type of people that we've consciously or unconsciously chosen to discount. The consideration that we grant another human being is "powerful!" Begin an active process in granting consideration to the people you encounter on a daily basis. This taps into Jesus' statement that what we have done to the least of humanity (accepted them or shunned them) we have done unto Him.

As you consider acts of consideration, oftentimes we can be much kinder to strangers than the intimate others in our life. Make daily efforts to show these professed loved ones that they, too, matter to you. Daily consideration of your partner will go a long way in producing the essence of "Consummate Love" (intimacy, passion and commitment).

Lastly, if the Abundancy of God's Love is meted out in the way of "consideration," so don't forget how important you are for self-consideration.

Hedonism, self-denigration and self-indulgence is the product of the lower self. "Love" as displayed in an act of consideration, comes from "praxis" (informed action) that is administered to ourselves and doled out freely to others. Choose acts of consideration on a daily basis that demonstrate the authentic love you have for yourself!

XI

Get Out of Yourself!

A man who isolates himself seeks his own desire;
He rages against all wise judgment.
A fool has no delight in understanding,
But in expressing his own heart.
When the wicked comes, contempt comes also;
And with dishonor *comes* reproach.
The words of a man's mouth *are* deep waters;
The wellspring of wisdom *is* a flowing brook.
It is not good to show partiality to the wicked,
Or to overthrow the righteous in judgment.
A fool's lips enter into contention,
And his mouth calls for blows.
A fool's mouth *is* his destruction,
And his lips *are* the snare of his soul.
(Proverbs 18: 1-7-NKJV)

The above passage, and indeed the bulk of the Bible, is written in patriarchal language with male dominant nouns and pronouns; thus, sometimes we forget how certain traits may equally fit both men and woman. Nevertheless, one seeking "his own desire" really does sound like the pursuit of males. Indeed, a self-indulgent, narcissistic woman appears to be an oxymoron. Yes, we can see arrogance, bravado, demanding, elitist, entitled behaviors in some men. There is a primordial biological determinant or social evolution that has men acting out "instrumental" tasks and roles. Men started our life's journey as hunters and gatherers to protect and provide for the family. Based upon Adam's disobedience and expulsion from the Garden of Eden, God informed Adam, *"Cursed is the ground for your sake: in toil you shall eat of it all the days of your life. Both thorns and thistles it shall bring forth for you."* (Genesis 3:17-18-NKJV) Survival was tough; thus, setting up this hierarchical difference between men (providers) and women (nurturers) made sense. This hierarchical system plays itself out when we look at the male's role in lessor species when the most dominant male is the one in charge and benefactor of privilege to copulate with each of the females he chooses; giving credence to Darwin's theory (survival of the fittest) strengthening the gene pool.

But what about women? They are not hairy, dominate or brutish people. They are not arrogant, demanding or insensitive. Aren't they the subject of schoolyard nursery rhymes of "sugar and spice and everything nice?" Aren't they the nurturers of the next generation; the homemakers to provide efficiency and order? Aren't they the expressive ones who are so in tuned with their emotional selves that author John Gray attributed women being from a totally different planet than men (*Men Are from Mars; Women Are from Venus*)? Whatever women are, it is hard to see women taking on attitudes, behaviors and personalities that are associated with the above passage or an entitled sense of narcissism but I am coming in contact with more and more such women.

The DSM-5 has a list of criteria about narcissism to justify a diagnosis for this disorder but broadly speaking this is a person that believes in his or her own "superiority" (oftentimes with little accomplishments or achievements to justify this superiority) and they lack empathy. It is strange, sometimes, because you'll get glimmers through their dogmatism that they do have the capacity to read others' behaviors accurately but that ability comes to a rapid halt when it comes to them. They tend to be demeaning of others, offering up slights and criticisms. They turn up the volume with boisterous and verbose interactions. Their lack of empathy makes them not only oblivious to the emotional/social needs of another they also appear to be deliberately cruel. Whether a direct tactic or in passive-aggressive form, they are poised for an attack. Communication is counterproductive, as their objective is the win the argument; thus, contradicting themselves in midsentence in order to get the win. Their work relationships suffer… their interpersonal relationships suffer; yet, they don't appear predisposed to modify their behaviors. It is as if they enter into a village, consume all of its resources and then burn the village to the ground before they leave.

In lessor forms of this disorder, in both men and women, is a self-indulgent feeling of entitlement that impairs healthy relationship bonds with others but it also sabotages their own efforts. Xia is a 42 years old, Hmong woman working at a food production company in Southwest MN. Xia has four adult children that reside with her. After her contentious marriage had folded Xia quickly forged a relationship with a 36 years old, Caucasian farmer, Chris. Chris was smitten by Xia as she presented with attractive features and frame that belies her 42 years of age. Chris' demeanor and reticence around women would have likely confined him to indefinite bachelorhood on his large farm, but Xia was shrewd and calculating. She enticed the relationship, married quickly and moved her family onto his farm.

Chris was a humble, generous and initially grateful man to have someone in his life and to be able to share his generosity to others. Unfortunately, in short order, Chris understood that Xia takes…takes…and takes with little regard for him, his property or his resources. Chris has learned that if he asked for anything ("Xia, could you bring me a cold beer," after a 12 hour day of harvesting while decompressing in front of the TV), Xia would become argumentative, resistant and complaining. She rifle's through his stuff when he is not around but complains vociferously if he asked to borrow something of hers. As pretty as Xia is, she belches loudly and throughout the day. When Chris is sleeping, she floods the room with light because she might want to trim a finger nail in the middle of the night. He has done well to maintain his livelihood and farm but Xia diminishes him with curt comments.

When this type of client presents for therapy, they are constantly using pejoratives about people in general (e.g., "idiots," "stupid," "dumb as a box of rocks," etc.). They'll have a sense of superiority without merit and will try to take control of the direction of the therapeutic session. It has been revealed to me during sessions that it is only the clients with this disorder (Narcissism) that will intercede when I'm illustrating psychoeducational information on the board as a way of undercutting me and over promoting themselves. Chris doesn't have the skill, temperament or inclination to have these ongoing social exchanges with Xia that produced conflict without resolution; thus, he kept withdrawing himself further from the relationship. If Xia had greater sensitivity, she might have cared about Chris withdrawing from her but she is accustomed of using up human resources and then simply moving on.

All social relationships are about mutual transactions. Any agreed upon transaction does have self-interest involved. The problem with this for most therapy seekers is that they do not understanding this transaction as a concept of love. As pointed out in the previous chapter, love transcends emotion and is a spiritual attribute and the Ultimate Essence of God. What we know about the "nature" of "spirit" is that spirituality has simplicity and is often counterintuitive. The simplicity in this spiritual law is borne out of the Golden Rule: To do unto others as you would have them do unto you (Matthew 7:12-NKJV). What makes it counterintuitive is our focus. We are countering our narcissistic impulses and putting the needs of another ahead of our own. When relationship transactions are built upon this level of exchange, it becomes a quality, health relationship!

Xia is not an "evil" person. Her self-interests do matter. She is a "child" of the Most High God and is "entitled" to dignity, respect, validation, honor, support, empathy, compassion, forgiveness and love. Somewhere along her journey, her path was skewed and she feels that she must attain these attributes by manipulation or dominance and once having done so, miserly hangs onto them. The tick bird rides upon the rhinos back to feed on the ticks and fleas embedded in the rhinos hide. The tick bird is lavishly fed and the rhino is relieved of the irritation from these insects. It is a symbiotic relationship with both parties benefiting but this is not true in the case of Xia and Chris. God didn't intend that any resource of abundance that He lavishly gives away would be possessed and hoarded. The God of Love, created us in Love, nourishes us in Love, protects us with Love, and sustains us with Love. He expects that what He is giving to us in abundance that we aren't stingy with in that we can't give this love away.

Perhaps it is an artifact of our times. The 21st Century certainly is paving the way for more equality and empowerment in women. As a person of color that has experienced within this society the adverse effects of a minority status, I would argue for nothing less than parity for all individuals but there appears to be a shift happening that is represented in pop culture reflecting a negative change. There are television shows like "Mean Girls" and "Pretty Little Liars" that point to this cultural shift. We have beautifully clad, reality star housewives, swearing like sailors, displaying themselves in an uncouth fashion and engaging in drunken brawls. Men have either lost their identity when it comes to being a "man" or the fear of loss in losing their partner is so palpable that we aren't standing up for our manhood anymore.

This does not bode well for couple's dynamics that I am seeing in therapy. The first woman, Eve, was described as a "helpmate" who was a part of Adam (rib) and stood at the side of Adam. Perhaps the Garden story was a precursor to what has become in that we were occupying a space with absolutely everything, yet with a selfish impulse to pursue more. As we are advocating more and more for our "entitlements" and "independent rights" within a relationship, these relationships are deconstructing. I met with an elderly widower the other day who continued to profoundly grieve the loss of his wife twelve years earlier. He was a farmer with nothing sophisticated or elegant about him but he talked about the bonding rituals in his marriage that created an unshakable intimacy and enduring partnership that those 12 years of physical absence has not broken.

While his wife was alive, the couple had decidedly different roles on the farm, with him caring for the livestock and crops, while she took care of the responsibilities within the home. (Doesn't this sound like a throwback to the past where gender roles were clearly delineated and hierarchical?) However, their joining ritual was to wash dishes together after the nightly meal. The task was mundane. Hey, it wasn't "date night" or a "trip to the mall," but it provided them with daily opportunity to check in with one another and build upon their partnership. They were able to see the value in being "other-directed" vs. "self-focused"; thereby, reaping the "fruit of love" from their "labor of love." The widower found it hard to let go of his partner because she truly was his "other half."

The confounding thing that I am seeing in this "sprouting" of narcissism within women is not so much that their focus is self-interest (indeed, all of us have varying degrees of ego-centrism). What is surprising me is the level of cruelty that they possess. If this is on par for the evolution of women seeking parity with men, just like the androgynist movement in the '70's, this too is a bad choice. The opening passage reveals that this focus upon ourselves can diminish our empathy and understanding for others, fosters contempt and displays wickedness. It is out of the condition of our hearts in how we forge transactions with others in our close relationships. More and more women seem to be losing sight of their hearts. Perhaps they are adopting the worldview of men to excel in the world as men traditionally have, but it is we, men, who need to enlarge our hearts and not for women to lose sight of theirs.

There is an ugliness of the self that we are giving into without much concern or hesitation; resulting in diminishing knowledge in our raison detre (reason for being); which is to Love God and to Love others. Transactions of love equate with greater mental health. Did you know that the notion of love can be a causal factor for anxious, depressive and/or psychotic symptoms? Did you know that the notion of love can ameliorate anxious, depressive and/or psychotic symptoms? My scientific minded colleagues would scoff at these notions, seeking "evidence-based, empirical, measurable facts" as a determinant for a "fragmented ego state," "distorted schema" or "disturbed mind" that creates anxiety, depression and/or psychosis. To my colleagues, I would ask of them to "show me a 'fragmented ego state,' 'distorted schema' or a 'mind' period; distorted or otherwise." We place a lot of faith in theorists, pharmaceuticals, and scientific methods that hasn't shown any greater efficacy than faith-based approaches.

The absence or the perversion of love is often a causal factor for psychological problems. Consider the ongoing effect of trauma, abuse, molestation, abandonment, over-involvement, neglect, etc., on a child that is only seeking a secure and loving environment. Therefore, love is vital and sought after with great intensity. It is replicated in song, poetry, novels, television, movies and our social interactions. We yearn to replicate love in our most intimate relationships with one another. This is certainly understandable that we would yearn to replicate the Essence of Love, from which we derive, in this physical world. People often have an idealistic, romanticized notion of love that doesn't help them with mate selection and retention. We ideally pursue a "love-based" relationship but because of our degree of spiritual, emotional and psychological differentiation, we are grasping at anything other than a love-based relationship.

I have had a number of clients come in for marital or couple's therapy, obviously struggling in their relationship. Our world is socially constructed; therefore, we will always see the world from the framework of our level of spiritual differentiation. Xia resides in the indifferent-heart realm where narcissism flourishes, pulling in the "good guy" Chris, who was striving to exist in the pure-heart realm but perhaps slipped into the craving-heart realm due to Xia's significant influence. I share with clients the following types of relationships in order for them to see what type of relationship that they are currently in and where they like to be (which is borne out in their actions vs. their statements). The 1st type of relationship listed is a love-based relationship. Most would say they want a love-based relationship but many will resist this type of relationship when they realize that they are not in the relationship to passively receive love but to take on the responsibility to create love. Xia receives but creates nothing of value for mutual exchange with Chris. If she had the tiniest bit of wisdom, one would think that Xia would at least "water" the "relationship garden" that Chris works so hard to produce but Xia can't get outside of her own self.

Love-based relationships require something from us in order to be "other-focused." Love doesn't permit self-absorption nor has an agenda of self-interests. It requires active involvement but our labor of love shouldn't be draining us; it should be replenishing us. There is the work that is necessary to produce a livelihood, but there is also the work of gardening, sculpting, auto repair, writing...etc., that rejuvenates us from the work of making a livelihood and there is the "work" of relationship development that soothes one's soul. Love-based relationships are the antithesis of narcissism that gets us outside of ourselves. I've referred to love as a form of praxis (informed action) because it is not about *feeling* (emotions) but *knowing* (awareness) and *doing* (action or consideration for the other). Love requires incredible courage and integrity. It is not designed for those of you who are weak. It requires that we become fully intact ego states, where we've claimed our value, worth and esteem; which then grants us the capacity to extend ourselves in loving connection to another.

Xia will clearly say that she loves Chris but she puts nothing behind her words. It is like trying to nourish one's self with an unlimited supply of marshmallows. Xia, like the marshmallow, may be puffy, sweet, and gooey that initially tastes great but has no nutritional benefit and can't sustain a person down the road. We can fall into relationships without much discernment or we can try to maintain a relationship under the guise of love, but love is not operating here. I teach my clients that we can forge unhealthy relationships under the misapprehension that we are generating love but the connection tends to be based upon "need, drama, anger, fear, guilt, shame, envy and obligation." Let's look at each of them below.

Need-based. Who doesn't want to feel "needed" in their partnered relationship? With mutual need and appreciation, this would likely be a good thing; however, "need-based" relationships are imbalanced. They can be manipulative and exploitive by the one who feigns weakness in the relationship. An individual in the relationship becomes woefully needy on the other person for his/her emotional survival. There can be many reasons that a need-based attachment remains (e.g., children, health, finances, etc.) but it is the "need" that forges an unhealthy bond verses the pursuit of love. There is no growth in this type of relationship because the growth that could be developed in a love-based relationship is sucked out of this relationship by the person with significant needs. There can be a complimentary type relationship where someone stays home and the other works. That's just fine, as the relationship is balanced by the complimentary roles with both individuals remaining whole. When one loses him/herself and latches onto another for survival, this would be an imbalanced, need-based relationship.

In the description of Xia and Chris' relationship, you might not think that someone as self-absorbed as Xia would have any needs. After all, she takes and takes and there would likely not to appear any real emotional damage within Xia if Chris finally "kicks her to the curb," but at the core of a self-promoting, arrogant, grandiose, selfish narcissist is an incredibly insecure individual. Though Xia "takes" with little consideration for Chris, she is also in great need for acceptance. Her ability to quickly find emotional detachment once she has dried up a source is just a way for her to be self-protective. Should Xia burn through the financial or emotional resources that Chris provides, she like a lot of men with narcissism, will reattached to another source that she will deplete.

Drama-based. Drama based relationships are fueled and stoked by adrenaline. There may be high emotional bursts with expressions of the words, "I love you," but the actions exhibited are anything but loving and the goal is to obtain that "fix" of adrenaline. It is not unlike the drug addict that needs the "fix" just to feel "normal"; the drama-based individual creates ongoing drama because anything else feels boring. The adrenaline rush may mean getting involved or enmeshed in other people's business. They stir the pot, yet feel as though they are the ones that are victimized. They indulge in gambling or shopping sprees. Their drama can include orchestrating sex outdoors, having affairs, hysterical emotional displays in public or constant criticisms and sniping just to keep the drama going. When the drama fades, so does the relationship because the person will be in need of a new fix.

Sandy and Tom was one such couple that was both drama-based individuals. They were enmeshed with a conflict-habituated relationship (a relationship type where the fighting is constant). There was no reports from either that Tom has ever strayed from his relationship with Sandy but Sandy's jealousy was so intense that she had to be present with Tom whenever he went out in order for her to monitor his interactions with other women. Should the cashier asks, in the presence of Sandy, if Tom found everything that he needed as he was checking out, that would produce heated conflict on the way home spurred by Sandy's notions that Tom lingered too long in an answer with the cashier or they were using coded language to confirm a sexual rendezvous. They "poked" the "relationship bear" constantly and jail wasn't a deterrent for either. Solomon advised that it is *"Better to dwell in a corner of a housetop, than in a house shared with a contentious woman."* (Proverbs 21:9-NKJV) Sandy is contentious but so is Tom! They both are fueled by adrenaline. Their relationship will destroy them as individuals and as a couple but neither will relent.

Anger-based. These types of relationships are interesting in that you'd think that people would run from a hostile or aggressive relationship. Ironically, these types of relationships often have a lengthy "shelf-life." They are venomous and attacking. Individuals are going for the jugular vein with name-calling, dehumanizing comments and character assassinations. One, or both, will ratchet up the intensity of anger emotions that can lead to violence but the relief comes during the "Honeymoon Stage" after this intense emotion has been spent. Anger arises out of failed expectation; along with issues of power and control. While immersed into ourselves we assume a power (the ability to impose our will upon another) and control (limiting another person's freedom) that is not within our prerogative to do (*"A fool takes no pleasure in understanding, but only in expressing his opinion"*). Anger can be the "emotional glue" that holds a relationship together but it is a contaminant that makes those involved psychological, emotionally, physically and spiritually ill.

I recall a couple who came to therapy with raw, venomous hatred for each other. They had four children born during the span of their marriage but none of the children turned out to be the husband's biological children. He'd call her the vilest names for her infidelities and her angry toward him manifested in unprotected sex with strange men that produced four children growing up in a household with no demonstration of love and a constant display of anger. As angry as they both are with each other, neither has worked up the courage to extricate themselves from this unhealthy relationship.

Fear-based. Participants within a fear-based relationship remain codependent or enmeshed due to insecurities within one or both of them. They teeter with thoughts of desperation that the relationship will end and they compromise themselves for the sake of the relationship that is not healthy for either person. Our greatest human need is acceptance; thus, our greatest human fear is rejection. I believe that this innate fear of rejection stems from our primordial fear of being rejected from the presence of God during the original sin. As we "sin" we "turn our back on God" and this dis-fellowship is painful. Replicated in our human interactions are fellowships (where we are connected to each other within a community) and the dis-fellowship that occurs when we are shunned. When we generate faulty notions of us being inadequate, incapable and insecure, those beliefs are triggered by the presence of someone else that threatens to leave us. God doesn't give us a spirit of fear and when we understand that God will never abandon us, we don't have to operate out of fear.

I have had countless clients that have operated by fear and desperately tried hanging onto a relationship long after it was too late. I wish that those individuals in a relationship who are so fearful when their relationship is ending would be better stewards of their relationship while they are in it. I wish the fear motivated them to provide care, concern and appreciation for their partners. I wish their fear triggered for them what their lives would be like after they've alienated and pushed their partner out of their lives. Fear-based individuals can concoct unsubstantiated fears of infidelities in their partners. They tax their partners with their unsubstantiated fears. A recent client was riddled with fears of infidelities by his spouse throughout their 11 year marriage. He surmised that she has cheated on him 20 different times with no shred of evidence for any of them. The fear of inadequacy within individuals does not often motivate them to change their actions prior to the collapse of their relationships and the flood of tears engenders little sympathy once their partner decides to walk away. Nevertheless, I urged this client to return home and operate out of his professed love vs. his fears. As he builds upon his own fidelity toward his wife, he'll be less likely to find infidelities within her.

Guilt-based. Ego-centric individuals (self-focused vs. self-absorb) may hang onto a relationship out of the experience of guilt. Guilt is an emotion where we feel badly about what we've done (or what we didn't do). When there is a loss, we feel guilty because we might have said something unkind that we weren't able to take back; or, we weren't there for our loved one when we know we could have been. The guilt that fuses us in an unhealthy way within an intimate relationship may result from an affair or maybe some physical abuse or maybe financial mismanagement or some other thing that makes us feel guilty. The problem with concepts like "guilt" and "shame" induced relationships is that it demands punishment. We punish ourselves and punish others by tenaciously hanging onto guilt and shame. Guilt is also leverage used by the non-offending party in a misguided attempt to keep the offending party in check.

The health and wellbeing of a couple's relationship requires wholeness of the individuals and parity with one another. Guilt will create an imbalance that will not allow the relationship to heal unless both parties choose to forgive. The couple that I highlighted as an example of anger-based relationships also had guilt and shame attached to it. The husband guilt-induced his wife for her affairs which she undoubtedly engaged in due to her anger toward her husband, but also out of her shame.

Shame-based. Another unhealthy indulgence in self-interest is shame. Shame is not a haughty self-promotion, like pride; rather, we focus on our perceived flaws. Shame caused Adam and Eve to hide themselves when they disobeyed God. With shame we are covering up ourselves with the "fig leaves" of life, hoping that no one will discover our flaws. In a couple's relationship, the shame we bring into the relationship keeps us attached in an unhealthy relationship because we believe no one else would want us. I met a woman with deep-seated shame issues that she was unwilling to let go of. She married a man who molested her daughters when they were children. In her shame, she initially denied her daughters' allegations. Ultimately the truth was revealed in a way that she could hear but it reactivated her shame because she didn't protect her daughters. Her compounding shame has not freed her from her husband and he treats her as worthless as she feels. If asked, "Why do you stay," her response is, "I love him." It is not love that attaches the two. The ugliness that she feels inside is reflected in her marriage but she won't let go. Her years of dysthymia (persistent depression) are adaptive responses to the life she lives. She can be free but she doesn't believe she deserves to be free.

Envy-based. In ego-centric fashion, we scan the lives of others to make faulty comparisons between them and ourselves. We envy our parents or the pastor's marriage and we may endure our own miserable relationship to reflect a façade that our relationship is great. Envy-based relationships can be relationships of pretense. They are maintained as long as one can sell the image that everything is OK but the relationship is often an emptied shell with no vitality within. Sarah didn't want to wait on God to work it out with her to conceive a child, so she gave her servant girl, Hagar, to her husband, Abram, to conceive a child. Subsequently, Sarah was envious of Hagar and instructed her husband to send Hagar and his son away. When we spend our time looking at what we don't have verses appreciating what we have, we devaluate the quality of the relationship that we do have.

Obligation-based. These are relationships that are forged and/or maintained out of obligatory reasons verses love. One might assert, "I married you in front of God, family and friends. Even though I can't stand the air that you breathe, I made this obligation and by gosh, I'm sticking to it!" We can remain obliged to stay together due to financial entanglements. We may have children in common or health concerns that bind us in a relationship where no love exists. Because relationships can be tough, there is a value to commitment within a relationship; however, if couples are knitted together strictly out of obligation, the value of love does not come into being.

When we are self-focused, thereby centering in on our own selfish desires we don't have consideration for others. We'll scoop up the kids each morning with cuddles and kisses to start their day. The dog greets us as if he/she hasn't seen us in years with boundless energy and affection. And then, we turn to the person we have selected to be our life mate and will barely speak. We may grunt an indifferent, "Good Morning," and our tone, attitude and behavior discounts our partner completely. Listen, I understand this. We get into unhealthy patterns of interaction and when the energy that comes from our kids and our pets is not forthcoming from our partner, we respond in kind.

If we don't appreciate someone, it is hard to "consider" them and then we stop doing so. We could easily make our partner a cup of coffee while we are making our own, but that requires consideration. The lack of consideration is a death knell in the coffin of a dying relationship. It can be resurrected but we'll have to shift our focus off of ourselves and place it upon others. Of course, someone like Chris might say that he poured significantly in the "well" of his relationship with Xia and the more he does, the more she takes. He would like for his partner to draw him water every once and awhile but this is not likely to be the case with Xia (*"When wickedness comes, contempt comes also, and with dishonor comes disgrace"*).

I'm going to shift a bit in my focus here, but I will tie it back in. My mother has staunch, theosophical beliefs. She doesn't strike me as being a fundamentalist in her views because I think of fundamentalists as narrower in their focus and more expressive in their views. That is, I talk with my mother every week, centering on three basic topics (family, God and religion) and I realize that at the moment of this writing, I can't tell you her stance on abortion. In all these years, the topic of abortion has never come up between she and I. Perhaps the topic is more political in nature, with strident views and opinions that leads to conflict and disengagement amongst others, which my mother tends to avoid. Perhaps I am doing some "linguistic hairsplitting" with the concepts above and we are all fairly "fundamental" in the beliefs that we endorse but one staunch view that my mother has is that "everything comes in threes."

Oh, my mother is not a numerologist by any stretch of the imagination but she looks at the world with the notion that good fortune or calamity comes in threes. The most recent evidence of that is that she and two of my brothers were each separately struck on icy wintry roads, by three separate motorists and none of the three motorists had auto insurance. Thus, this incident will be conformational and etched in her head as evidence of her belief in the series of threes. Of course, if a fourth or fifth incident were to occur, they would likely be dismissed because it doesn't align itself with her belief and if only two incidents occurred, she'll be scanning for a third.

Numerologists and astrologists will see patterns in numbers and will extract some meaning. In psychology, we may classify this as an "idea of reference" and look to see if it is consistent with a mental health disorder; however, this concept of "three" is very important educational piece that I present to clients when I am doing couple's therapy. That is, while doing individual therapy, the unit of analysis or the entity focused upon is clearly just one—the individual client. Nevertheless, when it comes to doing couple's therapy, standard rules of mathematics do not apply; resulting in the smallest unit of analysis for couple's therapy is "three." Perhaps my mother has something here when two events occur, she starts scanning for the third.

Frequently, the couple comes to the relationship as partners or as opponents and when they are sparring with one another, it does feel like there is only two boxers in the ring, squaring off with one another. However, the real damage that is done between couples is when the individuals involved fail to consider that there are three entities to a couple's relationship that must be equally considered. Oftentimes we have a greater singular focus upon ourselves when we enter into and try to sustain a relationship. We focus upon our needs, our wants, our desires, our expectations, our rules, our values, our way of growing up, our previous relationships, our ideals forged from romance novels and soap operas. With so much focus upon ourselves, it leaves little attention, resources or energy for our partner, who is the 2nd important entity in the relationship.

In a side note, I just had two couples referred to me due to their intransigence within couple's therapy and were hoping for a breakthrough with a different therapist, with the wife of one of the couple and the husband of the other telling me that their therapist told them that they had a "right to be selfish right now." I realize that the statement and/or the interpretation of the statement in a therapeutic session can morph significantly from its therapeutic intent during the initial context but we as therapists are not immune from a "self-promoting/indulgent" society so there may be some validity to what the clients were telling me but being self-focused is the cause of each of the concepts I've listed above that is devoid of a love-based relationship. As a result, we have individuals within the couple's relationship focusing on their own needs, minimizing the importance of their partner and they are oblivious of the 3rd entity of a couple's relationship; which is the relationship itself. The relationship is a "living, breathing" significant component in the trinity of a couple's relationship. Just like any "living" entity, it must be "fed, watered, nurtured and cared for." It is what Christ was conveying to the Samarian woman whom he asked her to drawn him water from the well but his exchange was to give her "living water" or "spirit" in which she would thirst no more.

Relationships are always bigger than the individuals involved. If we construct a basic triangle that represents the various entities of the relationship (i.e., you, the other and the relationship), we can apportion 33.3% to each entity that represents the whole. Noticed that the apportioned attributed to oneself is 33.3% or 1/3 of the whole. So, "Yes," you do have an importance in the couple's relationship that is being constructed but when you consider the "other" and the "relationship" itself (totaling 66.6%) 2/3 of the relationship focus is off of ourselves. Thus, one cannot be "selfish" in a relationship designed for "selfless" people.

What a difference it can make when we "get out of ourselves" and selflessly invest in the quality of our couple's relationship, attending to each of the entities that produce the whole. If you encounter a partner with a narcissistic personality disorder, the law of reciprocity (Golden Rule) will have little effect in balancing out the relationship. Whatever you give is taken with no intention for return. Indeed, you may even be chided for not giving more fully or frequently; thus, you are not doing the narcissist or yourself a service. In this case, reexamine what is needed in the relationship with your interest in mind and with a determination that you'll be advocating for yourself. For all others who want to change the dynamic of your devitalized couple's relationship, the exercise that I present below will be a weekly reminder to tap into those mutual transactions that will promote understanding and growth within your relationship. For those of you with a partner like Xia (a resource depleting relationship), I encourage you to attempt this exercise as well. If nothing else, it will help you identify the extent to which you want to continue to invest in your relationship if the outcome remains dubious.

Ripening the Fruit-Weekly Couple/Family Council

Council: An assembly of persons called together for deliberation or discussion.

A relationship, whether it is a couple's relationship or a family relationship, operates as a system. A system can be functional (in that it serves the need of the individuals involved) or it can be dysfunctional (in that it doesn't serve the needs of the individuals involved). When a system is not functioning well, the first tendency is to cast blame upon others in the system without seeing our role and responsibility in making a dysfunction system functional.

Weekly Couple/Family Council meetings help to get a relationship back on track and to keep it on track. It is not an opportunity for individuals to play the "blame game," but to genuinely chart a course for the wellbeing of the couple/family system.

The 1st step in this process is to believe in the basic core of humanity and integrity of all individuals involved. Even those who are behaving badly (perhaps even you), who yell, scream, curse, lie, steal and betray the couple/family system, do so because they are not getting their basic needs met, and they (perhaps even you) lack the knowledge and skills to ask for what you need.

The 2nd step is to set a specific date and time that will consistently occur with an expectation that all members will be present (e.g., Wednesdays at 6:00pm or Sundays at 10:00am). Set your kitchen timer for one hour and do not exceed the hour. All issues and concerns won't be resolved in an hour (and they are not meant to be), but we don't want the meeting to digress into endless ranting and raving.

The 3rd step is to select roles for the individuals involved. The "leader" will be the one that introduces agenda items, watches the clock to use time wisely and to ensure that everyone participates. Rotate leadership responsibilities at various meetings. Though children can serve in the leadership role if the meeting is structured and he/she is supported by a parent, younger children won't have the patience to endure an hour and they can be dismissed after calling the meeting together and doing a brief check in, if so desired. Assign someone the role of the "recorder." The recorder will enter brief minutes in a spiral notebook; which serves as the Couple/Family Journal. The rest of the individuals are "participants" and even the leader and recorder will participate in the family discussion.

The 4th step in the process is for the leader to do a brief check in with each participant. Ask each participant to rate the quality of their past week with a number from 1-10 (1 = the worst week ever; 10 = the best week ever). After the number is given, ask the participant why he or she has selected his/her number? This process should not be longer than 5 minutes, so leader, keep charge of the time. If a child states, "My week was a 1, 'the worst week ever' because mom didn't let me go to the movies with my friends," this in NOT to be challenged. This step is designed for honest identification and expression of overall feeling and no one needs to attack or defend anything here.

The 5th step in the process is for the leader to ask each participant (as well as contribute) to describe what each has specifically done during the previous week to have made the couple's union or the family system functional (or better)? Each partner in the couple's relationship and each member in the family have a responsibility to be thinking about and attending to the wellbeing of the couple/family unit. Children have a tendency to think that they ought to be catered to but they need to know that they have responsibilities in the healthy functioning of the family unit as well.

The 6th step. Establish or reassert couple/family goals (e.g., institute date night once a week or have the family enter a 4-H project at the State Fair next year). Individuals within the unit can establish or reassert individual goals (e.g., to be promoted at work in a year or improve a math course grade from a "C" to a "B" by the end of the semester). Determine how others can help with either the family goals, couple's goals and individual goals (e.g., granting mom an hour of uninterrupted time daily to work on a task for work or dad will sit down with Bobby to help him understand and complete math homework).

The 7ᵗʰ step. Establish and review the family/couple's rules, roles, and expectations. That is, a rule may be to call if you are going to be late; or homework is to be completed before talking on the phone or watching TV. Roles would be division of household labor—who is responsible for what? Expectations can be made explicit in statements like, "because we love one another we expect none of us will curse one another, yell at the other nor hit the other." Expectations about specific and private matters (e.g., sex, finances, medical, etc.) should be discussed by the parents separately from the children. Don't involve children in adult matters!

The 8ᵗʰ step. A healthy relationship requires healthy communication, so be assertive and ask for what you want. What is it that you need from your couple/family unit? Do you need more hugs or affection? Do you need words of encouragement? Do you need more individualistic quality time to process and decompress? Do you need mom or dad to be present at your recital or football game? Do you need Suzy to turn her music down by 9:00pm so that you can get the sleep that you need? Whatever you need, this is the time to ask loving family members to extend themselves by attending to one of your needs.

The 9ᵗʰ step. After assessing what it is that you want determine what it is that your partner or family needs and pledge to grant it. Be careful here when it comes to pledges. People in general and children specifically feel the betrayal of broken pledges. So, if you promise to play catch with your daughter when you come home from work, you must play catch. Don't promise things if you are unable to honor your commitment.

XII

The Whole is Greater Than the Sum of its Parts

Then God said, 'Let Us make man in Our image, according to Our likeness; let them have dominion over the fish of the sea, over the birds of the air, and over the cattle, over all the earth and over every creeping thing that creeps on the earth.' So God created man in His own image; in the image of God He created him; male and female He created them. Then God blessed them, and God said to them, 'Be fruitful and multiply; fill the earth and subdue it; have dominion over the fish of the sea, over the birds of the air, and over every living thing that moves on the earth.'
(Genesis 1:26-28-NKJV)

God's basic instructions for nature and humanity is that we become "fruitful" (productive) and expansive ("multiplying what we have produced"). This is replicated throughout the Bible in varying stories of God taking a "little bit of nothing" and creating a "whole lot of something" from it. Out of one human being (Adam), and there are others that dispute that Adam was THE original being, but from whatever humble beginnings that was, we now have a world population of over seven billion people! The population has multiplied. Similarly, a little boy, (Joseph) envied by his brothers, sold into slavery and ends up in prison due to no fault of his own is greatly positioned by God to later save his family (indeed Israel) from the famine and starvation. As this small band of Jews resided in Egypt, both as free people and then as slaves, their population swelled exponentially; thus, fulfilling God's command to be fruitful and multiply.

David, a little shepherd boy, with nothing more than a rock and sling, brings down a menacing giant and ultimately assumes the highest leadership role in Israel. Remember that David was the least of Jesse's sons and wasn't even considered by Jesse when Samuel sought to anoint a son of Jesse's to be king. Samuel rejected each of Jesse's sons and asked that Jesse send for the one that wasn't even considered (David), who would later rule Israel. With instruction from Christ, Peter takes his fishing boat out, having not caught a single fish prior to Jesus' instructions, has his nets overwhelmed and his boat nearly sank from the enormous bounty of fish they caught. I can imagine Peter's thoughts initially, "Hey, I'm a fisherman! This is what I do. We've been at it all day and today, there aint nothin' out there." However, based upon his obedience to Christ's instructions, Peter's efforts were "fruitful" and "multiplied" significantly (out of nothing came something).

We are made in the image of God and by God's example, He instructs us to take what He has given and make something of it. *"He who is faithful in what is least is faithful also in much; and he who is unjust in what is least is unjust also in much."* (Luke 16:10-NKJV) God created out of the void of nothingness a great universe. He has carved out planets and stars that would dwarf our own planet and sun. From the Earth of which we came, we too, are fed, nourished and comforted. After the rapid extinction of dinosaurs 65 million years ago, the "nothingness" of their extinction coagulating into pools of black, gooey, tar like substances underground, became the fossil fuel necessary to spark the industrial age. It continues to be the life blood of many economies that are thriving today. All around us, we bear witness to God's Universe where something comes from nothing; therefore, what are we unable to create using God as our example?

Many of us feel stuck by the limitations of our circumstances. Some assert that they didn't have an idyllic beginning where they were raised in a loving, two parent household. Their parents didn't have a modest income that would have allowed them to grow up in a safe, suburban community, on a neighborhood cul-de-sac, in a single family housing unit, with a white picket fence. Rather, they may have experienced single parent households, inner city living with urban blight and drug infested communities. They may have been adopted, relegated to foster care or detention centers. Surely there can be no fruit and prosperity with such auspicious beginnings. Hmm? What about celebrity notables like movie icon, Marilyn Monroe, software mogul Steve Jobs, fast food restaurateur, David Thomas, sports great Babe Ruth, comedian and versatile singer/actor, Jamie Foxx and songstress, "Blondie" herself, Debbie Harry are all people whose humble beginnings didn't dim the brilliance of their notable achievements. They may have felt like "nothing" while going through abuse and/or neglect, foster care, detention centers or adoptions but their perceived "nothing" has turned into "something."

We have biblical stories of individuals doubting their abilities; thus, expressing their limitations and flaws. How could anything great come from their limitations and perceived insignificance? Sarah doubted, at the age of 90, that she could be the mother of a new nation. Both Moses and Jeremiah doubted their capacity to lead because they had difficulties with speaking. God didn't absolve either man of their responsibilities because the expansive spirit of God doesn't reduce Himself down to the limitations of men. God honed Moses for forty years in the desert before sending him back to Egypt but He sent with him back without removing his speech impediment, supported by Aaron who assisted him. I'm sure that Moses must have thought of himself as "nothing" and certainly "unworthy" with his disability and with the discovery that he wasn't born into Egyptian nobility but a mere Israeli slave that he (by position) formerly oppressed.

Jeremiah was no different in perceiving his personal inadequacies verses aligning himself with the awesome Power of God. Jeremiah doubted God by inferring that God was mistaken in selecting him as a leader; stating that he was too young and (like Moses) couldn't speak. God informed Jeremiah that "*Before I formed you in the womb I knew you. Before you were born I sanctified you; I ordained you to prophet to the nations.*" (Jeremiah 1:5-NKJV) God is basically telling Jeremiah that out of "nothingness" (before he was even born) God already knew him and knew what he was ordained to do, despite his perceived limitations. Like Jeremiah, many of us succumb to our perceived inadequacies and the "humungous" obstacles ahead of us. I know I have! I don't mean to succumb to difficult challenges and I like to think that I know better but when I am out of partnership with God, thus, tapping into my own self (where fears and doubt loom), I can easily succumb to my inadequacies.

When clients present for therapy, one of the 1st things they focus on is what they don't have. They don't have a girlfriend (or boyfriend). They don't have family celebrations like they did while they were growing up. They don't have a job or they have a job that they don't like. They don't have compliance from their children. They don't have respect from their community. They don't have a high school education. They don't have a college degree. They don't have emotional stability. They don't have a new car. They don't have an iPhone. They don't have people to talk to and if they did, they don't have feelings of wellbeing, esteem and worth in order to talk with them. They don't have hope for a future or faith that they can get there. They don't have a vision of themselves as being good enough, smart enough, or attractive enough. God can help them transform their little into a lot but they don't value the "little" and they have little belief that they will be granted the "lot."

Harold Kushner captures these notions in his book entitled, *"When Bad Things Happen to Good People."* It is not merely the sense of loss or a feeling of deficit that an individual might have; it is also our tendency to turn on ourselves when this occurs. Kushner writes, "One of the worst things that happens to a person who has been hurt by life is that he tends to compound the damage by hurting himself a second time. Not only is he the victim of rejection, bereavement, injury or bad luck, he often feels the need to see himself as a bad person who had this coming to him, and because of that drives away people who try to come close to him and help him." We can manufacture in our heads a greater magnitude to the nature of our suffering than what is actually occurring. In doing so, (and throughout this book I have emphasized), "it is not as important the things that are happening to us but how our minds perceive what is happening to us."

Out of "nothing", we too, are created into "something." Of course, out of a clump of dirt (seemingly nothing), God animates into being the first man, Adam. If that biblical story breaches your notion of scientific credulity, consider your own birth as a process from nothing to something. In the undetectable seed to the human eye is the sperm and egg that has brought forth the person you've become. Cells multiplied and multiplied and multiplied to bring forth each of you. Thus, you've become a marvelous creation seemingly out of "nothingness." God's original instructions for humanity are being replicated all around us. Whether we see this in the activation of yeast in a bowl or the unfolding magnificence of the universe we see the production (and destruction); along with the expanding nature of things.

If God's injunctive is for us to produce (to be fruitful), what is it that we are to produce? Certainly, all things will produce its kind. That is, fish will produce fish, birds with produce birds and humans will produce humans but isn't there something more than that? "Yes." We are spiritual beings (made in the image of God); thus, we are destined to produce that attributes of God which are conveyed in the fruit of the spirit (e.g., Love, joy, peace, patience, kindness, gentleness, self-control, faithfulness, and goodness). It is no easy task producing these spiritual fruit because the material world entices us with hedonistic indulgences. We are in constant battle with the self in the pursuit of "joy" or the consumption of an "Almond Joy" candy bar. We long for "peaceful" coexistence or just another "piece" of that pecan pie. The 2nd part of God's injunctive is to replicate or multiple these fruit in our shared experiences with others. That is, once we are in receipt of God's "Favor," because we are aligned with His Will, we are to give of our "fruit" and dispense the "seeds."

Rusty is a 25 year old, narrow framed, but strikingly tall (6'4") Caucasian male. He wears his hair long and sports a lengthy mustache and straggly beard that hardly covers up some stridently effeminate features. He has a flaccid grip when he shakes hands, with smooth skin that conveys he has not engaged in a single moment of manual labor. Rusty asserts that he is heterosexual and indeed relocated to SW Minnesota from the West Coast in hopes of solidifying a three year old, Internet relationship with a woman he had met. When he arrived, it is not clear to me why he didn't join with his Internet love but he found himself without resources, leaning on the generosity of an older guy who subsequently confined him to the house where he was to remain nude and forced to share the same bed.

Rusty was able to break free of the older guy's dominance and control but he was isolated and alone in an unfamiliar community before he had his mental collapse.

After being hospitalized, Rusty came to me and I gave him a diagnosis of Major Depressive Disorder (MDD) and Attention Deficient Hyperactive Disorder (ADHD). I also assigned a diagnosis of Posttraumatic Stress Disorder (PTSD) due to Rusty's social history. His mother had her own mental health issues and committed suicide when Rusty was young. His mother was a prostitute and Rusty was the product of one of the encounters his mother had had. Rusty reported that his mother used every illegal drug known to man and then some. She was yet another mother living her life with significant toxic shame issues, along with substance abuse issues, who passed Rusty around as a sex object for money or drugs. When babies are put in harm's way by the mother or father who are obliged to protect them we can find many ways to be upset with Rusty's mother. However, Rusty's mother was a product of her own lived experiences and when she could no longer face her condition, she aborted her own life through an act of suicide. Rusty negatively judges his mother for the abuse, neglect and abandonment he has had to endure; however, for the rest of us to judge his mother negatively serves no purpose and may call into question our own spiritual level of development *("He who is without sin among you, let him throw a stone at her first."* John 8:7-NKJV).

The circumstances of Rusty's life have created his confusion about who he is and what he is here to do but Rusty is not alone in his quest. Most of us do not have a clue as to who we are and what we are here to do but it is not because we haven't been told. The Biblical Book of Genesis tells us that we are made in the image of God and whatever God is, we contain. If we did a DNA swab of you, the reader, Jabari, my son, and myself, the genetic markers would identify me as the biological father of my son because whatever DNA configuration that is within me will be reflected in him to the degree that the evaluator of the test would know with certainty that he is my son. He is smarter than I am and more creative than I am but the uniqueness of who he is doesn't discount the fact he is a part of me. A DNA analysis is a biological marker to distinguish one physical human being from the other but God Breathed His Spirit in the nostrils of man to animate us on this life's journey and there is no distinction of spirit (per se). There is a distinction that results from one's awareness of his/her level of spiritual differentiation but our individual spirit has no distinction from others or from God.

Though our individual uniqueness does not discount the fact that we are the children of the Most High God, in human form, we receive a biological inheritance from our parents that in some ways predestines us. That is, tall parents tend to produce tall children. Obese parents tend to produce children on the trajectory of obesity in their adulthood (if not in their childhood). With human characteristics notwithstanding, we are spiritual beings and we do have a spiritual inheritance that come from God and each are pure attributes. God cannot pass down what He doesn't possess, even if He could think to do otherwise. That is why each and every time we seek forgiveness, God grants it immediately and without condition. Luke, (17:4-NKJV) instructs, *"And if he sins against you seven times in a day, and seven times in a day returns to you, saying, 'I repent,' you shall forgive him."* We might have to haggle with our human counterparts for the ability to be forgiven but no such haggling is needed for God. In our limited capacity to enlarge our hearts to have a fuller experience of love, God has not granted us anything less than love. He doesn't barter with us, in that He'll only love us if we love him back. He doesn't measure love out piece by piece for those whom we might think does most deserve love. God just Loves!

As we are developing the attributes of spirit, we are arriving at the apex of Abraham Maslow's Hierarchy of Needs—Self Actualization. We are coming into the "realization of our actual selves"; which are spiritual beings made in the image of God. This is an important transformation because we no longer see ourselves as "Ugli fruit" with blemishes and flaws being passed over by others. We are inseparably connected to the Most High God. When our frame of reference changes, so does our trajectory on the spiritual differentiation scale change. We can move closer to God or further away. There is the benefit of choice that God grants to us freely to decide our course in life. It is the gift from a Loving Entity that allows us the freedom to reject the very God that has created us.

Rusty didn't believe in God. He couldn't fathom a great entity or intelligence that put all of what we know into motion; while lovingly watching over us and protecting us. I understood Rusty's disconnection from the Ultimate. In his lived experience, his father was one of the many "Johns" his mother engaged in sex with for money or drugs. Certainly, the Johns weren't seeking to have a child with a prostitute and I doubt that Rusty's mother was trying to get pregnant at the time. So, Rusty comes into this world unwanted by both biological parents and though his mother maintained custody of him for a while, Rusty's experience of being passed around to other Johns did not convey to him that he was ever loved. When someone throws out the notion that there is a wise, loving, caring and protective God existing in our daily lives, Rusty rejects it wholeheartedly. Earlier, I asked the reader to extend compassion to a mother who would exchange her child for drugs or money. We now must extend understanding for Rusty, the adult, who cannot find within himself it plausible to believe in a Loving God.

Once Rusty's living situation was stabilized; thus, his basic needs (according to Maslow) were being met (e.g., food, clothing, shelter as well as his safety needs), his depression rapidly abated. He got on stimulant medication that helped him with his concentration and distractibility. In some ways, Rusty was "good to go" but he kept coming to therapy. I believe Rusty saw me as a "surrogate father" in whom he was seeking guidance, validation and love. "Love" is a controversial word when it comes to professional and client relationships but in that moment, that 50 minute hour, perhaps once a week, the client is in a "safe holding environment" where they are validated, affirmed and perhaps for the first time in their lives they feel as if they matter; this is love.

I'm replicating for Rusty what he should have received from his parents. I replicate for Rusty, God's surrogate, even though he denies God's existence and the experience of God at a micro level. I'm replanting and watering the seeds that will produce each of the fruit of the spirit. Though Rusty denies his spiritual essence (and understandably so) he is intuitively aspiring for each and every fruit of the spirit. He may not have seen a good example of love during his formative years but he was inclining toward love; which brought him to Minnesota. Rusty was yearning for a loving connection and he nurtured an Internet relationship with a woman for three years. He felt love for her and he felt that she loved him. Rusty had hopes and aspirations that not only came up short, but failed miserably.

Rusty initially came to me for therapy due to his "mental collapse" (depression). In addition to love, Rusty, like all of us, was seeking the fruit of spirit of "peace." Rusty lived a chaotic life with sexual abuse, neglect and ultimately abandonment when his mother decided to end her own life and though he doesn't cry out to God he is in pursuit of peace. He aspires for peaceful coexistence with others but also within himself. Certainly, getting some of his basic needs met provides some peace but Rusty has lived a trauma-filled life; thereby, he has internalized a belief of himself as unworthy. His peace will come when he can reconcile his past without personalizing the negative things that has happened to him. It would be easier if we could talk directly about God to find some meaning in his suffering but he is not there with God; however, he is still inclining toward peace.

Despite Rusty's physiological, emotional, psychological and spiritual insults, he appears to embody the spiritual fruit of kindness, gentleness and goodness. He appears to be a good man. He is thoughtful, personable and other-focused. Though it may have been an impulsive endeavor on Rusty's part to leave the West Coast for an Internet romance that didn't really materialize when he arrived, he was motivated by "feelings" of love within him and the desire to comfort the woman he understood to have been assaulted and he dropped everything to be by her side. He continues to grieve in session because he can't figure out why she drastically changed from the person he knew via Internet for three years to a woman who vehemently despises him? She refuses to talk with him at all, threatens to involve the police if he persists and will glare at him with disdain if she happens to see him in the community.

I suspect, and I really don't know because Rusty doesn't have a theory as to what could have happened to cause her to switch so drastically, but I believe she learned of Rusty's experience with the older guy he moved in with. She may not have been able to wrap her mind around the notion of the guy that she was interested in was compelled to remain nude in the household and sleep naked in the same bed with the older guy. There were no charges filed, thus, Rusty might assume that few people are privy to his ordeal but in a small community, people's secrets don't stay secret, so she may be aware of what transpired. I have moved slowly with Rusty and thus far, he hasn't revealed to me that there was any sex exchanged between the two of them but based upon what has been reported, it is hard to imagine that there was no sexual interaction between Rusty and the older guy. However, what is for certain is that his situation is a replay of the same sexual exploitation that occurred to him as a child.

Faith is another fruit of the spirit. The Bible informs us that, *"...faith is the substance of things hoped for, the evidence of things not seen"* (Hebrews 11:1-NKJV). Rusty has no faith in an unseen God but he is not devoid of faith. He had the faith to forge a relationship with someone he met online. It was his faith (and of course love) that compelled him to come to Minnesota. Of course, Rusty has trust issues that has been reactivated based upon the occurrences in his life since he has moved to Minnesota but he continues to hope that he can have a relationship that defies any of the experiences that he has previously had. Despite the chaos of Rusty's childhood and the ongoing chaos that seemingly continues in his young adulthood, Rusty has a small measure of faith and hope that his life can be different. He has spoken to me about going back toward the West to join with some healthy, loving family members in Wyoming. Perhaps they will provide him with a degree of structure and stability to develop a healthier foundation in order to mature into the man that he wants to be.

Faith is a spiritual fruit but it is needed from a psychological perspective to pull people out of their depression. Given that depression contains negative attributes of self, negative attributes of others and negative attributions of one's future, faith is the antidote to remaining within a depressive state. Returning to God's example in creating "something" out of "nothingness," we have to have a measure of faith to know that no matter what our current life situation is, we too, can create "something" out of the perceived "nothingness." When accessing faith *("...the substance of things hoped for and the evidence of things not seen*") we change our negatively skewed focus, empowering our capabilities; while we honor God's directives to be fruitful and multiple.

Whether or not Rusty can comprehend of a Loving (Omnibenevolent), Knowledgeable (Omniscient), Powerful (Omnipotent) and All-present (Omnipresent) God, he intuitively pursues joy. Even a drug user, within his or her distortions, will pursue the next "fix" in effort to simulate joy. Nevertheless, a purer form, higher level, thus healthier level of joy can be pursued and obtained. "*These things I have spoken to you, that My joy may remain in you, and that your joy may be full.*" (John 15:11-NKJV) Solomon references joy in the following: "*You will show me the path of life; In Your presence is fullness of joy; At Your right hand are pleasures forevermore.*" (Psalms 16:11-NKJV) Joy is the satisfaction and contentment of life. It is what psychologist, Eric Berne's reference to in his notion of "I'm OK and You're OK." He suggests that distortions occur when we have the views of "I'm OK but You're not OK," or "I'm not OK but You're OK," or "I'm not OK and You're not OK." I'm made in the image of God; I have to be OK. You are made in the image of God; you have to be OK (or as God expressed upon His creation of the universe and human beings on the sixth day "…it was very good"). I dare say that we can find joy in our suffering if we knew who we are and why we are here.

The fruit of "patience" and "self-control" for Rusty and others to pursue is important because they symbolize the notion of maturity. Rusty was a bit impulsive when he left the West Coast on behest of a woman he really didn't know. He came without resources; thus, putting him in harm's way and exploited by an older guy who had his own prurient self-interest in mind. He didn't accumulate a "nest egg" to draw upon in case things went awry (as they did). He didn't have a plan in place, even if he felt motivated by "love" because, "love" as "praxis" is informed action. He didn't calculate what needed to have happened but responded out of his "adolescent mentality." Though 25 years old, Rusty's emotional development was stymied a decade or more previously due to the various traumas he endured. Also, without appropriate models for his maturity, Rusty was trying to figure it all out on his own. Nevertheless, James instructs, *"My brethren, count it all joy when you fall into various trials, knowing that the testing of your faith produces patience. But let patience have its perfect work, that you may be perfect and complete, lacking nothing."* (James 1: 2-4-NKJV)

Whether Rusty or any of us are aware that there is an intuitive (in tune with) alignment between God and us, Rusty and we are intuitively pursuing the essence of spirit in our desire for spiritual fruit. If we are producing fruit in line with God's injunctive to "be fruitful and multiple," what does it mean to "multiple" our production? In the most basic terms we are to give bushels of our fruit away in our association with others; thereby, giving others the seeds of which they can produce their own fruit. In our casual encounters, we can spread the seeds of "gentleness, kindness and goodness." As mental health providers, when we encounter people who have been traumatized like Rusty, we'll have to ingest the fruit of "patience" because their healing is not likely to come quickly. We grant the "fruit of love" in validating and affirming their stories. Rusty would ultimately have to forgive his mother for letting him down and not being the type of mother that any person would deserve, but he was steeping with hatred and resentments and it'll take patience if he is going to arrive at forgiveness.

Christ has taught us that it is *"better to give than it is to receive"* (Acts 20:35-NKJV) and this furthers the notion that out of a little bit of nothing comes a whole lot of something. God is a God of Abundance and He gives liberally to us with the expectation that we replicate this generosity in the lives of others. Luke (6:38-NKJV), *"Give, and it will be given to you: good measure, pressed down, shaken together, and running over will be put into your bosom. For with the same measure that you use, it will be measured back to you."* Consider that one tiny little seed can produce a single plant with numerous fruit. From each fruit is a wealth of seeds that can produce numerous plants. As you can imagine, a grove of citrus bearing trees can be produced from one tiny little seed. However, in our limited human understanding, we view life as a depletion of resources. If the resources of this world are scanty and destine to run out, it makes sense to even fight vociferously and aggressively over scanty resources.

The human flesh hoards resources, thus we might misconstrue God's injunctive to "be fruitful and multiple." The human ego convinces us that "I gotta get mine!" We are self-indulgent in our pursuit of pleasure and we are self-indulgent when we focus upon our misery. As co-creators with God we can pull from seemingly paltry resources and tap into an abundance. I am not endorsing the prosperity gospel that is being preached by a number of the televised ministers that we are seeing in this current generation. Perhaps they have it right and I'm missing it completely but Jesus informs, *"Children, how hard it is for those who trust in riches to enter the kingdom of God! It is easier for a camel to go through the eye of a needle than for a rich man to enter the kingdom of God."* (Mark 10:24-25-NKJV) If the image of living a godly life is like John the Baptist, a disheveled, wild man of the wilderness, eating locus and honey and ultimately beheaded, who would want to live this type of life? But I think spiritual beings are mindful of their accumulations and what they are actually giving away; adhering to the spiritual injunctive that it is better to give than to receive.

Another spiritual concept that we find replicated in the Bible is that of "attending." David was attending to sheep before called upon to defeat Goliath and then become the king of Israel. In the book of Matthew Jesus asks what man would not attend to the sheep that has fallen into a pit on the Sabbath. When we attend to something, we are focused upon it or we are watching over it or we are investing into it. The things that we attend to in life will grow; whether we are attending to the things related to our higher self or the lower self. *"Watch and pray, lest you enter into temptation. The spirit indeed is willing, but the flesh is weak."* (Matthew 26:41-NKJV) As long as Rusty continues to attend to the narrative of his life script, which he has a legitimate right to be upset with; while refusing to tap into the Ultimate Source (God) in order to replenish his soul with what has been depleted from him, he'll remain lost, confused, angry and depressed.

Attending to the spiritual fruit will develop our harvest, moving it from seeds to fruit bearing plants (or trees) and diminish the attributes of the lessor self. Conversely, attending to the lower self will multiply the hedonistic cravings in our life; thereby, foregoing our peace and joy. Pay attention to the type of spiritual being that you would like to be while on this earth. Ascertain your meaning, purpose, direction and connections. Discern that you are indeed the child of the Most High God; thus, you need not be diminished by anything on this earth. Having knowledge of God, we know that that "whole is greater than the sum of its parts" but the "parts" have tremendous power also. You have tremendous power! We may be labeled an "Ugli fruit"; perhaps thumped and bruised along the way. However, let us start accumulating our wealth, by first identifying that we are aligned with the Source—made in the image of the All Mighty God. Secondly, obey God's original instructions to be "fruitful and multiply."

Ripening the Fruit-One Percent

Most of us squander or disregard the little things in our lives but it is the accumulation of little things that produce our wealth. Benjamin Franklin touted the importance of a "penny saved is a penny earned"; thus, we can achieve greater resources by paying attention to the little things. In terms of accumulating financial resources for our retirement, we are being instructed by financial strategists to just increase the amount we are saving from each paycheck by one percent, which we'll barely notice, but will bode well by the time we retire. This is sound advice no matter what we are trying to produce and multiply.

Those with meager resources always tell me that they don't have the money to save. A client tells me that the cost of a pack of cigarettes for her is $8.00 in the State of MN; thus, she makes periodical trips to an Indian Reservation in South Dakota to purchase cigarettes at a reduced cost. I have no idea what the cost of cigarettes is in the State of MN; thus, I looked online and was informed that the average cost is $5.62. Let's use this figure (though I surmise that the client's assertion is more accurate), the client is smoking a pack of cigarettes a day at $5.62 x 30 days a month, resulting at a cost of $168.60. That is a lot of money spent on a bad habit! However, let's just take away 1 of 10 of her cigarettes a day for the entire month. That is 9/10 of $168.60 = $151.74. This is a savings of $16.86 per month. If we can put this amount away in a coffee can or savings jar, in a year the person who "can't save anything" has saved $202.32.

I've urged people (and indeed have done so myself) to consider if they are making purchases of groceries each week to write your check for $20.00 over the amount and put that $20.00 away faithfully. The annual result of this effort is a savings (considering 52 weeks in a year) of $1040.00! What a savings for the person that asserts that he or she can't save anything.

As you are considering savings for yourself, I want you to also consider what monies that you can donate. A tithe is often considered 10% of your income. Perhaps your income level will allow you to tithe 10% or more of your income and that is great, but I am talking to those who believe that they can't tithe anything. The spiritual law of abundance demands that we give something away. How about disciplining yourself to one percent? If your monthly income is a $1,000.00, one percent is only $10.00 and we'll likely spend $10.00 for lunch at a local fast food establishment. You must get into the habit of sowing seeds (especially financial seeds) into the world. God will bless your "little" with both a recursive and reciprocal feedback loop.

Aside from money, give 1% of yourself away during the day, week, month and year. Make the call that you've been avoiding to make over the years. Shovel your neighbor's sidewalk when it snows. Say, "Hello" to the stranger you would never talk to. Send a note of gratitude to a boss identifying the employee that treated you well. There is much you can do and what little you do can pay huge dividends in the lives of others (and yourself).

Afterword

The challenge that clinicians will have and a challenge that I continue to have is how do we join these seemingly disparate disciplines of theosophy (faith-based) and psychology (empirical-based) together to give credence to the spiritual essence within us? The challenge of those who are suffering and in need of our help is to see themselves beyond their physical limitations and to access the power of spirituality that resides within. There will be clients that resist the notion that they are spiritual beings. There will be clients that resist our efforts in helping them reclaim their higher selves. There will be those who deny the existence of God. And, there will be those who are lost and confused and have no idea what to think. This was a challenge that Christ had and a challenge He knew would befall his disciples. He instructs, *"If the household is worthy, let your peace come upon it. But if it is not worthy, let your peace return to you. And whoever will not receive you nor hear your words, when you depart from that house or city, shake off the dust from your feet."* (Matthew 10:13-14-NKJV)

Emotions and intellect; along with indulgences in sense desires makes us fundamentally human. There is value in being human…It is an undeniable gift! The human body has five sense receptors that allow us to bring in the sensations of the physical world. We taste, touch, hear, smell and see; which, is then experienced and interpreted by our emotions and intellect. There is functional utility and seemingly great cooperation between the mind and physical body to experience this physical world. If this was all that we were, we wouldn't have so many people worldwide yearning for God, worshiping God and experiencing God. From our earliest beginnings, whether evicted from the "Garden" or first walking upright as a biped being, we've hungered for a relationship with God.

My hope for the reader, having now read "*The Ugli Fruit: Tapping the Inner Spirit for Greater Mental Health*," is to have reminded you of your spiritual essences that takes precedence over your fleeting thoughts, emotions and physical being. It is a reminder that our dis-fellowship from God can cause the development of our physical and psychological maladies and can keep us stuck in our physical and psychological maladies. We are fundamentally spiritual; therefore, our emphasis while enjoying the experiences of this world ought to be on "spirit." Our degree of spiritual differentiation informs us and reflects for others the efforts we are making to abide in spirit. Our focus upon spirit can give us abiding peace in the midst of infirmities to our bodies, discord with others and disequilibrium within our minds.

As service providers (ministers, therapists or caring individuals), we have a duty to access the spirit, if we seek to promote fundamental change in the lives of others. We ought to "risk" living authentically spiritual lives (not a moralistic, self-righteous one of religiosity) and "risk" sharing what we know about spirituality and God without dogmatic imposition but also without trepidation. We won't always be received well in our efforts but a "seed" doesn't have a chance to grow in another person's garden if we hoard the "seeds" ourselves. Whether those in the helping profession are "seed sowers" or "path pointers" we can't prepare the garden for anyone else and we can't take anyone where they don't want to go. Indeed, God doesn't take anyone where they don't want to go. Healing and change is possible. A loving God wants healing and change to occur. If we can arrive at the notion that we are more than what the "Ugli fruit" represents, we will have a more pleasant life experience upon this earth; while honoring God's directive to "be fruitful and multiple."

Glossary

Abraham-Patriarch and progenitor of Jews, Christians and Muslims. Originally called Abram but at the age of ninety-nine, he and his wife, Sarah (90 years old) conceived a child and God changed Abram's name to Abraham that meant, "Father of many nations."

Adam-Biblical character of the Old Testament and the first human creation by God. Through disobedience it was attributed to Adam who led humanity into original sin; Whereas, Jesus has been referred to as the 2nd Adam in leading humanity into salvation.

Ambiguous Loss-Concept of Dr. Pauline Boss when loss is not definitive and the author of a similar titled book.

Amen, Daniel-Author and medical doctor, psychiatrist and brain disorder specialist who has written 15 books and is the director of the Amen clinic. His 1st and perhaps the most notable book is, *"Change your Brain: Change your Life."*

Berne, Eric-Author (notably, *"Games People Play"*) and 20th Century Psychiatrist who created Transactional Analysis that focused upon social transactions between people.

Bradshaw, John-Author and motivational speaker who earned a degree in theology and psychology with notable books like *"Homecoming"* and *"Healing the Shame that Binds You."*

Boss, Pauline-Author of *"Ambiguous Loss: Learning to Live with Unresolved Grief"* and professor emeritus at the University of Minnesota.

Connection-Essence of Spirit

Craving-heart Realm-The mid-range of spiritual development upon the spiritual differentiation scale

David-A biblical hero from the Old Testament who slew the giant, Goliath, and ascended to king of Israel.

Direction-Essence of Spirit

Diagnostic Statistical Manual 5th Edition (DSM-5)-A manual for clinicians that cluster symptoms, defines parameters and codifies mental health disorders.

Dyer, Wayne-A prolific author of 40 books (notably, *"The Erogenous Zone"*) and spiritual teacher in the 20th and 21st Century.

Egocentric-Centering thoughts and understanding of our world from the perspective of self.

Emmons, Henry-Psychiatrist and author of such books like, *"The Chemistry of Calm"* that focuses on drug-free alternatives for dealing with anxiety.

Empirical-Observable, measureable and objective notions of reality.

Entropy-The essence of impermanence that leads to death, destruction and decline.

Faith-A theological construct of allegiance, fidelity and adherence absent of empiricism.

Faith-based-A foundation of experience and belief bolstered by faith.

Frame of Reference-Criteria and/or values which judgments are made.

Frankl, Viktor-Notable psychiatrist and author (notably, *"Man's Search for Meaning"*) who endure imprisonment in Nazi concentration camps.

Franklin, Ben-One of the original founders of the United States adept in science, writing, politics, invention, etc.

Fruit of the Spirit-The attributes of God with nine specifically mentioned in Galatians as love, peace, faithfulness, gentleness, kindness, joy, self-control, goodness and patience.

God-Creator and Sustainer of the entire universe.

Goliath-A menacing warrior and Philistine giant of Gath, represented in the Old Testament, who was defeated by a boy with rocks and a sling.

Gray, John-Author/lecturer and relationship expert and noted for the book, *"Men are from Mars: Women are from Venus."*

Grief-A reaction to impending and actual loss. The process of redefining one's self during the aftermath of the loss.

Harry, Debbie (Blondie)-New wave/punk rock songstress of the '70's & '80's.

Hedonistic-Pleasure seeking and self-indulgent lifestyle, often devoid of spiritual inclinations.

Histrionic Personality- Distinctive characteristics (e.g., superficial, overly emotional) that culminates into a psychological disorder as described in the DSM-5.

Impermanence-Absent of any permanent state and represented in all things within the material/physical universe.

Indifferent-heart Realm-Early stages of spiritual differentiation

Inertia-A state of rest and motion that retains its state unless impacted by an external force.

James-Original Disciple of Christ.

Jesus-One third of the God trilogy and progenitor of Christian Faith.

Jeremiah-Anointed prophet of God in the Old Testament.

John-Original Disciple of Christ.

Jonan-A biblical servant who initially defied God by refusing to go to Nineveh to inform them of their impending demise.

Joseph-Biblical hero sold into slavery by his brothers but rose to prominence to later save his brothers; thus, saving the tribes of Israel.

Kubler Ross, Elisabeth-Psychiatrist with a focus on death and dying with a similarly titled book who identified the five stages of the grieving process.

Kushner, Harold-Rabi and author of the notable book, *"When Bad Things Happen to Good People."*

Leaf, Caroline-Physician and author of the notable book, *"Switch on your Brain."*

Logan, Lara-CBS News correspondent

Logotherapy-Therapeutic approach created by Viktor Frankl that implies that life has meaning with any and all circumstances in life.

Loss-The absence or reduction of what one was previously experiencing.

Luke-Original Disciple of Christ

Maslow, Abraham-Psychologist known for the Hierarchy of Needs (e.g., physiological, safety, belonging, esteem & self-actualization).

Mark-Original Disciple of Christ

Meaning-Essence of Spirit

Micro level-Social transactions at an individual level.

Morrison, Randy-Pastor of Speak the Word Church International in Golden Valley, MN.

Moses-Biblical emancipator of the Israelites held in bondage for 400 years.

Narcissistic Personality-Distinctive characteristics (e.g., grandiosity, self-absorption) that culminates into a psychological disorder as described in the DSM-5.

Newton, Isaac-17th Century mathematician, physicist, invention, author, etc.

Nineveh-Biblical city that Jonah was dispatch to by God.

NASW (National Association of Social Workers)-Professional organization for social workers.

Obama, Barak President-The current and 44th president of the United States and the 1st African-American president.

Paul-Apostle of Christ and prolific writer of much of the New Testament

Peter-Original Discipline of Christ

Praxis-A sociological concept between theory and practice or "informed action" which I have associated with abstract concept of love that comes into fruition with discernment (vs. emotional reactivity) followed by action.

Prayer-A method of communicating with God.

Psychoeducation-Empowering education focused upon individuals with mental health issues, symptoms and disorders.

Pure-heart realm-The last developmental stage on the spiritual differentiation scale

Purpose-Essence of Spirit

Samuel-A biblical prophet in the Old Testament

Sarah-Wife of patriarch, Abraham, and matriarch of the "chosen" people

Saul-Persecutor of Christians prior to his conversion to Apostle Paul

Self-Actualization-The highest level of attainment of Maslow's Hierarchy of Needs; thereby, realizing one's actual/authentic self.

Serenity Prayer-An anonymous prayer often cited in treatment facilities: "God grant me the serenity to accept the things I cannot change. The courage to change the things I can change and the wisdom to know the difference."

Schema-Earlier mental constructions that shapes a person's psychological trajectory throughout life (i.e. an unlovable schema impairs one's psychological wellbeing and mate selection choices).

Scientific methods-A modernistic worldview moving away from faith-based orientation to empiricism.

Sherwood, David-Author

Social construction-Socially relative constructs to perceive the world that suggests that no independent, objective realty exists.

Stahl, Leslie-CBS News Correspondent

Steinberg, Robert-Psychologist focusing on interpersonal/close relationships who has identified "Consummate Love" embodying three distinctive, yet connecting concepts "intimacy, passion and commitment."

Transaction-An exchange based upon formal/informal contracts.

Toxic Shame-A concept referenced by John Bradshaw of poisonous shame.

Vanzant, Iyanla-21st Century spiritual teacher, minister, lawyer, author and TV personality.

Whitaker, Carl-20th Century Psychiatrist and symbolic-experiential therapist.

Worldview-A subjective point of view in how one sees the world (e.g., Christian or Western worldview).

References

Amen, D. (1998) Change your brain change your life: The breakthrough program for conquering anxiety, depression, obsessiveness, anger and impulsiveness. Three Rivers Press. NY, NY.

Boss, P. (1999) Ambiguous loss: Learning to live with unresolved grief. Harvard University Press. Cambridge, MA.

Bradshaw, J. (2005) Healing the shame that binds. Health Communications Incorporated. Deerfield, FL.

Efran, J., Fauber, R., (2015) "Spitting in the client's soup: Don't overthink your interventions." Psychotherapy Networker P., 31-37, 46-48.

Emmons, H. with Kranz, R. (2006) The chemistry of joy: A three-step program for overcoming depression through western science and eastern wisdom. A Fireside Book. Simon & Schuster. NY, NY.

Frankl, V., (2006) Man's search for meaning. Beacon Press. Boston, MA.

Holloway, A. (1998) Break the chains-free the heart: A spiritual pathway through healing, transformation, and mental health. Beaver's Pond Press, Inc. Edina, MN.

Holloway, A. (2008) Fruit of the spiritual: A primer for spiritual-minded social workers. iUniverse Press. Chicago, IL.

Kubler-Ross, E. (1969) On death and dying. Scribner. NY, NY

Kushner, H. S. (1981) When bad things happen to good people. Anchor Books. NY, NY.

Leaf, C. (2013) Switch on your brain: The key to peak happiness, thinking and health. Baker Books Publishing Group. Grand Rapids, MI.

Love, C. (2013) They loved with a closed fist. Dark Planet Publishing. www.Darkplanetpublishing.com.

Sternberg, R., Love Triangle. In Ashford, J. B. & LeCroy, (2006) Human behavior in the social environment. Brooks/Cole. Pacific Grove, CA.

Sherwood, D. A. (1997) The relationship between beliefs and values in social work practice: Worldviews make a difference. Social Work and Christianity, Vol. 24, No. 2 (Fall) 115-135.

Strong, J. (1996), The new strong's exhaustive concordance of the bible. Thomas Nelson, Inc. Nashville, TN.

The Holy Bible, New International Version, (2011). Biblica, Inc.

The Holy Bible, New King James Version, (1982), Thomas Nelson, Inc.

The New Revised Standard Bible, (1989). The Division of Christian education of the National Council of the Churches of Christ in the United States of America.

The Revised Standard Bible, (1971). The Division of Christian Education of the National Council of the Churches of Christ in the United States of America.

Zastrow, C., (1999) The practice of social work. Brooks/Cole Publishing Company. NY, NY.

Zukav, G. (1989) The seat of the soul. Free Press. NY, NY.

Index

About the Author

"*The Ugli Fruit: Tapping the Inner Spirit for Greater Mental Health*," is Dr. Al L. Holloway's third book that focuses upon the importance of spiritual awareness and development to foster greater mental health. He has authored, "*The Fruit of the Spirit: A Primer for Spiritual-minded Social Workers*", which operationalized the abstract concept of "spirit" making it practical and useful for clinicians to develop greater spiritual awareness in themselves and that of the clients they serve. Additionally, he authored, "*Break the Chains – Free the Heart: A Pathway through Healing, Transformation and Mental Health*" that placed the emphasis on psychologists vs. social workers to consider spirituality as a vital part of therapeutic change.

Dr. Holloway is a psychologist and clinical social worker and resides in Marshall, Minnesota, where he provides therapy to those with mental health disorders that range from anxiety or depression to severe and persistent mental illness. He works with couple's, families and those with comorbidity (i.e., chemical health issues and mental health issues). He has severed in this capacity for the past 10 years at Western Mental Health Center. Previously, he has worked as an Adjunct Professor at the University of Minnesota and was a tenured professor at the University of St. Thomas for 10 years.

Printed in the United States
By Bookmasters